Bandwagoning in International Relations

China, Russia, and Their Neighbors

Dylan Motin
Kangwon National University

Series in Politics

VERNON PRESS

www.vernonpress.com

In the Americas:	*In the rest of the world:*
Vernon Press	Vernon Press
1000 N West Street, Suite 1200	C/Sancti Espiritu 17,
Wilmington, Delaware, 19801	Malaga, 29006
United States	Spain

Series in Politics

Library of Congress Control Number: 2023951277

ISBN: 979-8-8819-0070-0

Also available: 978-1-64889-833-4 [Hardback]; 978-1-64889-858-7 [PDF, E-Book]

Cover design by Vernon Press with resources by macrovector on Freepik.

Table of Contents

Acknowledgments

I must express my sincere gratitude to all whose support and encouragement made the completion of this book possible. The initial idea behind it originates from my time as a research fellow at the Institute for Far Eastern Studies in 2021. The Institute nurtured my interest in the China-North Korea relations puzzle and thus launched me on the path of writing this monograph. Special thanks go to Kuyoun Chung, my thesis advisor. I bandwagoned to her unrelenting revisionism, which greatly improved the argument. I am also grateful to several of Kangwon National University's faculty, who offered valuable feedback. The two anonymous reviewers' contribution is also deeply appreciated. Most importantly, none of this would have been possible without the unwavering support of my parents. Note that an earlier version of the argument and fourth chapter were presented during the '2022 Voice of Youth' research contest of the Asia Society Korea.

List of Figures

List of Tables

Chapter I

Introduction

1. The Bandwagoning Conundrum

A significant part of the International Relations (IR) field focuses on how states choose whom to follow or oppose. Realist scholars are in relative agreement that military capabilities explain alignment decisions but disagree on what these decisions are. There are two main schools on whether states balance or bandwagon with superior military power. The first school believes that bandwagoning is infrequent, and states choose to balance most of the time. The second expects that states facing a stronger military force will bandwagon and balancing is rare. Why do some states bandwagon with threatening great powers? What forms take bandwagoning? Do a great power's military capabilities push neighboring states to balance or bandwagon? Are military capabilities sufficient to explain bandwagoning? If not, what other factors can? Why do some states bandwagon more intensely than others? This book addresses these questions by studying the behavior of contemporary China and Russia's neighbors, two great powers engaged in intense security competitions for mastery in Asia and Europe, respectively.

The stark contrast in how Ukraine and Belarus responded to Russian pressure illustrates the problem. Russia has tried to stymie Ukraine's rapprochement with NATO and reestablish domination over Ukrainian foreign policy since the 2014 Maidan Revolution. In late 2021 and early 2022, the Russians massed a significant part of their military around Ukraine's borders. A Russian onslaught appeared imminent, and NATO members — including the United States — had made clear that military intervention on Ukraine's behalf was off the table. Yet, this threat of an impending onslaught failed to convince the Ukrainians to cave in and drop their Westernizing orientation, and Russia ultimately had to invade the country.

The opposite case is Ukraine's northern neighbor, Belarus. Belarus long tried to keep Russian power at bay and refused Russia's frequent requests for greater military integration and military bases in Belarus. The Belarusians used actual or potential rapprochement with Western states as a bargaining chip to resist Russia's overwhelming power (Götz 2023; Vieira 2014). However, after a domestic political crisis in 2020, numerous Western states heavily sanctioned Minsk, destroying any leverage Belarus could have over Moscow. As put by one observer, "the door was closed towards the West, and [Belarusian president Lukashenko] had only one option: Russia" (Sullivan 2022). After that, Belarus wholeheartedly threw in its lot with the Kremlin and even backed the Russian invasion of Ukraine. Why do some like Ukraine refuse bandwagoning in the face of overwhelming military power while others like Belarus cave in? Belarus now works in lockstep with Russia, even supporting Moscow's invasion of Ukraine. However, Armenia, Serbia, and those bandwagoning with China, like North Korea or Cambodia, appear unwilling to take orders from Beijing and Moscow, and all maintain greater foreign policy autonomy. Why do some bandwagoners keep their distance from Beijing and Moscow?

Alignment designates a formal or informal commitment to support another state's security policy (Walt 1987, 12–13). To bandwagon means to align with the strongest power, entrust it with one's security, and support its foreign policy goals. The bandwagoning state usually hopes to reap benefits from its loyalty or at least avoid subjugation. Bandwagoning implies trusting the stronger state's benevolence since the bandwagoner is left with few means to resist it (Mearsheimer 2014, 162–163; Walt 1987, 19–21). Bandwagoning is the polar opposite of balancing on the spectrum of foreign policy choices. To balance means finding allies (external balancing) or increasing one's military capabilities (internal balancing) to deter or possibly defeat the most powerful state (Morrow 1993; Waltz 1979, 118). Internal balancing imposes costs on the balancer's economy and society while finding allies is relatively inexpensive, but one can never be sure that allies will ultimately come to help (Mearsheimer 2014, 156–157; Parent and Rosato 2015; Walt 1985, 5–6). Although bandwagoning and balancing are ideal types and can come in many nuances, this dichotomy offers a starting point to discuss alignment.

Foreign policy alignment is again at the forefront of International Relations due to the return of great power politics. China and Russia have joined the long list of potential regional hegemons willing to revise the balance of power and dominate their neighborhood. Although "in the 1990s or 2000s, one could imagine that the world was becoming more peaceful and cooperative; states such as China and Russia appeared largely to accept the international lay of the land" (Colby 2021, x), Beijing and Moscow built up their military capabilities during the 2000s and 2010s to possess the most formidable military forces of their respective region, Asia and Europe. As per Blagden and Porter, "in Russia and (especially) China, there are regional actors with both reason to find it tempting and sufficient capability to at least contemplate region-wide coercion in pursuit of dominance" (2021, 44). Specialists in military affairs confirm that the growth in Chinese and Russian military capabilities is the factor driving military developments in Asia and Europe (IISS 2022, 6). Therefore, the two regions make ideal contemporary cases to test hypotheses about alignment because both have a clear potential hegemon. Did China and Russia's newfound military power bring them allies? How committed are these allies?

China and Russia's coercive diplomacy enabled by their improved militaries offered them some success. Russia notably acquired Crimea from Ukraine, a strategic piece of real estate, and Beijing grabbed a few islands in the South China Sea. Yet, Beijing and Moscow also provoked a backlash. Various Asian states like Australia, India, Japan, and Vietnam, along with the United States, reacted to Chinese pressure by increasing their military effort and cooperation (Christie, Buts, and Du Bois 2023; Luttwak 2012). Russian actions had a similar effect across Europe and reinvigorated NATO (Graef and Kühn 2022). This cursory glance would suggest that China and Russia's military capabilities failed to compel most of their neighbors to bandwagon with them. Nevertheless, a handful of states, such as Belarus or Cambodia, still chose to follow Beijing and Moscow. How to explain this handful of bandwagoners' choice?

This study sheds new light on whether states prefer to balance and bandwagon, a longstanding debate within IR and realism. I argue that military capabilities alone usually fail to explain why and how minor powers bandwagon with great power threats. Specifically, this answers two related questions in order to create a neorealist theory of minor power bandwagoning. First, what explains bandwagoning, a seemingly rare and dangerous strategy? Second, what concrete forms take bandwagoning and why?

Theoretical expectations about alignment weigh on scholarly debates concerning the future of international politics. Some neorealist scholars claim that structural incentives push states to balance against threats and that bandwagoning is only a last-resort option (Labs 1992; Walt 1987; Waltz 1979). For example, while Mearsheimer (2010) expects China's neighbors to balance Beijing's growing power, others see Asian states as likely to submit to Chinese hegemony (Ross 2006). Indeed, numerous scholars and decision-makers believe that bandwagoning is historically widespread while balancing is rare (Jakobsen 2022, 111–134; Jervis 1991; Powell 1999; Schroeder 1994; Schweller 1994; Slater 1987). Snyder (1991, 3) notices that "most imperial strategists defending far-flung commitments have feared falling dominoes and most rising challengers have anticipated bandwagon effects." Recently, some believed that the Afghan government's fall in 2021 would embolden China and Russia to disregard American security commitments worldwide and convince U.S. allies to switch sides (Cunningham et al. 2021; Maley 2021). The present book contributes to this lively academic debate. Furthermore, although scholarship on past cases of great power bandwagoning is consequential, compelling theorizing about why and how some minor powers bandwagon with China and Russia remains lacking. This work thus helps to understand alliance formation and cohesion in the background of the intense security competitions ongoing in Asia and Europe.

The bandwagoning-balancing debate has significant policy implications. China, Russia, and their relations with their neighbors and the United States are probably the most discussed issues by foreign policy observers and practitioners. If bandwagoning is widespread, China and Russia can employ a "focused and sequential strategy" to dismantle actual or potential balancing coalition using the right mix of cajolement, inducement, and pressure (Colby 2021, 23–26). The potential hegemon can play on collective action problems to their full extent, offer inducements, and use ruthless tactics to reach hegemony (Hui 2004; 2005). Once powerful enough, it can finally move to claim regional hegemony. Those still willing to resist, now isolated, could be swiftly destroyed. Even if a last-hour balancing effort takes form, the potential hegemon can unleash its full military might against the shaky and unprepared coalition. In a bandwagoning-dominant world, divide-and-conquer strategies are highly efficient, and dominos fall. Those willing to forge anti-hegemonic coalitions in Asia and Europe — foremost, the United States — would face tremendous difficulties and need to devolve considerable resources to reassure China and Russia's neighbors.

Conversely, if balancing predominates, Beijing and Moscow will have difficulty pushing regional states away from the anti-hegemonic coalition. Coercion is unlikely to preclude states from balancing, and the potential hegemon will need to provide expansive inducements and make costly concessions to reassure or allure its neighbors, if possible at all. In a balancing-dominant world, most states resist to the bitter end like Ukraine. Balancers like the United States need not fear much that allies will defect and dominos do not fall. However, this comes with a risk; the potential hegemon has little choice other than war to break the anti-hegemonic coalition because it may never be able to dominate its neighborhood otherwise. Hence, this discussion can help devise more efficient strategies for an era of intense security competition.

2. The Existing Literature on Bandwagoning

Only a few scholars have proposed typologies of bandwagoning. To simplify, the vast literature on alignment can be divided into three branches. Composed of defensive and offensive realism, the first, neorealism, sees bandwagoning as rare. The second, labeled here as hegemonic realism, sees bandwagoning as widespread. The last encompasses non-realist approaches and argues that domestic politics or ideas determine alignment. I primarily build on neorealism to develop a novel theory that contradicts hegemonic realism. Non-realist approaches are used to extract alternative explanations to this study's argument.

2.1. *Types of Bandwagoning*

Students of bandwagoning often treat it as a single type of behavior. However, concepts such as balancing and bandwagoning are always ideal types. Like balancing does not imply unremitting hostility and confrontation, bandwagoning rarely means full and loyal alignment (Walt 1988, 282).

The few scholars who theorized bandwagoning generally differentiate offensive and defensive bandwagoning. Offensive bandwagoners align with the threat to accomplish their own foreign policy goals or freeload off their stronger ally's efforts. Defensive bandwagoning is close to appeasement. One aligns with the threat to avoid becoming its next target (Snyder 1991, 129; Walt 1985, 7–8). Schweller (1994, 93–103) builds on this offensive-defensive distinction to make a bestiary of bandwagoning types. For him, bandwagoning minor powers take three forms: 'lambs,' 'jackals,' and 'piling-on bandwagoners.' Lambs are status quo states that bandwagon only to appease the threat and avoid its wrath. Jackals follow the threatening great power to share the spoil of victory and use its support to accumulate power. Piling-on bandwagoners are states that join the winning side of a war to get a share of the spoil.

Nevertheless, the distinction between offensive and defensive motives remains artificial, as both generally coexist (especially in an offensive realist view). If a minor power has no realistic option to resist, it may reluctantly bandwagon to avoid trouble and still hope to reap some benefits in the process. If the minor power is likely to suffer regardless of whether it bandwagons or not, it may be better off bandwagoning now and securing as many benefits as possible before either the potential hegemon or a third threat turns against it. Also, seemingly offensive policies can have defensive motives. A minor power could temporarily appease the potential hegemon to gain time to expand and accumulate power before switching side and betraying it (Eckstein 2023). Therefore, defensive and offensive bandwagoning are not absolute categories; what matters is the relative importance of defensive and offensive motives.

2.2. Neorealism

Although offensive and defensive realists disagree on states' ultimate motives and the frequency of balancing, they concur that states seldom bandwagon with threats (Levy and Thompson 2005). For Waltz, "secondary states, if they are free to choose, flock to the weaker side; for it is the stronger side that threatens them. On the weaker side, they are both more appreciated and safer" (1979, 127). Mearsheimer claims that "bandwagoning is employed mainly by minor powers that stand alone against hostile great powers [and] have no choice but to give in to the enemy, because they are weak and isolated" (Mearsheimer 2014, 163). However, in contrast to defensive realists, offensive realists consider buck-passing a prevalent strategy (Mearsheimer 2014, 157–162; Motin 2022e). Whenever possible, states avoid balancing to the full extent and instead free-ride on the balancing efforts of others. Indeed, in line with offensive realist predictions, Kaufman, Little, and Wohlforth (2007) demonstrate through a groundbreaking historical study that although balancing behaviors generally occur, buck-passing is also widespread.

For offensive realism, states want to maximize their share of world power because it is the safest way to guarantee one's survival in a dangerous world. States are revisionist when they can, and status quoits when they must (Labs 1997).[1] All great powers at least hope to dominate their corner of the world. Offensive realists foresaw more than two decades ago that China would translate its growing wealth into military power and attempt to gain regional hegemony over Asia (Mearsheimer 2001, chap. 10). In the offensive realist view, "China and Russia, like other great powers throughout history, are primarily revisionist in their intentions, or at least other states' political leaders must assume that they are in order to protect their own security" (Hancock and Lobell 2010, 146–147). If China and Russia are potential regional hegemons, then Asian and European states have a deep-seated interest in counterbalancing them. Indeed, a potential hegemon threatens to end the foreign policy autonomy of many regional states — and sometimes their very existence.

In that background, bandwagoning is risky because it increases the potential hegemon's odds of reaching hegemony and terminating the bandwagoner if it pleases. Bandwagoning is a dangerous choice even if the potential hegemon does not reach hegemony since the bandwagoner is left alone and with few options against a far stronger state. Already, Machiavelli recommended that "a prince must beware never to associate with someone more powerful than himself so as to attack others, except when necessity presses" because even if "you win, you are left his prisoner, and princes should avoid as much as they can being at the discretion of others" (1985, 90). At best, the bandwagoner is forced to please the potential hegemon; at worst, it could become a mere satellite or end up outright annexed. Defensive realists generally expect little bandwagoning because it means putting one's survival into a stronger state's hands. This violates defensive realism's assumption that states primarily seek security. Some, like Posen, expect a degree of bandwagoning, but balancing will ultimately prevail:

> small, weak states [will] bandwagon because they have little choice. Some second rank, but still consequential, powers may also bandwagon with the greatest states in a gamble to improve their own positions. All these behaviors are observed, but unless we are to attribute the ultimate failure of all aspiring hegemons on the Eurasian landmass in modern times to chance, balancing has ultimately happened. Balancing is accomplished mainly by small coalitions of the most capable powers

---

[1] A related argument concerning military posture is Cooper (2016).

and is ultimately backed with enough force to exhaust or destroy the expansionists. (Posen 2006, 155)

Nevertheless, Waltz's baseline defensive realism is relatively indeterminate about alignment choices due to its high level of abstraction. Also, neorealists usually focus on relations between great powers because they are the heavyweights of international politics. Although neorealism compellingly explains relations among great powers, minor powers' behavior has garnered comparatively less attention. Adding other variables than the sheer global distribution of power is thus necessary.

Walt (1987) filled that gap by explaining alignment through four variables: aggregate power, geography, offensive military capabilities, and threat perception. He mostly tests his balance-of-threat theory on Middle Eastern and South Asian minor powers living far away from great powers (Walt 1987; 1988). This is problematic because minor powers' alignment in great power-deprived regions is *structurally indeterminate*. Minor powers have a large array of threats to consider: neighboring minor powers, coalitions of minor powers, faraway great powers, and even faraway secondary powers with power projection capabilities. Therefore, the behavior of minor powers distant from a great power is less amenable to generalizations about balancing or bandwagoning (Snyder 1990, 122–123). There are few reasons to expect much bandwagoning in regions without great powers. A minor power is unlikely to acquire enough military capabilities to force regional states to bandwagon. If a minor power gains a clear lead, even limited interventions from outside powers would be enough to restore the balance of power (Montgomery 2016). Therefore, cases comprising a neighboring great power threat are more amenable to test propositions about bandwagoning.

Furthermore, Walt's four variables can be improved upon. First, although aggregate power likely matters, some states with considerable power potential lack actual military capabilities and thus do not provoke balancing reactions (Motin 2021). Second, geography and offensive power are intricated; one can hardly consider them in isolation. A state with large offensive capabilities against a neighbor will often lack the means to attack a faraway state. Terrain features can also greatly diminish offensive power. Third, threat perception as an independent causal variable is inconsistent with neorealism. In Walt's theory, a state could choose to balance against another not because it poses a material threat but because it boasts a different ideology or regime type (Legro and Moravcsik 1999, 36–38; Narizny 2017).

States move on the balancing-bandwagoning spectrum following changes in the balance of power. Generally, states do not balance much when a potential threat is weak. Balancing turns widespread when the threat becomes formidable, and bandwagoning becomes rare. However, balancing disappears when the threatening state reaches hegemony (more than 50% of a region's share of military power) because any resistance is futile at this point (Fiammenghi 2011). As put by Snyder:

> the balancing tendency will become stronger as an aggressor gains repeated increments of power and will become irresistible, logically, when an aggressor is on the brink of acquiring half of the power resources in the system, for beyond that point it will be able to dominate the entire system. (Snyder 1990, 108)

2.3. *Hegemonic Realism*

Other realist scholars are less sanguine about the frequency of balancing (*Table 1.1*). They believe the Athenians who once told the Melosians: "the dominant exact what they can and the weak concede what they must" (Thucydides 2009, 302).[2] In their view, lesser states yield to great powers and eschew balancing; they easily cave in when threatened (Carter 2022). For Ross (2006; 2021), military power is a necessary and sufficient condition to compel bandwagoning. Therefore, he expects China's neighbors to submit to Beijing as Chinese military capabilities grow. Indeed, when a great power expands, neighboring states jump on its bandwagon, either voluntarily or pushed by domestic forces supporting accommodation. If a great power becomes powerful enough, minor powers will want to break existing alliance arrangements with the declining side in favor of hedging, neutrality, or bandwagoning (Castillo and Downes 2023). Dean Acheson illustrates that fear well; a victory of the pro-Soviet forces in the Greek civil war, for him,

> would infect Iran and all to the east. It would also carry infection to Africa through Asia Minor and Egypt, and to Europe through Italy and France, already threatened by the strongest domestic Communist parties in Western Europe. The Soviet Union was playing one of the greatest gambles in history at minimal cost. (Acheson 1969, 219)

Hegemonic stability theorists expect most states to bandwagon with the strongest power. First, the hegemonic power provides other states with public goods like security and economic governance, thus incentivizing bandwagoning. Second, balancing is highly costly for most states; hence, only formidable rising powers (or hegemonic challengers) will take the risk to balance. Rosecrance and Lo (1996) argue that balancing is far from automatic, and states will readily

---

[2] In a case in point, the small island of Melos refused to cave in to Athens's threats and chose to resist to the bitter end.

bandwagon if the rising hegemon is accommodative. As put by Gilpin (1981, 30), "to some extent the lesser states in an international system follow the leadership of more powerful states, [...] subordinate states frequently form alliances with the dominant powers and identify their values and interests with those of the dominant powers."

States may also resort to bandwagoning to maximize power since "balancing is an extremely costly activity that most states would rather not engage in" while, oppositely, "bandwagoning rarely involves costs and is typically done in the expectation of gain" (Schweller 1994, 93). Furthermore, states may sense which way the wind is blowing and decide to prevent future losses by joining the winning side early. Therefore, "like a ball rolling down an incline, initial success generates further success, not greater resistance" (Schweller 1994, 92). Revisionist states will want to ally with other revisionists to share the spoils of expansion and correct the international order. Hence, Schweller answers Walt that states often bandwagon, not for lack of a better choice but to maximize power. A variation of the hegemonic school contends that only great powers tend to balance, whereas minor powers neighboring great powers are reduced to bandwagoning, the safest option to survive (Levy 1989, 231). For Sweeney and Fritz (2004), great powers balance as much as they bandwagon, and thus, minor powers should logically tend to bandwagon even more than them. An investigator affirms that,

> Instead of moving to the side of the less powerful and thereby helping to restore the balance, [small states] tended to comply with the demands of the more powerful and thus to accentuate any shifts in the balance of forces caused by changing fortunes of war or prospects of ultimate victory. Viewed in this way, the small state's characteristic behavior may be described as "anti-balance of power" while that of a great power is characteristically "pro-balance of power." (Fox 1959, 187)

Table 1.1. Minor power behavior in realist theories

	Defensive realism	**Offensive realism**	**Hegemonic realism**
Balancing?	predominant	widespread	rare
Bandwagoning?	rare	rare	predominant
Buck-passing?	rare	widespread	N/A

2.4. *Non-Realist Approaches*

Non-realist scholars reject the distribution of power as an explanatory variable and analyze state behavior through individual- and domestic-level theories (Waltz 1959). Among them, liberal scholars usually emphasize the role of trade and international organizations. Liberals consider security competition counterproductive and costly due to the opportunity costs of cooperation that does not happen. They argue that charm and trust-building yield better results over the long run than military power (Axelrod and Keohane 1985; Gallarotti 2011; Larson 1997; Nye 2004). Also, they contend that cooperation is generally rewarding and the most rational choice (Axelrod and Keohane 1985; Larson 1997).

Specifically, liberals believed globalization imposed on Beijing and Moscow to focus on international trade, apolitical transnational issues, and the pursuit of ideas and norms. By extension, they did not expect Asian and European states to balance the rise of China and the return of Russia. They failed to understand that globalization and the liberal international order themselves were outcome variables of U.S. primacy and that balance-of-power politics would come back as new powers appeared (Allison 2018; Ripsman 2021). Therefore, China and Russia's rise as potential regional hegemons and the resulting balancing behaviors by their neighbors at first stunned liberal thinkers, convinced that power politics and the defense of the national interest were things of the past (Mearsheimer 2018; 2021).

Even if balancing and bandwagoning are not liberal concepts, one can extract alternative explanations from liberalism. Liberals believe alignment originates from two potential sources: domestic politics and economic intercourse. First, liberals expect balancing against unalike states and alignment with like states (Haas 2005; Kaufman 1992; Strüver 2016). For Owen (2001; also, Deudney and Ikenberry 1999), liberal democratic states do not balance against the United States due to their shared liberal ideology. On the contrary, some liberals believe that democratic states will oppose autocratic powers like China and Russia (Selden 2016). Relatedly, Schweller (2004) argues that elite consensus on the threat's identity must exist for balancing to happen. Domestic concerns influence alignment decisions, and internal threats to a government's survival can push it to bandwagon with an external threat to gain its backing (Barnett and Levy 1991; David 1991; Lee 2017). Consequently, the empirical part will test the domestic regime type as an alternative explanation. Second, liberals argue that economic intercourse with a potential threat can limit or cancel balancing outright (Chan 2012; He and Feng 2008; also, Medeiros 2005; Papayoanou 1996). Going one step further, one may argue that intense economic intercourse can force bandwagoning. Indeed, Han and Paul (2020) believe that economic links with China will force accommodation and neutralize balancing tendencies. I will test this alternative hypothesis too.

Constructivists focus on how interstate interactions construct states' identities and how identities inform foreign policy (Wendt 1999). Perceived similarities in identity or ideology should push toward alignment (Owen 2005). Constructivist scholars qualify Asia's international culture as 'Lockean' (Moore 2013); even if conflicts and tensions persist, states do not fear for their survival, which social norms guarantee. Therefore, there is no reason to expect much balancing dynamics in the face of China's rise. In Europe, although constructivists see the potential for discursive conflict between Russia and its neighbors, there is nothing to preclude inter-subjective understanding either (DeBardeleben 2012). Constructivists believe Asia and Europe are Lockean systems where power politics has disappeared and expect little balancing against Beijing and Moscow.

Furthermore, a strand of constructivist scholarship expects East Asian states to promptly bandwagon with China. It argues that China has been a benevolent hegemon in East Asia for many centuries, and Asian states are culturally used and ready to accept hegemony, contrary to European states. China's neighbors should readily embrace Chinese hegemony, and power politics would not occur because China is a benevolent and non-expansionist great power per nature (Kang 2003b, 2005, 2007; also, Hui 2018; Meng and Hu 2020). Therefore, for these scholars, theories based on the European-Western experience cannot apply in the Asian context (Kang 2003a; Hsiung 2009). Yet, few Asian states decided to bandwagon with China. In addition, popular distrust of China is widespread in Japan, South Korea, and Taiwan (Devlin and Huang 2020; Yonhap 2021; Zhou 2021). Also, this book's case selection circumvents this problem by including both Asian and European states. I will nonetheless test the East Asian bandwagoning hypothesis. One could extend such a constructivist argument to the European case and imagine that states culturally close to Russia would also see Moscow as a benign hegemon; this will be tested too.

3. The Argument and Its Importance

This book proposes the first fully-fledged neorealist theory of minor power bandwagoning. It builds on prior realist claims that military capabilities are an essential variable to predict alignment but argues that military capabilities alone are insufficient to explain it. Military capabilities are here conceptualized as the threat severity — the conventional military balance between the potential hegemon and the target state. This study's second variable is third conflict. Conflicts with thirds are diplomatic confrontations between at least two minor powers (that do not include the potential hegemon) plausibly able to erupt in war. The third variable is great power assistance: diplomatic, economic, or military support emanating from a great power (that is not the potential hegemon) toward a regional state. This refers here to U.S. assistance.

This work shows that the best predictor of bandwagoning with a potential hegemon is the mix of a conflict with a third and the unavailability of U.S. assistance. In contemporary Asia and Europe, states that combined these two variables *all* bandwagoned with China and Russia between 2008 and 2022. Going one step further, I analytically divide bandwagoning between three possible outcomes: *full alignment, survival accommodation,* and *profit accommodation.* Profit accommodation ensues when a minor power is confronted with third rivals and low U.S. assistance but is not under direct threat from China or Russia. Survival accommodation occurs when the former two conditions combine with a high threat severity. Full alignment occurs under the same three conditions, but tensions with third rivals are intense, and the United States is not only unsupportive but hostile. Overall, the empirical part demonstrates that changes in these three variables are closely related to changes in the minor powers' level of bandwagoning.

This book has other qualities beyond solving the immediate research puzzle. It is a new addition to the neorealist research program and eliminates one of its blind spots. In doing so, the theory remains parsimonious because it accounts for only three causal variables: threat severity, conflict with a third, and great power assistance. This parsimony allows significant predictive power and generalizability (Waltz 1979, chap. 1). Therefore, it travels well to other cases where minor powers faced potential hegemons. Coincidentally, this research supports the insights of geography-sensitive realists like Walt or Mearsheimer by showing that alignment is better conceptualized at the regional than at the systemic level.

Finally, the argument offers significant policy recommendations. Are the few bandwagoners the beginning of a trend or the high tide of Chinese and Russian success? I conclude that minor power alignment with Beijing and Moscow is no destiny compelled by coercive power, economic interdependence, or traditional sympathy. Instead, bandwagoning is a choice influenced by how foreign — and especially American — leaders approach the neighbors of China and Russia. Whether a state aligns with the Kremlin or the Zhongnanhai is in big part an American choice, and states gone to the Chinese and the Russians are often self-inflicted wounds. Thus, even small U.S. steps to improve relations with minor powers and overcome enduring conflicts among regional states could favorably alter the balance of power and influence.

4. Definitions and Scope

This section defines essential concepts, justifies the case selection, and explains the empirical strategy. Chapters Three and Four focus on cases from contemporary Asia and Europe, the only two regions where potential hegemons currently exist. The concept of potential hegemon applies only at the regional/subsystemic level (here, Asia and Europe). A potential hegemon possesses a significant lead in military capabilities and is formidable enough to compete with the two next most powerful states in tandem and possibly even beat them (Mearsheimer 2014, 44–45). For Colby (2021, 8), "an aspiring hegemon […] is powerful enough to plausibly establish hegemonic control [and] the most powerful within a region by a considerable margin." Also, in the contemporary era, a potential hegemon must possess a credible nuclear deterrent since a balancing coalition counting a nuclear state would easily obliterate a non-nuclear potential hegemon (Mearsheimer 2014, 5). A potential hegemon thus has a significant lead in military power over any regional state but possesses less than 50% of its home region's military capabilities.

Potential hegemons are usually willing to use coercion and war to reach regional hegemony because they are dissatisfied with their home region's political and military order and wish to change it. The existing balance of influence does not reflect the potential hegemon's actual power (Schweller 1994, 87). Typically, the potential hegemon recently emerged from a position of weakness to acquire formidable military capabilities but is surrounded by hostile powers, their armed forces, and their allies. Also, coveted tracts of lands, resources, or strategic locations that could secure and improve its position escape its control (Colby 2021, 6–13; Harris and Marinova 2022). The endgame of potential hegemons is regional hegemony: the possession of an overwhelming share of the military capabilities in its corner of the world. A regional hegemon can shape its neighbors' foreign, defense, and economic policies to its liking and extract additional resources from them. With its neighborhood under control, the likelihood of survival of the hegemon dramatically increases. It becomes able to meddle in other regions' affairs because it is secure in its own backyard (Colby 2021, 6–15; also, Allen 2018). Modern cases of potential hegemons are Habsburg Spain, Louis XIV's France, Revolutionary France, Wilhelmine Germany, Nazi Germany, Imperial Japan, and the Soviet Union (Motin 2022a).

China in Asia and Russia in Europe are potential hegemons because they are the only states with a credible path to regional hegemony. Brazil looked like a rising power during the 1990s and 2000s but failed to develop the military capabilities necessary to race toward regional hegemony. It lacks the power to defy the two next regional powers (Motin 2021). Similarly, many saw South Africa as a rising power during the 2000s and 2010s. However, by this study's definition, it is neither rising nor a power. India is probably the closest call; it has significant military capabilities and even a nuclear deterrent. Nevertheless, China is the most potent power in Asia, not India. Therefore, India is not a potential hegemon. During the 1990s, some envisioned Germany and Japan as potential hegemons (Mearsheimer 1990; Waltz 1993), but both failed to develop significant military capabilities. Since the nineteenth century, the United States has been the Western Hemisphere's regional hegemon, so this study does not concern it (Elman 2004; Mearsheimer 2014; also, Butt 2013).

Potential hegemons are a particular subset of great powers. The only great powers of the post-Cold War era are the United States, China, and Russia, in that order. Great power is a concept used at the systemic or global level. It is a state that "must have sufficient military assets to put up a serious fight in an all-out conventional war against the most powerful state in the world." Although it needs not to be strong enough to defeat that most powerful state, "it must have some reasonable prospect of turning the conflict into a war of attrition that leaves the dominant state seriously weakened, even if that dominant state ultimately wins the war" and "a nuclear deterrent that can survive a nuclear strike against it" (Mearsheimer 2014, 5). Great powers "have a superior military potential, which even with a moderate rate of mobilization generates commanding ready military strength" or are "endowed with a moderate potential in terms of manpower and other resources, [but] mobilize to a greater extent than do states of comparable military potential" (Knorr 1970, 21). It is "a state which could insure its own security against all comers" (Rothstein 1968, 296). This book discusses states that do *not* match this definition and are consequently called *minor powers*.

The 2017 U.S. *National Security Strategy* and 2018 *National Defense Strategy* classified China and Russia as great powers (U.S. Government 2017, 25–35; U.S. Department of Defense 2018) and "herald the return of great power competition, identifying China and Russia as long-term strategic competitors that are challenging U.S. interests and the balance of power in Europe and the Indo-Pacific simultaneously" (Simón, Desmaele, and Becker 2021, 96; also, Allison 2020). Thus, 2017 can be used to mark the transition from unipolarity (1992–2016) to tripolarity (Mearsheimer 2019, 8).

This study focuses on contemporary regions that count potential hegemons since potential hegemons are the most threatening states to populate the international system. A potential hegemon is a great power that informs most of its weaker neighbors' foreign policy because it is the only state with a realistic chance of claiming regional hegemony. Potential hegemons endanger the survival of numerous states simultaneously. This elicits widespread dread and intense balancing reactions and makes local or even major wars likelier (Mearsheimer 2014; Rosato 2011). In a balancing-dominant world, the potential hegemon should be the target of numerous states' balancing efforts due to its significant lead in military power. In a bandwagoning-dominant world, the potential hegemon's military capabilities should suffice to force most weak neighbors to bandwagon.

Some may argue that balancing or bandwagoning is a cultural trait more than a strategic choice. Indeed, as mentioned earlier, some constructivist scholars believe that Asian states have an inherent tendency to bandwagon. Therefore, including Asian and European cases helps control for the civilizational variable (Volgy et al. 2017). Furthermore, liberals and constructivists make the case that economic intercourse renders security competition unlikely. China is a preeminent trading power, while Russia is far less so. Therefore, whether or not economic intercourse cancels power politics can be controlled using both Asian and European cases.

Chapters Three and Four delimitate the relevant regions (or subsystems). Contrary to others like Buzan and Wæver (2003) or Zimmerman (1972), 'region' is used here in a purely geographic, mechanical sense. The two chapters show that China and Russia are potential regional hegemons in Asia and Europe because they possess superior military capabilities. Although the two chapters discuss numbers, numbers alone do not suffice to assess the actual balance of power. Students of international security have sophisticated methods of evaluating balances of power; however, exhaustive net assessments (Mahnken 2020) and campaign analyses (Tecott and Halterman 2021) are outside the reach of this study. These are data-intensive and resource-consuming endeavors.[3] It also requires numerous assumptions on specific scenarios and military operations. Instead, I collect data concerning the main items of military power for both cases. Chapters Three and Four use military expenditures based on power purchasing parity (PPP) data to account for military spending.[4] Furthermore, I describe the major evolutions of the Chinese and Russian militaries, notably in terms of morale, training, doctrine, experience, weaponry, and socio-economic mobilization capabilities, and relate them to the dynamics of their regional neighborhoods.[5]

After that, Chapters Three and Four test the theory through a focused comparison of the foreign policy of Asian and European states that chose bandwagoning (analytically divided between full alignment, survival accommodation, and profit accommodation) between 2008 and early 2022 (the beginning of the Ukraine War). I investigate the evolution of my three variables and the bandwagoners' foreign policy to understand their foreign policy choices during this period. Indeed, regional states should have started to adjust their foreign policy during that time frame, as Chinese and Russian military capabilities rose during the 2000s and 2010s, and it became clear to most that China and Russia were the most formidable states in their respective neighborhood. Furthermore, 2008 represents a symbolic milestone, as many saw in the financial crisis the beginning of a shift from unipolarity to multipolarity. Finally, liberal and

---

[3] For example, see Barrie et al. (2019) and Shlapak and Johnson (2016).

[4] Appendix 2 expands on this methodology.

[5] This is similar to Ross's (2006) method. A case for mixing quantitative and qualitative analyses is Roche and Watts (1991).

constructivist scholars often argue that the contemporary era differs in essence from previous eras and, therefore, realist scholarship does not apply because it often grounds itself in pre-1945 cases. The present book tests hypotheses about alignment in recent cases, so this potential criticism cannot apply.

Each case study describes the severity of the military threat (high or low threat) posed by the two potential hegemons to the bandwagoner. For that, I analyze the balance of military power between China or Russia and each state. I then trace the presence and evolution of third-rival conflicts and U.S. assistance. Chapters Three and Four overall represent a comparative study of seven cases, all states that bandwagoned with China or Russia between 2008 and 2022 with varying intensity. These represent the entire universe of regional states that bandwagoned with either Beijing or Moscow and should thus provide solid findings (Appendix 1, *Table A1.1*). These cases are Armenia, Belarus, and Serbia for Europe; Cambodia, Myanmar, North Korea, and Pakistan for Asia. They are the states that experts generally see as bandwagoning with either China or Russia.[6]

Chapters Three and Four are thus a focused comparison tracing the impact of the three causal variables throughout all the cases (George and Bennett 2005, part 2; also, Bennett and Elman 2007; Levy 2008; Mahoney 2012). For each case, this study employs diplomatic history, decision-makers' declarations, and secondary sources to trace my causal mechanisms. Because each case offers several observations, the case studies provide numerous data points to test the theory. Furthermore, Chapter Five discards alternative explanations extracted from the existing literature and several context-based potential counterarguments. Therefore, the within-case analysis represents a 'doubly decisive test' (Collier 2011): the case study strongly confirms the hypotheses, while the most likely alternative explanations are weakened. I then check whether the theory can travel to Cold War cases to explain them convincingly. This method reaffirms the theory's causal inference and allows for generalization.

5. Plan of the Book

This book proposes a new neorealist theory of why minor powers align with neighboring potential hegemons. Specifically, it aims to elucidate why and to what extent some states choose to bandwagon with China and Russia. Chapter Two explains my three variables — threat severity, conflict with a third, and great power (U.S.) support — to build a coherent theory and offer testable hypotheses. Chapters Three and Four demonstrate first that China and Russia are potential hegemons in their respective region, Asia and Europe (which are

---

[6] This case selection method resembles that of Chung (2009) and Chung and Kim (2023).

delimitated). Second, they list the states that bandwagoned with China and Russia and trace the presence of the book's causal variables in each of them. Chapter Five summarizes the findings, discards the most prominent alternative explanations, checks whether the theory travels well to other historical cases, discusses policy implications, and proposes avenues for further research.

Chapter II

A Neorealist Theory of Bandwagoning

This chapter explains why and when some minor powers bandwagon with a potential hegemon while most others do not. It also proposes a typology and theory of bandwagoning intensity. The first part describes the principal alignment choices available to minor powers facing potential hegemons and considers why bandwagoning is the most unattractive. This shows that threat alone explains bandwagoning poorly since states have an inherent interest in balancing. The second part conceptualizes threat severity, the explanatory variable most realist theories consider essential. The third and fourth parts discuss the two remaining causal variables, conflicts with thirds and great power assistance. The last part combines the three variables to form a single theory and extracts testable hypotheses from it. This new theory provides a nuanced explanation of why and how some minor powers decide to bandwagon with China and Russia.

As hinted throughout the first chapter, geography matters tremendously to explain alignment choices, and potential regional hegemons are the most dangerous type of great powers for minor powers. Minor powers will care deeply for regional balance-of-power politics and give only an afterthought to world affairs (Chabbi and Lim 2013; Walt 1987).[1] Therefore, the present theory applies only at the regional level and if said region contains a potential hegemon. It cannot scale up to the global level.

1. Alignment Strategies and the Rarity of Bandwagoning

1.1. *Main Alignment Strategies*

States adapt their foreign policy strategy following changes in the balance of power; the distribution of military capabilities shapes states' intentions (Zakaria 1998, 9). Geography also contributes to making some strategies more likely than others. The three main strategies available to states are listed below, from the least to the most appealing.

Bandwagoning. A state with no hope to resist or deter a threat can choose to entrust it with its security and instead support its ambitions. The bandwagoner

---

[1] Prominent non-realist scholars also consider regions as the dominant level of analysis (see Buzan and Wæver 2003).

hopes to receive a share of the spoil, or at least be destroyed last, in exchange for its loyalty. Bandwagoning is a risky choice. Great powers rarely bandwagon because they generally have enough staying power to put up a good fight. Bandwagoning is unlikely when balancing opportunities exist but can become unavoidable when the aggressor is too formidable to balance against (Mearsheimer 2014, 162–163). Although punishment for bandwagoning may not come swiftly, a bandwagoning state loses control over its destiny and may ultimately pay the price for failing to balance (Waltz 1997, 915).

Balancing. Balancing is a state's attempt to increase its relative capabilities or find allies to deter or potentially defeat an aggressor. Making allies that fear the same threat is an inexpensive way to balance. However, one can never be sure of its allies' commitment and utter motives. Furthermore, coalition warfare is always less effective because of the hurdles inherent in international coordination. Alliances are hard to establish and manage but easy to break. States also balance by mobilizing more domestic resources and increasing their military capabilities. Although this is the safest way to balance, it can impose a heavy burden on the economy and society (Mearsheimer 2014, 156–157; Morrow 1993; Parent and Rosato 2015; Walt 1985, 5–6).

Buck-passing. States have a powerful incentive to let others bear the cost of balancing and avoid wasting their own resources. Buck-passing entails free-riding on the defense efforts of others and shifting the burden of balancing onto them. The buck-passer understands that the aggressor is a severe threat but still takes the risk of eschewing or delaying balancing efforts. The buck-passer may ramp up internal mobilization and even reinforce relations with the balancing coalition but will avoid confronting the potential hegemon head-on. Therefore, it does not balance to the full extent and generally strives to maintain cordial relations with the threat to deflect attention away (Mearsheimer 2014, 157–162; Olson and Zeckhauser 1966).

Buck-passing originates from a collective action problem. When one's full contribution is not mandatory to provide the public good (the balance of power), it is tempting to free-ride on the efforts of balancing states. The attraction of buck-passing depends on the details of the military balance and geography, which "helps identify the likelihood of buck-passing in multipolar systems: common borders promote balancing while barriers and buffers encourage buck-passing" (Hancock and Lobell 2010, 149; also, Blankenship 2021). Buck-passing is most alluring when the threat is distant geographically or when another more directly endangered state — a buck-catcher — is available.

Furthermore, buck-passing can improve one's position. It leaves balancing powers weakened because they must contain or eventually fight the threat on their own. The buck-passer hopes "that other states, even singly, will be able to stalemate the aggressor without assistance" and also "that the process of fighting will be debilitating even for a victorious aggressor. Such an aggressor will pose a reduced threat to buck-passing onlookers who remain at their full, prewar strength" (Christensen and Snyder 1990, 145). Therefore, a buck-passer can eschew the cost of conflict and tilt the balance of power in its favor. Nevertheless, buck-passing is not risk-free; the buck-passer can end up alone to face an empowered aggressor if the buck-catching states fail to contain it. Thus, if the potential hegemon keeps gaining ground, buck-passing will become increasingly risky, and most states should engage in balancing.

Finally, some states may defy structural incentives and refuse to choose between bandwagoning, buck-passing, and balancing. Geographic distance can encourage states to pay no attention to power politics and simply hope to be left alone. Also, some states may adopt alternative strategies due to specific domestic particularities or beliefs. Very weak states are more likely to use such strategies, which often come in two forms: hedging and hiding. Hedging aims at eschewing "clear-cut alignment with any great power, and in turn creating greater uncertainty regarding which side the secondary state would take in the event of a great power conflict" (Lim and Cooper 2015, 709). The hedging state maintains similar levels of security cooperation with the bandwagoning and the balancing coalitions and makes little military preparation against the potential hegemon. Hiding means avoiding power politics and alignment in the hope of keeping trouble away. A notable form of hiding is neutrality; the neutral state limits its security relations with all sides and portrays itself as an impartial observer (Schroeder 1994, 117).[2]

1.2. Why Do Weak States Balance Despite an Overwhelming Threat?

I make the case that bandwagoning is rare while balancing and buck-passing are widespread. Therefore, this section argues that resisting a potential hegemon remains a safer choice than bandwagoning, despite the threat. Neorealists agree that bandwagoning is a dangerous policy. There is no shortage of historical cases where bandwagoning did not end well for the bandwagoner. For instance, Numidia became a loyal ally of a rising Rome from the Second Punic War (219–202 B.C.) onward. Betting on Rome worked initially, as Numidia benefited from Roman protection and expanded its territory. But once Rome gained hegemony over the Mediterranean region during the first century B.C.,

---

[2] Some scholars proposed the concept of 'soft balancing': a form of balancing conducted through diplomatic consultations, international organizations, or economic competition but which eschews military build-ups and alliances (Pape 2005; Paul 2005; 2018). However, stretching the concept of balancing in that way complicates distinguishing it from normal diplomatic friction or other strategies like hedging (Lieber and Alexander 2005). Therefore, I leave it untouched here.

it became free to turn against Numidia, which was ultimately annexed in 40 B.C. (Hoyos 2015; also, Bailey 2018; Walsh 1965). Even if the potential hegemon does not physically harm the bandwagoner, it can compel it to support its bid for hegemony, which usually comes at a high cost.

To bandwagon implies some confidence that the potential hegemon will not conquer or harm the bandwagoner. In other words, the bandwagoner must expect the potential hegemon to remain benign. However, states cannot guess with certainty others' intentions, present and future (Rosato 2021). Uncertainty about intentions pushes towards balancing, the safest option. Even if the potential hegemon refrains from aggressive behavior, neighbors are still likely to fear it since "the state to whom victory would give hegemony passes for aggressive, whatever are the intentions of those who govern it" (Aron 2004, 94). A balancing state may incur costs as high as destruction, but a bandwagoning state is nearly certain that its foreign policy autonomy will decrease or even disappear altogether. Furthermore, the bandwagoner endangers its sovereignty by giving the potential hegemon opportunities to penetrate its state apparatus and society. The potential hegemon becomes more able to interact with the bandwagoner's political leadership, bureaucrats, and soldiers. It also has more opportunities to build loyalties among civil society and businesspeople (Andersen 2011). It possesses even more leverage to pressure the bandwagoner's leadership if it is allowed to base troops in the country. This penetration can serve to twist the arm of the bandwagoner or, if required, elicit a regime change to place a more servile government in charge. If penetration is successful enough, the bandwagoner loses its foreign policy autonomy and becomes a mere extension of the potential hegemon.

Why do minor powers generally eschew bandwagoning? Despite an unfavorable balance of power, why do they still resist a potential hegemon? Weak states may hope to survive despite their lack of military capabilities, and only states in a desperate position will resort to bandwagoning. Weak states may find four main reasons to choose balancing despite fearful odds.

First, a state may have the potential to balance internally. It can hope to grow its capabilities successfully and reduce its vulnerability over time. Reforms may boost the economy and increase the tax base, ultimately offering more resources to the military. Furthermore, if the weak state possesses a decrepit or inefficient military, it can try to modernize it, optimize its strategies, and reduce the waste of resources (Layne 1993). Indeed, structural incentives push states to emulate efficient practices and reject inefficient ones in the same way the market pushes companies to adopt the most productive strategies. States modernize their militaries and copy the best practices of their neighbors to balance efficiently (Sechser and Saunders 2010). In the long run, states that fail to extract resources from their societies are punished by falling behind in international competition or even disappearing from the map (Zakaria 1998).[3] Weak governments can also use the mobilization strength of nationalism to increase the state's resource-extracting capabilities (Mearsheimer 1990, 20–21; Posen 1993; Roy 2019, 61; Taliaferro 2006). Historically, some weak states have been able to assemble potent military forces. Interwar Czechoslovakia built a large and modern army. North Korea musters a formidable military apparatus relative to its resources. Israel is small in size and population but maintains a military feared by its neighbors. Furthermore, the minor power does not need to balance against all the components of the potential hegemon's capabilities but only against those most threatening to its survival. For example, an island state can afford to focus its limited resources on coastal and air defense. Inversely, direct neighbors will likely forgo building a strong navy and concentrate their efforts on land forces (Lobell 2018).

However, this option implies that states have an untapped potential for both economic and military growth — namely, a sizeable population. Therefore, growth potential matters little for very small states of a few thousand or a few hundred thousand people. In addition, relative strengthening is workable only if the potential hegemon is relatively stagnant compared to oneself. If it is growing quicker, the prospects for improving the balance of power are slim. In theory, a minor power willing to grow can expand by conquering neighbors. But armed expansion is dangerous when a potential hegemon lurks nearby. The potential hegemon benefits from its neighbors fighting each other instead of balancing. The potential hegemon could even join forces with the neighbor under attack to defeat the attacker more easily than it could have alone. Thus, wars of conquest are most likely to remain the preserve of the potential hegemon and its allies. One thinks of the 2022 invasion of Ukraine.

Second, the stagnation or decline of the potential hegemon can incentivize weak states to balance. Schweller (1994, 96) suggests that states ride the "wave of the future" and may shift to bandwagoning if they perceive the hegemon as winning. The reverse may be true; weak states have more incentive to resist a hegemon if they believe it will fail. A minor power can perceive that the potential hegemon is losing and gets emboldened to balance either due to the hegemon's internal weakness or the balancing coalition's prowess. In that case, it makes sense to delay bandwagoning as long as possible and wait for the decline of the potential hegemon.

Third, a minor power may hope that the prospects of fighting a potent and enduring insurgency will be enough to deter the potential hegemon. Even if the

---

[3] Thoughtful discussions of state socialization and trial-and-error learning are Feinstein and Pirro (2021), Popescu (2017; 2018), Resende-Santos (1996), and Sinnreich (2014).

potential hegemon is well-positioned to conquer the minor power, it may fear the costs of fighting a counter-insurgency war for many months or years. According to this logic, "the prospect of waging a prolonged war for hearts and minds will convince a potential aggressor that an invasion is unlikely to work at a price it is willing to pay" (Lee and Hunzeker 2022). Not only would it cost dearly in blood and money, but it would also immobilize a significant part of its military, limiting its ability to expand further or even defend itself. Even if the minor power doubts that the prospect of insurgency will deter the potential hegemon, it could still hope that the insurgency will force it to withdraw from its lands over the long run. This is notably the three Baltic states' strategy to deter Russia (Flanagan et al. 2019; Petit 2023; Stringer 2021).

Nevertheless, states are not equal in their ability to muster a credible insurgency. A state's population may have ethnic links or cultural proximity with the potential hegemon. Alternatively, recently founded states and multiethnic societies may lack the strong nationalism that glues more ancient or homogenous states and thus be easier to subjugate. Aging societies may also prove more conquerable, as citizens of military age are less numerous. Furthermore, most states forbid the possession of military-grade weapons by civilians, rendering insurgency less potent. Remote geography can complexify attempts to obtain weapons from the outside world. In fact, scholarship suggests that insurgencies generally impose limited costs on a conqueror and that determined occupants generally extract benefits that outweigh costs (Liberman 1996; also, Van Evera 1999, chap. 5; Weisiger 2014). Hence, the important takeaway is not that insurgencies are likely to defeat the potential hegemon but that some minor powers may believe they are.

Fourth, a minor power can bet that a war will turn to its advantage despite an unfavorable prewar balance of power. It may believe it can defeat an attack or deny victory long enough to discourage the potential hegemon from pushing on. Weak states sometimes defeat stronger powers (Sullivan 2007). Great powers can under-commit to a war against a minor power, while the minor power will commit its resources to its full. Also, a minor power will sometimes receive support from abroad in quantity large enough to level the playing field. Thus, despite a significant power gap, a minor power may survive the onslaught. China withheld the superior Japanese from 1937 up to 1945. During the 1939–1940 Winter War, Finland contained a Soviet offensive despite the Soviet Union's overwhelming superiority. In 1979, Vietnam pushed back a Chinese attack. In 2022, Ukraine fared better against Russia than most had expected.

According to hegemonic realists, bandwagoning can increase one's security. But the reverse appears more accurate: bandwagoning increases the potential hegemon's ability to reach hegemony. Indeed, the bandwagoner places its military capabilities, economic might, and territory in the potential hegemon's hands. By adding warfighting capabilities and enlarging its geographic reach, the small ally bolsters its coercive power and thus its ability to compel more states to bandwagon.[4] Alternatively, a potential hegemon can 'milk' its satellite states for resources to increase its power resources to support its bid for hegemony.

Going one step further, allying with a potential hegemon is more dangerous than allying with an 'average' great power. It differs from the abandonment-entrapment dilemma of traditional alliance politics (Snyder 1984) because, within standard alliances, the partners share at least some common interests. A 'proxy-betrayal dilemma' replaces the traditional abandonment-entrapment dichotomy. A potential hegemon does not fear entrapment; it may even prefer its allies to pick fights with others and create instability to weaken and distract its adversaries. Iran's Foreign Minister Mohammad Zarif once confessed that Russia secretly tried to sabotage the 2015 nuclear deal because Moscow opposed normalization between Iran and the West (quoted in Katz 2021). The intentions of the Kremlin are transparent: it sees Tehran as a cock fighting the Westerners and distracting them away from balancing against Moscow.[5] In a similar fashion, Beijing has paid only lip service to anti-North Korean sanctions and has been reluctant to rein in North Korea for a sound strategic reason: if it were not for Pyongyang, Seoul, Tokyo, and Washington would have all latitude to focus solely on China (Blank 2021; Motin 2022c, 2022d). Abandonment is not a significant worry for the bandwagoner either; the danger of betrayal is more salient. The bandwagoner allies with the potential hegemon to avoid the costs of balancing. But it is left powerless to resist the potential hegemon's will. Thus, its primary concern is not abandonment but ending up as the potential hegemon's next target.

2. First Variable: Threat Severity

2.1. *Threat and Alignment*

This section defines threat and explains why offensive capabilities matter to understand alignment, even if not the sole factor. In international relations, power can be defined as "the inability to inflict [...] cost on another country's high-value interests, including territorial integrity and political survival, lives of its citizenry, and economic prosperity" (Ross 2006, 367). Hence, power primarily entails land military power. Ground forces represent the heart of power because human life and activity overwhelmingly take place on land (Mearsheimer 2014, chap. 4; Parent and Rosato 2015). Since the ultimate test of power is war, latent resources like population and wealth help little on the day of the battle (Aron 2004, chap. 2). Therefore, power is foremost the available

---

[4] For a discussion of coercion by proxy, see Bowen (2019).
[5] China and Russia likely think of each other the same way.

land military capabilities. Land power is necessary to seize and secure territory. In addition to allowing human life and economy, territories also offer natural resources of all types. The larger the territory, the more one has options to deploy military forces or withdraw if a war goes poorly. Due to that, states fiercely defend their territory. The British strategist Julian Corbett explained that

> since men live upon the land and not upon the sea, great issues between nations at war have always been decided — except in the rarest cases — either by what your army can do against your enemy's territory and national life, or else by the fear of what the fleet makes it possible for your army to do. (Quoted in Grygiel 2021, 103).

Naval, air, cyber power, and space operations can matter tremendously, but only to the extent that they support land power. Indeed, neither ships, aircraft, cyber tools, nor spacecraft can conquer and secure territory (Schinella 2019). Wars become contests of resolve when decisive land operations are not possible because air, sea, cyber, and space power can harm and destroy but not conquer. Such capabilities can inflict great pain, but a determined opponent can choose to continue fighting nonetheless (Pape 1996). On the contrary, the enemy's resolve matters less in a land war since the victorious side can seize control of the other's territory, destroy its state, and dissolve its military. Therefore, this study discusses, at times, air and naval power (especially in the chapter on Asia), but only to the extent it enables and augments land power.

The most powerful counterargument is that nuclear weapons rendered land power obsolete. Nuclear weapons offer the ability to damage the core of an enemy state without defeating it on the battlefield first. Some could thus claim that the nuclear revolution made seizing and holding territory unnecessary. First, most states appear to disagree and continued maintaining and modernizing their ground forces despite the introduction of nuclear weapons in 1945 (Bowen 2021; Lieber and Press 2020). As clear with the recent Russian invasion of Ukraine, states still view territorial control as paramount. Second, a nuclear strike may not suffice to eliminate an adversary. The target state may survive a nuclear strike, recover, and continue fighting. Tactical nuclear strikes have a limited impact on alerted, dispersed, and sufficiently protected ground troops (Miller 1985). Although a superior nuclear enemy may destroy one's nuclear arsenal in a single strike (Cote 2019; Lieber and Press 2017), ground forces are hard to swiftly destroy but can be quickly regenerated.[6] Additional land operations would be necessary to vanquish for good a stubborn enemy state. Third, a would-be invader can complicate its own task by using nuclear weapons.

---

[6] For a discussion of the fungibility of military power, see Lobell (2023).

Radioactive fallouts impede further military operations and destroy many valuable economic assets and infrastructures. Fourth, nuclear weapons represent the ultimate deterrent. An aggressor would recoil at depleting its nuclear arsenal for fear of decreasing its deterrent power and becoming vulnerable to an attack. Fifth, debilitating a sizeable enemy state demands using numerous nuclear weapons. However, nuclear detonations can create climate disruptions of planetary proportions, affecting both the attacker and the target (Xia, Robock, Scherrer et al. 2022).

Military power enables coercion, intimidation, threats, or limited force to prevent a behavior or gain concessions from another state. Coercion means pain or the promise thereof. Scholars usually identify two types of coercive diplomacy: deterrence and compellence (Biddle 2020). Deterrence aims to convince the target state not to engage in some behavior — often a military offensive — and compellence aims to force a new behavior. Both deterrence and compellence can be tools for a potential hegemon in its quest for regional hegemony and, therefore, need not be distinguished here. Coercive diplomacy often serves to remind the target to accommodate and respect the coercer's interests. The more one possesses coercive power — the ability to cause pain — the cheaper and the more effective coercion is (Boulding 1963).

Indeed, growing one's military power has an obvious advantage when employing coercion: "the less costly threats or inducements are to the sender, and the more costly or valuable they are to the target, the more credible and effective they will be" (Legro and Moravcsik 1999, 17). Nothing works better than military threats to convince another state of the seriousness of one's requests (Katagiri and Min 2019). For example, scholarship shows that the most potent nuclear powers make more credible threats because they appear readier to risk escalation (Kroenig 2018). The more powerful a state is, the more carefully one must craft its policies toward that state. Many states may feel the urge to self-censor their foreign policy when confronting a military juggernaut next door. They anticipate a violent response from the potential hegemon and thus refrain from harming its interests because of "the implicit threat to use [force] that is communicated simply by a state's having it available for use" (Art 1980, 5–6, fn. 2). Alignment choices occur in the shadow of, and in relation to, the potential hegemon's military power.

Contrary to Walt's (1987) balance-of-threat argument, there is no need here to account for the perceived intentions of the threatening states, as China and Russia's revisionist intentions are clear to most. China and Russia's quest for regional hegemony already pitted them against numerous weaker neighbors. As Roy (2019, 51) noticed, "China began to exhibit more assertive foreign-policy behaviour around 2009, a trend that has accelerated since Xi became China's paramount leader in 2012." In 2011, a Chinese ship fired toward Philippine fishing boats near the disputed Spratly Islands. In 2012, China seized the Scarborough Shoal, claimed by the Philippines, and began building islands in the Spratly and Paracel Islands the year after. In May 2014, a major showdown started with Vietnam when the state-owned China National Petroleum Corporation moved an oil rig into waters claimed by Hanoi. Anti-Chinese riots erupted in Vietnam, and gunfire was exchanged across the China-Vietnam land border, raising fears of war. Beyond the South China Sea, Beijing increased its incursions in Japanese waters after the Japanese state purchased land on the Senkaku Islands in 2012. High-profile border incidents between China and India in 2017 and 2020 threatened to degenerate into a broader conflict.

In 2007, Russia suspended compliance with the Treaty on Conventional Forces in Europe, showing its dissatisfaction with the post-Cold War balance of military power on the continent. Diplomatic and military incidents between Georgia and Russia multiplied throughout 2007 and 2008. At the April 2008 Bucharest summit, NATO promised the Georgians they would one day join the Alliance. The Russians then prepared for war, and when the Georgian army entered the separatist province of South Ossetia in August 2008, Moscow took the occasion to invade Georgia. The intensity of Russian coercive diplomacy increased after that. The Ukrainian Crisis of 2014 saw Russia annex the Crimean Peninsula and Russian troops enter Eastern Ukraine, where they fought the Ukrainian army masked as local separatists.

2.2. *Operationalizing Threat*

The potential hegemon must have the most formidable offensive land capabilities in its home region. In addition, the potential hegemon must also possess the air power to allow and support land operations. If the target is outside the reach of land forces, one may need the airlift capabilities to project ground troops to the target's territory. Advancing on land may be slow if one cannot bomb the enemy and impossible if the enemy maintains air superiority. Furthermore, naval power is a prerequisite to reach a target lying across a sea or an ocean. One must defeat the enemy's fleet, establish superiority over its shores, and land troops on its beaches. A potential hegemon may also need the naval capabilities to strike otherwise out-of-reach targets and may want to use its landing capabilities to open new fronts or unblock a stalemate on land. Conversely, the potential hegemon needs enough sea power (or sufficient land-based missile and air power) to ensure that nobody lands on its shores, gets close enough to strike important targets, or disturbs land operations. Furthermore, (contemporary) potential hegemons should want to possess significant space and cyber capabilities. The cyber and space domains are new layers that combine with the traditional three others (Gartzke 2013; Schneider, Schechter, and Shaffer 2022). Satellites enhance one's reconnaissance, targeting, and communication capabilities, while anti-satellite weapons deny these to the enemy. Cyberattacks can harm the enemy's economy and perturb its weapon systems and logistics.[7]

However, military capabilities alone tell little of a state's offensive power unless colored by geography. Geography matters tremendously because "the distribution of power explains whether or not the minor powers try to buck-pass, then geography accounts for the identity of the buck-passers," specifically, "weak states in close proximity to the great power realize they have little choice but to form a coalition" while "states that are further away from their adversary, or separated from it by other states, mountain ranges, or large bodies of water, are not as fearful of being conquered and are therefore more likely to pass the buck" (Rosato 2011, 35; also, Gray 2006, chap. 9; Walt 1985, 10–11; Webb 2007). Indeed, geography can negate a potential hegemon's superiority in military capabilities. Terrain features like seas, mountains, deserts, jungles, dense forests, lakes, and rivers can help defend against a stronger invader (Mitchell 2018). Large urban areas can also become formidable obstacles (Bracken 1976). The reverse is true, and plain terrain with few obstacles magnifies a potential hegemon's superior firepower.

To summarize, the threat severity is the relative capability of the potential hegemon to conquer a minor power's territory. It accounts for the offensive power of the potential hegemon, the military capabilities of the defender, and the impact of geography. In the empirical part, I will describe the military balance between the potential hegemon and each bandwagoner and assess whether the threat severity is high or low.

High. The potential hegemon is likely able to conquer the target state in totality or at least its core territory, and the attack can begin on short notice. The conventional balance is the most unfavorable when the potential hegemon can perform a blitzkrieg on the target state. A blitzkrieg succeeds when the attacker's armored forces penetrate the rears of the defender and move fast enough so the defender's forces cannot regroup and stop the breakthrough. The attacker can then attack the defender's lines of communications and essential targets to destroy the enemy's warfighting capacity. A blitzkrieg avoids the bloody and lengthy battles of an attrition war, which entails high costs to the attacker for an uncertain outcome (Mearsheimer 1983, chap. 2; also, Reiter 1999). However, in the cases studied here, an attrition war can still be attractive due to the sheer disproportion of power between a potential hegemon and its

---

[7] Although usually not decisively (Maschmeyer 2021). Gartzke remarks that "whether an actor can benefit from cyberwar depends almost entirely on whether the actor is able to combine a cyberattack with some other method — typically kinetic warfare — that can convert temporary advantages achieved over the internet into a lasting effect" (2013, 57–58).

weak neighbors. In some cases, a potential hegemon will be able to overrun a weak neighbor even if a blitzkrieg is unworkable because of the defender's terrain or force posture. The target state may still turn the fight into an attrition war but would probably lose within weeks or a few months.

Low. The potential hegemon can harm the target state but has no straightforward path to conquer it or its core territory. Typically, the potential hegemon will only be able to capture border areas or peripheric territories on short notice. The potential hegemon might be able to conquer the target state if it mobilizes all its capabilities, but this would take a multi-month effort, if feasible at all. Due to distance or natural barriers, the potential hegemon may only have the means to hit the target state with air and sea power, standoff weapons, or raid it but will be unable to conquer and hold its core territory.

In the case studies, I investigate threat severity in two steps. First, I describe the material threat severity for each case. Then, I analyze primary and secondary materials to confirm that decision-makers perceived the same threat severity.[8] This two-step method is necessary for the theory to remain falsifiable. Indeed, a neorealist theory rests on the explanatory power of material capabilities (Narizny 2017). Thus, one must show that decision-makers react to material threats in ways predicted by the theory. If one focuses only on threat perception without first giving their own assessment of the military balance, then the theory becomes unfalsifiable.

3. Second Variable: Third-Party Conflict

A conflict with a third is a diplomatic confrontation with a neighbor (that is not the potential hegemon) severe enough to influence the alignment decisions and orient the military posture of a state. When embroiled in a conflict with a third, a state may bandwagon for security to avoid the potential hegemon's wrath or for profit to gain the upper hand against the third. A conflict with a third creates a path dependency. The rise of a potential hegemon pushes states to reorient their military posture to oppose it. But conflicting states have their armed forces already arrowed toward each other. If one of the two rivals decides unilaterally to reorient its force posture towards the potential hegemon, the second state may use the opportunity to attack the first one or blackmail it to extract large concessions. Furthermore, one of the two may conclude that it could gain the support of the potential hegemon to solve the conflict on favorable terms before turning to balance if needed.

The potential hegemon has an obvious interest in fueling conflicts among neighbors. Endorsing a neighbor in a dispute with a third state is a cheap and

---

[8] A defense of such methodology is Martin (2003; also, Telhami 2003: 108–109).

attractive way to divide actual or potential balancers and further its hegemonic bid (Crawford 2011, 172). If the potential hegemon has a bone to pick with the said third state in the first place, the target state becomes a welcomed addition of military strength.[9] The target state may even turn into a partner in coercion, helping the potential hegemon promote its interests (Smetana and Ludvik 2019). Even if the potential hegemon has no quarrel with that third state, it benefits from its neighbors fighting each other instead of pushing back against itself.

During the 1960s, the Soviets benefited from the Cypriot dispute to stir up conflict among NATO members by alternatively supporting Greece against Turkey and then Turkey against Greece. During the late 1970s, the Soviet Union backed Vietnam in its claims over the Spratly Islands with the hope of turning Hanoi into an enemy of China (Crawford 2011, 173–174). More recently, China has taken the party of North Korea against South Korea and Pakistan against India, while Russia helped Belarus in its feud with Lithuania and Poland.

On the systemic level, the logic of minimum winning coalitions helps explain that minor power states can refuse to join a strong balancing coalition because it could infringe on their interests or even their survival (Riker 1962; Walt 1985, 5–6; Waltz 1979, 127). Consider a situation where a potential hegemon A possesses 45% of the system's total power while states B and C each have 25%, and minor power D has 5%. If D joins a balancing coalition with B and C, the B-C-D coalition will successfully overpower A, but then B and C will be free to treat weak D as they please. Due to this logic, states are likely to remain wary of security cooperation with threatening neighbors, even in the face of a hegemonic threat (Byun 2022).[10]

Note that third rivals need not be recognized or established states. Parties in a civil war are often proto-state since they are political entities controlling a territory, a population, and maintaining an army. Like conflicts with third states, civil wars distract governments from focusing on international threats (Mishali-Ram 2022). A state threatened by a rebel army approaching its capital will have little energy for balancing against a potential hegemon. Contrary to 'omnibalancing' theorists (David 1991), who see states as balancing against internal political opposition, this book's addition of rebel armies does not violate the neorealist core. In neorealism, legal or symbolic recognition matters little. What counts is whether a political entity has effective control over a territory. In that sense, the Houthis in Yemen, the Libyan National Army, the Tigray People's Liberation Front, and the Wa State in Myanmar are no less states

---

[9] Consider China's growing support for Pakistan against India over the Kashmir issue (Kurita 2022).

[10] However, in the long run, the fear caused by the potential hegemon should alleviate or even extinguish preexisting conflicts, like the fear of the Soviet Union pushed France and Germany closer or rendered the China-Taiwan conflict dormant during the 1970s–1980s.

than France or China. Unrecognized states and territorial entities also obey the logic of anarchy. Ignoring real-world actors for the sake of legalism or symbolism risks misrepresenting states' calculations.

All the bandwagoning states under study confronted third rivals on an enduring basis. The empirical part traces the intensity of third-party conflicts and notes the period where third conflicts grew in intensity or winded down. I rank conflict intensity from low to high depending on the probability of war. 'Low' denotes relatively cordial relations marked by diplomatic engagement. 'Medium' implies limited contacts, hostile rhetoric, and sometimes limited border skirmishes. 'High' describes intense tensions where diplomacy is inexistent, and war appears possible.[11]

4. Third Variable: U.S. Assistance

The last explanatory variable is U.S. assistance. For Asia and Europe, the United States is an outside great power. The assistance of a third great power like the United States can matter for two reasons. First, a state neighboring a potential hegemon may want assistance from a great power to increase its odds of survival against this threatening juggernaut. Second, support from a third great power counteracts the allure of appealing to a potential hegemon's backing against a third.

The ablest state to deter or eventually defeat a great power is another great power. Other minor powers can provide support, but they are unlikely to match what can provide a great power. Security guarantees from minor powers will probably not suffice to deter a potential hegemon. Hence, great power assistance matters enormously when deciding whether to bandwagon with a potential hegemon or resist. Conversely, other great powers generally have a deep-seated interest in ensuring that a potential hegemon does not turn into an actual one. Even a great power located in a distant region like the United States will fear the rise of a regional hegemon because it could become powerful enough to project significant power toward the Western Hemisphere (Mearsheimer 2014, chap. 7; Motin 2022b; Walt 2018; also, Thompson 1992). The more an ally promises to be helpful during a general war, the more the third great power will accept to give significant inducements to keep it away from the potential hegemon (Crawford 2014). A great power balancer can go to great lengths to reassure minor powers that may defect to join the potential hegemon (Blankenship 2020).[12] Rosato makes this point well:

---

[11] The category 'very high' is used in the case of Armenia only, which experienced open warfare with Azerbaijan.

[12] Reassurance seeks "to influence another actor's behavior by alleviating a perceived source of insecurity and/or giving the actor a greater sense of security" (Knopf 2012, 378).

an offshore balancer is least secure when another region is dominated by a single state, it wants as many competing power centers as possible in that region. Therefore, it is likely to welcome and promote the formation of any formidable minor power coalition. (Rosato 2011, 28)

The balancing great power can also help by allaying conflicts between minor powers, thus reducing the allure of bandwagoning and alleviating the collective action problem. A state willing to balance against a potential hegemon but embroiled in a third conflict will be wary of reorienting its military posture away from the preexisting rival. A great power can give security assurances against the third rival, hence diminishing the cost of balancing against the potential hegemon. The great power can also push the third state toward restraint and accommodation so that the other is free to balance (Choi and Alexandrova 2020). If no great power is willing to support a weak state facing both a third rival and the potential hegemon, it is left in a desperate situation. Bandwagoning becomes a reasonable option, however risky.

Among potential great power allies, offshore (like Britain for modern Europe) and extra-regional ones (like the United States for contemporary Asia and Europe) are especially attractive. An extra-regional great power can provide support while being geographically distant enough not to threaten regional states' survival (Mearsheimer 2014, chap. 7; Schuessler, Shifrinson, and Blagden 2021).[13] Indeed, there is ample evidence that states do not balance against offshore great powers (Elman 2004; Levy and Thompson 2010). Note that a balancing coalition counting a single great power will be more cohesive and more able to reduce intra-coalition conflicts since it has a clear leader (Choi 2021).

The most potent and reassuring type of assistance is a significant military presence on the ground (Blankenship and Lin-Greenberg 2022; also, Lee 2021). Great power can also improve a balancing state's odds by providing military support like weapons, money, technologies, training, and intelligence. Weapons notably provide reassurance and bolster the client's combat capabilities without the giver risking being dragged into a war it does not want (Yarhi-Milo, Lanoszka, and Cooper 2016). Great power can increase others' capability to balance by bolstering their economy (Beckley, Horiuchi, and Miller 2018; Blackwill and Harris 2016). Great power support also matters in more indirect ways. It can help create multilateral arrangements and institutions to maximize

---

[13] However, if extra-regional great powers are busy with power competition near their borders, they are unlikely to provide much support against a potential hegemon (Elman 2004). Also, this does not mean that alliance with the United States does not come with strings attached (Cha 2010), but simply that aligning with Washington does not threaten a state's survival in the way aligning with Beijing or Moscow does.

the balancing coalition's military and economic efficiency. Multilateral institutions put the states of the balancing coalition on the same page and thus increase their ability to resist the potential hegemon. Economic institutions aim to bolster the growth of the balancing states, and military institutions aim to harmonize military strategies and doctrines and improve interoperability (Creswell 2002; Mearsheimer 2019, 9–11; Rosato 2011). A small amount of great power reassurance is sometimes enough to harden a minor power's resolution to balance, and even remote prospects of great power assistance can push a minor power to resist an aggressor:

> For a weak state to balance against a strong aggressor, the former seems to require only a Great Power's willingness to provide assistance in the immediate future. Weak states need the hope that the aggressor will ultimately be defeated to balance against it. That the weak state might suffer considerable destruction in the meantime rarely affects this inclination to balance. (Labs 1992, 393)

In all the cases under study, U.S. assistance generally remains low. The empirical part traces when U.S. assistance for each bandwagoner increased or decreased. U.S. support is ranked from medium to none (medium, low, none). Medium support implies a low level of economic and military aid, occasional high-level contacts, and non-confrontational declarations. Low support sees almost no material aid, but diplomacy continues. No support denotes the total absence of high-level diplomacy or even favorable rhetoric. In some cases, the United States is outright hostile, threatening to use force or oust the target government.

5. Argument and Hypotheses

In a region comprising a potential hegemon, as a general rule, most of the potential hegemon's neighbors will either balance against it or choose buck-passing depending on specific situations, while only a handful of neighbors will bandwagon. But when does bandwagoning become likely? The likelihood and intensity of bandwagoning can be predicted by variations in the three variables introduced in this chapter (*Figure 2.1*). Although all forms of bandwagoning share the absence of balancing behaviors against the potential hegemon, at this stage, it becomes necessary to divide bandwagoning into three different types: accommodation, full alignment, and captivity (*Table 2.1*).

Figure 2.1. Explaining bandwagoning

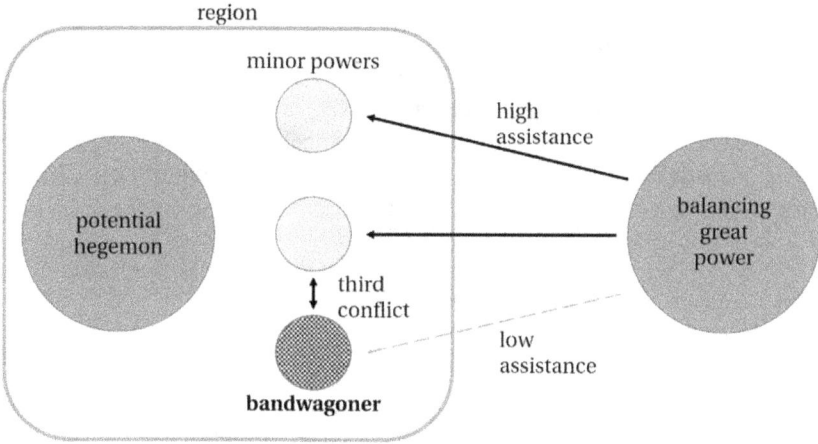

region

minor powers

high
assistance

potential
hegemon

balancing
great
power

third
conflict

low
assistance

bandwagoner

Table 2.1. Level of bandwagoning

Level	Type	Description
low	accommodation	mostly aligned, but maintains a distance
high	full alignment	closely aligned, limited relations with balancing states
total	captivity	totally aligned, foreign policy autonomy lost

The loosest form of bandwagoning is *accommodation.* The accommodating state has the potential hegemon for its principal security partner and may even have troops on its soil. However, the accommodator maintains substantive relations with actual or potential balancing states. Its foreign policy does not always align with the potential hegemon, sometimes leading to open criticism or low-key disputes. *Full alignment* means to ally closely with the potential hegemon and follow its foreign policy preferences loyally. The bandwagoner will maintain only poor relationships with balancing states. Conflicts and disagreements with the potential hegemon remain rare and muted. *Captivity* means that the state lost its sovereignty in foreign policy-making to the potential hegemon. Typically, this happens when the potential hegemon penetrates the state apparatus to the extent that significant decisions are impossible without its consent.[14] The risk of captivity is what makes bandwagoning such a dangerous choice for minor powers. The potential hegemon is now in charge; a captive state enters a hierarchical relation with it. This hierarchic relation allows for a level of trust unlikely in normal interstate relations.[15] In that case, this book's theoretical framework does not apply anymore since a captive state's foreign policy is decided elsewhere. Therefore, I do not investigate cases of captive states. *Table 2.2* relates bandwagoning and accommodation to the three causal variables.

Table 2.2. Alignment choices toward a potential hegemon

Threat severity	Third conflict?	U.S. assistance?	Outcome	Cases
high	yes	none	full alignment (1)	Belarus (2020–2), Myanmar (2021–2)
high	yes	low	survival accommodation (2)	Belarus (2008–20), Myanmar (2008–21)
low	yes	none/low	profit accommodation (3)	Armenia, Cambodia, North Korea, Pakistan, Serbia
any other combination			balancing, buck-passing, etc.	all others

Full alignment (1). If fear leads to balancing, hopelessness leads to full alignment. A minor state confronting an imminent threat, embroiled in a third conflict, and deprived of great power assistance faces odds so poor that it becomes likely to fully bandwagon. Conflicts with thirds already complicate balancing efforts against the potential hegemon by immobilizing a minor power's limited resources elsewhere. Furthermore, the minor power receives no relief from the United States — which may even be overtly hostile — and is left to its devices to confront both the third rival(s) and the potential hegemon. Finally, said potential hegemon has an overwhelming military advantage over the minor state and can probably subjugate it on short notice. Therefore, the minor state is in a desperate situation because it has no bargaining power against the potential hegemon and

---

[14] The member states of the Warsaw Pact during the Cold War belong in that category.
[15] Discussions of hierarchy in IR are Butt (2013), Lake (2007) and Nexon and Wright (2007).

no realistic way to deter it either. In that case, preventive total bandwagoning is preferable to subordination or outright destruction at its hands.

Survival accommodation (2). When the threat is high, the natural tendency is to balance to counter the threat. However, the state is embroiled in third conflicts that endanger its security and has to survive with limited U.S. support. This poor situation leaves the minor power with little solution other than to appease the potential hegemon and "seek safety by getting on the bandwagon of an ascending power, hoping somehow to escape complete subjugation once their powerful 'friend' has gained supremacy" (Wolfers 1962, 124). Nevertheless, working relations with the United States offer some bargaining power and the hope of more considerable support in the future or in a crisis. The main difference between accommodation and full alignment comes from the potential hegemon's inability to compel the minor power to align closely with its preferences. The potential hegemon's overwhelming power threatens to compel the minor power to fully bandwagon with it, but the minor power tries hard to maintain its foreign policy autonomy. While the potential hegemon can *dictate* to a full bandwagoner, it can only *suggest* to an accommodator. Minor powers faced with the full might of a potential hegemon face an immediate existential threat. For those states, solving or at least allaying third conflicts and gaining U.S. support is more urgent than for less threatened minor powers. Therefore, survival accommodators should tend to offer concessions to third rivals or the United States more often than profit accommodators, who have more leeway to pursue other interests.

Profit accommodation (3). When the threat is remote, avoiding a costly balancing effort and buck-passing is the natural tendency. However, the state is embroiled in third conflicts that endanger its security and has to survive without support from the United States. In such a weak position, accommodating the potential hegemon becomes attractive; it is better to be in bad company than alone. Because the potential hegemon has limited military options against the minor power (due to its formidable military or geographic distance), the minor power can maintain a high level of foreign policy autonomy. This type of accommodation relates to Schweller's (1994) 'bandwagoning for profit' because the minor power uses the potential hegemon's support to further its own goals. Conversely, (1) and (2) are akin to 'bandwagoning for survival.' When the potential hegemon's threat is less severe, minor powers should feel more strongly threatened by preexisting third rivals. Also, receiving U.S. assistance is less urgent since a swift defeat at the hands of the potential hegemon is a more distant prospect. In such a case, the profit accommodator is in less of a hurry to terminate third conflicts or receive more U.S. assistance since the threat is less immediate. Because it has more freedom, it will likely ask for concessions from third states or the United States before shifting sides. Therefore, one would expect profit accommodators to align with a potential hegemon primarily due to threats from third rivals and less due to the lack of U.S. support (*Figure 2.2*).

Figure 2.2. Alignment intensity with a potential hegemon

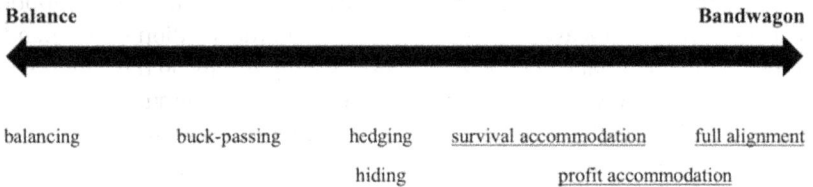

To summarize, the intensity of bandwagoning varies alongside the threat severity, the intensity of third conflicts, and the level of U.S. assistance. This book describes bandwagoning intensity by listing all major shifts of each bandwagoner's policy toward the potential hegemon. The empirical part classifies bandwagoning as increasing when the bandwagoner seeks the potential hegemon's support, voluntarily accepts greater influence, or takes the initiative to support the potential hegemon's foreign policy. Conversely, bandwagoning decreases when the bandwagoner limits the potential hegemon's influence, actively reduces political and military interactions, criticizes the potential hegemon, or seeks better relations with rivals of the potential hegemon. Based on this discussion, a set of hypotheses can be extracted and tested:

H1. Bandwagoning should be a minority choice among regional states.

H2. The best predictor of bandwagoning with a potential hegemon is the combination of a conflict with a third and the absence of great power assistance.

H3. Changes in the severity of third conflicts and the level of great power assistance should be correlated to alignment shifts.

H4. When threat severity is high, third conflicts are intense, and great power assistance is nonexistent, the minor power should choose full alignment.

H5. Survival accommodators should be more willing than profit accommodators to make concessions to rivals and the United States.

H6. For-profit accommodators, shifts in alignment should correlate closely with the severity of third conflicts.

Chapter III

Cases in Europe

1. Background

This chapter treats Europe as a regional grouping coherent enough to be studied in isolation from the other regions of the world. Europe is delimited by the Ural Mountains in the East, the Mediterranean Sea and the Lesser Caucasus Mountains in the South, the Atlantic Ocean in the West, and the Greenland Sea in the North. Although it possesses lands on the European continent, Turkey is not considered a European state because the core of the Turkish state centers on Anatolia. The Vatican is also excluded, being a state only in name. Inversely, the study includes the unrecognized small states of Eastern Europe. Although they do not exist in international law, they are *de facto* states.

Russia is primarily a European power. Although Russia's territory spans both Asia and Europe, the core of the Russian state is its European part. Three-fourths of the population and the overwhelming majority of the economic activity are concentrated there, as well as most of the country's military capabilities. Except for the Mongols in the thirteenth century, all the existential threats to the Russian state came from its western borders (notably Poland, Turkey, Sweden, France, Germany, and NATO). Nowadays, Russia does not fear China much. Although Russia directly borders China, the European core of Russia is several thousand kilometers away from China. A continental-scale land attack originating from Asia to invade Russia is a nonstarter. Russia knows that Asian states cannot threaten its survival as European states can. During the 1930s, before Germany became a formidable military power, Japan was the most powerful threat to the Soviet Union (Haslam 1992, chaps. 1–4). Nevertheless, even then, the Soviets kept maintaining most of their military to guard their European borders.

2. Balance of Power

This section justifies that Russia was the strongest power, and ultimately a potential hegemon, in Europe between 2008 and 2022. It first describes its military capabilities in numbers before discussing them in qualitative terms.

2.1. *Quantitative Discussion of Power*

This section argues that Russia had the strongest military force in the region during the period, at least in numbers. Data from the 2011 and 2021 editions of

The Military Balance are used to count the total military personnel, the ground troops, the main battle tanks, the armored fighting vehicles, the artillery pieces, and the combat aircraft of the leading European powers — Russia, France, Germany, Italy, Poland, the United Kingdom, and Ukraine (*Tables 3.1* and *3.2*). For Mearsheimer (2014, 45), a potential hegemon is a great power markedly stronger than any other great power and potentially potent enough to defeat two opponents in tandem. Although Russia was the sole great power in Europe for the period, I apply this standard to the regional level. Russia was the strongest state in Europe between 2008 and 2022, far above France or Germany. In 2010, Russia already had almost twice as many ground troops as France and Germany combined and more than twice as many troops as the two combined in 2020.

Table 3.1. Balance of conventional forces in Europe, 2010

	Total personnel	Ground forces*	Main battle tanks**	Armored fighting vehicles	Artillery***	Combat aircraft****
Russia	1,046,000	406,500	3,310 (18,000)	18,730 (14,500)	6,167 (21,695)	1,449
France	238,591	133,100	254	4,149	375	289 (10)
Germany	251,465	105,291	768 (384)	4,201	824	318
Italy	184,609	109,500	320	3,332	965	255
Poland	100,000	48,950	946	1,576	1,136	115
U.K.	178,470	109,440	325	2,727	688	189
Ukraine	129,925	73,753	2,988	4,460	3,351	211
Russian percentage	49	41	37 (78)	48 (62)	46 (79)	51 (51)

Source: International Institute for Strategic Studies. 2011. *The Military Balance, 2011.* Abingdon: Routledge.
Note: Weapons in store are indicated within parentheses. Percentages have been rounded.
* Including special forces, naval infantry, and airborne forces, excluding paramilitary forces.
** Including naval infantry and airborne forces, excluding paramilitary forces (Russian paramilitaries hold significant heavy weaponry).
*** Including rocket artillery, excluding paramilitary forces (Russian paramilitaries hold significant heavy weaponry).
**** Including naval aviation, excluding training aircraft and strategic bombers.

Table 3.2. Balance of conventional forces in Europe, 2020

	Total personnel	Ground forces*	Main battle tanks**	Armored fighting vehicles	Artillery***	Combat aircraft****
Russia	900,000	361,000	3,330 (10,200)	15,047 (14,500)	5,689 (22,985)	1,083
France	203,250	116,900	222	3,135	265	249
Germany	183,500	63,400	245 (78)	2,121	262	228
Italy	165,500	99,700	200	1,426	976	213
Poland	114,050	61,650	808	2,064	719	94
U.K.	148,500	90,100	227	1,299	637	162
Ukraine	209,000	156,500	987 (1,132)	2,091	1,960 (83)	125
Russian percentage	47	38	55 (78)	55 (71)	54 (85)	50

Source: International Institute for Strategic Studies. 2021. *The Military Balance, 2021.* Abingdon: Routledge.
Note: Weapons in store are indicated within parentheses. Percentages have been rounded.
* Including special forces, naval infantry, and airborne forces, excluding paramilitary forces.
** Including naval infantry and airborne forces, excluding paramilitary forces (Russian and Ukrainian paramilitaries hold significant heavy weaponry).
*** Including rocket artillery, excluding paramilitary forces (Russian and Ukrainian paramilitary forces hold significant heavy weaponry).
**** Including naval aviation, excluding training aircraft and strategic bombers.

Furthermore, the IISS' data likely underestimate Russia's ground troop numbers. According to the IISS' *The Military Balance 2021*, the Russian army counted 280,000 troops and the U.S. Army 485,000. Although the Russian figure represents more than the French, British, and German armies combined (respectively 115,000, 83,000, and 63,000 troops), it remains far from the U.S. one. But this way of counting is faulty and misrepresents Russia's true power. Army aviation, airborne, support, and railway troops are not counted as army personnel in Russia while they are in the U.S. Army. Therefore, Russian ground forces for 2020 would be closer to 470,000 if the American way was taken as a yardstick (Binkov 2021). This is close to the U.S. figure and the equivalent of four French, six British, or seven German armies.

Data for military spending tells a similar story (*Figure 3.1*). Russia enjoyed a clear lead over its European competitors for the whole period. After 2012, Russian military expenditures were always at least twice as large as any other state. Russia has hovered between 150 and 200 billion dollars after 2014, while no other European state reached the 70 billion mark.

Figure 3.1. Military expenditures in Europe, 2008–2020, PPP (billion USD)

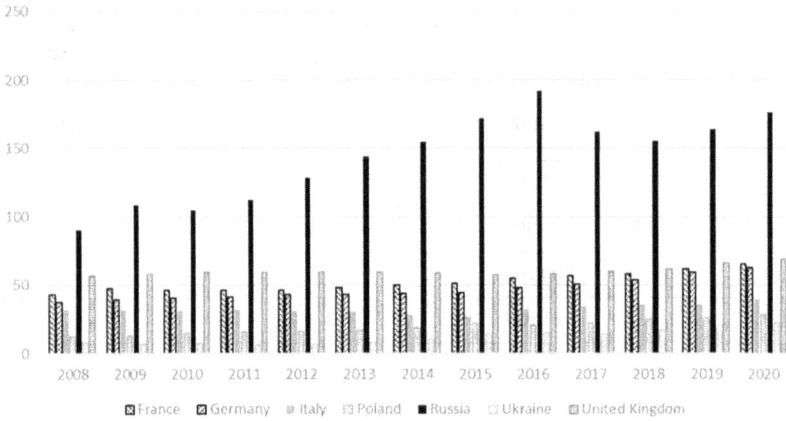

Source: The author's calculation, based on World Bank. https://data.worldbank.org/ (accessed 2022, January 22).

Russia also appears to be the most populous European state. Its population equals France and Germany combined, and it possessed for the period around 30% of the total population of the seven leading European states (*Table 3.3*). To conclude, in terms of numbers, Moscow constantly had more military power than any other European state and more than any tandem of them. Nevertheless, numbers do not tell the whole story and must be contrasted by qualitative considerations.

Table 3.3. Population of the main European states, 2010, 2020

	2010	2020
Russia	142,849,468	144,104,080
France	65,027,505	67,391,582
Germany	81,776,930	83,240,525
Italy	59,277,417	59,554,023
Poland	38,042,794	37,950,802
U.K.	62,766,365	67,215,293
Ukraine	45,870,741	44,134,693
Russian percentage	29	29

Source: World Bank. https://data.worldbank.org/ (accessed 2022, January 5).
Note: Percentages have been rounded. These numbers do not reflect Russia's annexation of Crimea in 2014 and the subsequent Ukrainian loss of Donetsk and Luhansk.

2.2. *Qualitative Discussion of Power*

The collapse of the Soviet Union in 1991, the economic malaise that ensued, and the overall lack of leadership in the new Russia led the Russian military to the brink of collapse. The First Chechen War (1994–1996) saw the Russian army crippled by weak command, faulty tactics, and low morale. The 1998 economic crisis almost completed the military third-worldization of Russia. But Vladimir Putin's rise to power in late 1999, combined with a long-term increase in oil prices, gave Russia the political impetus and the money to start rebuilding its power.

The resurrection of Russian power during the 2000s was magnified by the decline of the military capabilities of most other European states. While the Russians poured significant money into their military after 2000, the Europeans reaped the 'dividends of peace' by decreasing their spendings and scraping large numbers of troops and weaponry. Even if West European militaries had a considerable advantage in terms of training, morale, and technology at the beginning of the period, they abandoned their ability to fight large conventional wars while the Russians were rebuilding it (Meijer and Brooks 2021).

The quality of Russia's military quickly improved after the 2008 Georgia War as budgets increased, training and exercises became more systematic, and newer weapons entered into service. Many European militaries have little actual combat experience, and those which have conducted mostly counter-insurgency warfare (notably Britain and France). Meanwhile, Russian forces acquired extensive experience in both irregular (the Chechen and Syrian campaigns) as well as high-intensity conventional warfare (the Georgian and Donbas campaigns). Furthermore, significant reforms were adopted in 2010. They notably restructured the officer corps and military education, reorganized the military commands and created four new Joint Strategic Commands to replace the old military districts, outsourced maintenance, catering, and similar services to commercial providers, transformed paper units into permanent readiness units, reorganized the reservist training system, and increased the share of professional soldiers (Jesse 2020, chap. 3; Kashin 2021, 906–907).

Other factors favor Moscow still more. Russian units are heavier in terms of artillery, armor, and air defense, while equivalent Western units are generally lighter and more oriented toward counter-insurgency operations. Russia continued the Soviet practice of using airborne troops as the spearhead for offensive operations. Therefore, the Airborne Troops branch was high in priority for modernization and training. It not only received modernized airdroppable infantry fighting vehicles but also became heavier by introducing tank companies after 2015 (Elfving 2021). European militaries lack a similar capability for rapid and massive deployment. Moscow also progressed by leaps and bounds in electronic warfare and has a lead over all its potential European opponents (McCrory 2020). The Russians possess extensive tactical nuclear strike capabilities, while no European state does. Finally, the balance of power shifted all the more in Russia's favor thanks to the decreasing U.S. presence in Europe. While close to 115,000 U.S. military personnel were present in Europe around 2000, only 64,000 were left in 2015 (Kane 2016, 5).

Russia is not and has never been a competitive trading nation but always succeeded in remaining among the great powers of the world; Russia is what Sokoloff called the 'poor power' (1996; also, Fuller 1992). However, trading nations are the first to suffer when international trade collapses. Russia has abundant natural resources, a large pallet of industrial capabilities, and is self-sufficient in the defense sector. Although Russia may not be the next China, it can sustain prolonged security competition. To do so, the most important is to maintain a weapon industry capable of furnishing up-to-date weaponry in sufficient quantity and without relying on foreign suppliers.

Shortly after Putin's rise to power, and motivated by the U.S. withdrawal from the Anti-Ballistic Missile Treaty in 2002, Moscow focused on rejuvenating its capabilities in weapon development and production, at first primarily in strategic weapons. During the 2000s, Russia accelerated the production of newer ballistic missiles. Moscow maintained a high level of research and development expenditure relative to weapons procurement. The 2008 war with Georgia gave Russia an additional impetus to accelerate the reform of the weapon industry. Syria served as a shooting range to test and improve Russian equipment (Kashin 2021). Russia also strives to compete in newer fields, such as artificial intelligence (Edmonds et al. 2021). Despite delays in production and setbacks due to the loss of its Western and Ukrainian suppliers after 2014, there is little doubt that the Russian military industry can easily sustain its ground, air, and strategic forces.

Regarding shipbuilding, one can see the glass as either half empty or half full. The shipbuilding industry was slow to catch up with more efficient trends in construction techniques during the Soviet era, while the lost years of the 1990s and 2000s nearly killed Russia's potential in the sector. Putin naturally tried to salvage Russia's capability to produce large, advanced ships of all types by pouring money into the sector. According to the State Armament Programme 2011–2020,

> the Russian shipbuilding industry was required to deliver 24 submarines and 54 surface naval ships in the main categories by 2020. In order to handle this task, the shipbuilding industry needed to modernise their

industrial parks in parallel. However, as of January 2018, the industry had only succeeded in building 10 submarines and 16 surface naval ships, with a total displacement of some 127,000 tonnes. [...] In comparison, China managed to build 37 analogous naval ships, with a combined displacement of almost 240,000 tonnes, and the United States, 24 ship units with a displacement over 370,000 tonnes, in the same period. (Malmlöf 2021, 21)

On one side, Russia failed to build as many ships as it wished to and fell in this regard far behind China and the United States. But on the other, Moscow managed to launch numerous new ships — much more than any European state — despite the structural weaknesses of the shipbuilding industries and its limited budget.

Russia's armies still have major deficiencies: many of the rear units rely on conscripts, and units in central and Asian Russia lagged in modernization. It is also unclear how far from its border Russian logistics can support combat forces (Connable et al. 2020; Vershinin 2021). However, Moscow maintains by far the strongest army in Europe, and this superiority increased between 2008 and 2022.

3. Case Selection

The European region counts seven largely unrecognized states: Abkhazia, Artsakh, the Donetsk People's Republic, Kosovo, the Luhansk People's Republic, South Ossetia, and Transnistria. All of them except Kosovo bandwagoned with Russia. However, Russia helped create five of them (Abkhazia, the Donetsk People's Republic, the Luhansk People's Republic, South Ossetia, and Transnistria), which are led by Russian officials and take orders from Moscow. Therefore, these five proto-states can hardly be considered fully functional states and are captives of the Kremlin. Lastly, Artsakh is a small breakaway proto-state of Azerbaijan and depends on Armenia for its sustenance. Since Artsakh depends on Armenia for its survival, and Armenia bandwagons with Russia, Artsakh bandwagons with Russia by extension. Among non-captive states, only Armenia, Belarus, and Serbia experienced both a third conflict and hostile relations with the United States or lost U.S. support during the 2008–2022 period (Appendix 1, *Table A1.2*).

There is a consensus that Armenia is a close ally of Russia, although it maintains foreign policy independence (Delcour and Wolczuk 2015; Kopalyan and Ohanyan 2022; Shirinyan 2019; Ter-Matevosyan et al. 2017; Vasilyan 2017). Experts agree that Belarus mostly aligned with Russia, although it kept its distance from Moscow until 2020 (Cepurītis 2017; Golts 2017; Götz 2023; Muzyka 2021; Nizhnikau and Moshes 2020). Serbia is often described as the European state the closest to Russia outside the former Soviet Union. For Clark (2018), Serbia is "pro-Russian and anti-NATO." Yet, alignment is not total, and Belgrade maintains margins of maneuver vis-à-vis Moscow (Galeotti 2018; Kraemer 2022).

4. Armenia

Armenia is a small, landlocked state located in the Caucasus region. It borders Artsakh, Azerbaijan, Georgia, Iran, and Turkey and has around three million people. Armenia became formally independent in 1991 when the Soviet Union collapsed. Despite ups and downs, Yerevan remained aligned with Russia throughout the 2008–2022 period, but it never fully bandwagoned with Moscow. The Armenian case is important for this book's theoretical claims since the country experienced a shift from autocracy to democracy. *Innenpolitik* theorists would expect democratization to push Armenia away from authoritarian Russia. It can thus help check whether domestic regime matters to explain bandwagoning.

4.1. *Threat Severity*

Armenia is ill-prepared to face a great power onslaught. The Armenian military is overall small, with around 40,000 troops. Although the Armenians have extensive combat experience, the army still rests on conscripts, and most weapons lack modernization. The air force is weak and unable to sustain high-intensity warfare. The defeat during the 2020 war against Azerbaijan compelled Yerevan to engage in major reforms of its military (IISS 2022, 181–182).

Armenian geography neither favors nor disadvantages a Russian invader. Northern and Eastern Armenia, where a Russian invading force would come from, is mainly mountainous. Lake Sevan would complicate the approach of the capital from the Northeast. However, the only major city is Yerevan, and Armenia is a tiny country. Furthermore, winter is relatively mild, even if snowfalls can be abundant in mountainous areas. All in all, Armenia would appear unlikely to survive a Russian invasion.

Yerevan finds its salvation in its distance from Russia. Indeed, the two are non-contiguous and separated by Azerbaijan and Georgia. Neither of them is an ally of Russia; therefore, Moscow would have a hard time staging an invasion of Armenia from their territory. It would likely need to conquer at least one of them beforehand, making a successful blitzkrieg against Armenia difficult. Unsurprisingly, there is little trace that Armenian leaders perceive an existential threat emanating from Russia.

4.2. *Third Conflict*

Armenia's archenemy is Azerbaijan. Azerbaijan has been in conflict with Armenia over the Nagorno-Karabakh region since the fall of the Soviet Union, and the two waged war in 1992 and 2020. The period between the end of the first war in 1994 and 2008 was relatively calm. However, major skirmishes occurred in March 2008 in Nagorno-Karabakh as Armenia went through internal upheaval. The situation calmed down until another major clash over Nagorno-Karabakh happened in February 2010. Further major skirmishes occurred in June and September.

The intensity of violence decreased, although fatalities during border clashes kept occurring throughout the next few years. Peace negotiations took place in June 2011, although the Russian-hosted talks led nowhere (Sputnik 2011). However, these normalization efforts did not last. 2014 saw increasing violence after July, with Azeri forces shooting down an Armenian helicopter in November (Agayev and Khojoyan 2014). Deadly skirmishes continued the following year. Due to this continuous fighting, the Armenians explained in December 2015 that the ceasefire was crumbling and warned of war (Ergan 2015).

In April 2016, violent clashes with heavy weaponry (the so-called Four-Day War) erupted at the Nagorno-Karabakh border. It ended a few days later with a ceasefire agreement signed under Russian auspices. Tensions went down, although regular skirmishes kept occurring. The 2018 regime change in Yerevan opened the door to renewed diplomacy with Azerbaijan, and numerous high-level meetings occurred throughout 2019.

Everything changed in mid-2020. In July, battles with heavy weapons happened all around Armenia's borders. Between September and November 2020, Armenia and Azerbaijan waged an open war over Nagorno-Karabakh. The war killed thousands and ended with a decisive Azeri victory. Relations soon recovered from that nadir. In January 2021, Azerbaijan and Armenia agreed under Russian auspices to deepen economic exchanges and build transborder infrastructures, and the first meeting of the Russia, Azerbaijan, and Armenia trilateral group to normalize Armenian-Azeri relations took place (Daily Sabah 2021). However, after May 2021, fierce skirmishes occurred up to the end of the period, and Azerbaijan seized more Nagorno-Karabakh territory.

4.3. *U.S. Assistance*

As Shirinyan noticed (2019, 14), "Western detachment from Armenia has been unintentional but persistent." Armenian-U.S. relations never gained much traction but varied in intensity with each passing American administration. The relationship started on a poor footing. In December 2008, the United States accused Armenia of providing weapons to Iran, which ultimately ended up in the hands of Iraqi insurgents. The Americans threatened to sanction Yerevan (Guardian 2010). Yet, afterward, the Obama administration pressured Turkey to open its border to Armenia and normalize relations with Yerevan, although with little success (Shirinyan 2019, 15–16). In July 2011, the United States agreed with Armenia to hold bilateral military exercises (Radio Free Europe 2011). The American and Armenian presidents met in April 2010, and Secretary of State Hillary Clinton visited Armenia two times, in 2010 and 2012 (Ministry of

Foreign Affairs 2022). The Armenian president visited Washington in May 2015, where he signed a trade deal with the United States (Sahakian 2015).

Armenian-U.S. relations declined under the Trump administration. In May 2017, the U.S. government announced it would cut aid to Armenia by around 70% (Armenian Weekly 2017). In September 2018, Donald Trump promised to increase American assistance to Armenia to support its democratization process (Harutyunyan 2019). However, when U.S. National Security Adviser John Bolton visited Armenia in October, he warned Yerevan that the United States would not turn a blind eye to Armenia's transborder trade with Iran. Defiant, the Armenian Prime Minister Nikol Pashinyan made clear the next month that Armenia would maintain its relations with Iran (Radio Free Europe 2019a). In January 2019, Washington sanctioned an Armenian company dealing with Iran (Bne IntelliNews 2019). Therefore, the Armenian prime minister criticized in March the lack of U.S. support for his country despite its recent democratization (Harutyunyan 2019). In July, the parliament speaker complained of American pressure to enforce the sanctions on Iran (Radio Free Europe 2019a). Visibly, his plead was ineffective, and further sanctions hit Armenian companies in August (ARMENPRESS 2019). During the 2020 war, the United States showed no sign of supporting Armenia and paid little attention to the conflict (Safi and Borger 2020).

The Biden administration appeared more sympathetic toward Armenia, at least in words. In April 2021, President Joe Biden used the word "genocide" on the Armenian Genocide Remembrance Day, a symbolic victory for Yerevan. However, little additional cooperation took place.

4.4. *Armenian Behavior Toward Russia*

Armenia is a founding member of the Russian-led Collective Security Treaty Organization (CSTO). Russia maintains a military base at Gyumri, near the Georgian and Turkish borders. Russian border guards also help secure Armenia's borders with Iran and Turkey. The period started with a close relationship. In October 2008, the Armenian president received his Russian peer to discuss increased cooperation (President of Russia 2008), only two months after the Russo-Georgian War of August. However, this soon shifted, and Armenia joined the EU's Eastern Partnership, launched in May 2009.

But mid-2010 saw a realignment with Russia. In August, Russian President Dmitry Medvedev visited Yerevan. Armenia agreed to extend the Russian military presence in the country until 2044 and asked Russia to participate in building a new nuclear reactor. On this occasion, Armenian officials affirmed that the deal would guarantee Armenian security in case of war with Azerbaijan (EURACTIV 2010).

Yerevan veered off course in mid-2011, however. In June 2011, the Armenian president stated to the Parliamentary Assembly of the Council of Europe that "the people of Armenia have made their historic and irreversible choice. [...] For us, it is a homecoming to the European civilization and cultural realm, to which we belong" (quoted in Ter-Matevosyan et al. 2017, 341). In July, Armenia agreed to plan joint bilateral military exercises with the United States for the first time. Yerevan started negotiating a partial free trade agreement with the EU in March 2012.

2013 saw the Armenians returning to growing alignment with the Russians. In April 2013, Armenia signed a memorandum of understanding with the Russian-led Eurasian Economic Commission. In June, Moscow and Yerevan signed a treaty to enhance military and technological cooperation. In September, the Armenian president met with Vladimir Putin and announced Armenia would join the Moscow-led Customs Union, thus dropping the Association Agreement with the EU. Security concerns towards Azerbaijan profoundly influenced Armenia's decision to join the Union. As an official stated, "the security issues of Armenia can be considered resolved after the decision was made to join the Customs Union" (Ter-Matevosyan et al. 2017, 345). Putin visited Armenia in December to sign numerous cooperation agreements. Yerevan also agreed to expand the Russian military presence in the country.

In March 2014, Yerevan voted against the UN General Assembly resolution to condemn Crimea's referendum for joining Russia. In September, Russian and Armenian troops conducted a joint military exercise on Armenian soil. During the maneuvers, they simulated an attack from "Ottomania," a barely veiled reference to Turkey (Kaghzvantsian 2014). In October, Armenia signed a treaty to join the Russian-led Eurasian Economic Union and became a member in January 2015. In December, Armenia and Russia agreed to form a joint air defense system. In November 2016, Moscow announced that the two states would create a joint military command. According to the agreement, the Armenian military could be placed under the command of a Russian general during wartime (Moscow Times 2016).

Yerevan changed course once again in 2017. Armenia and the EU signed a Comprehensive and Enhanced Partnership Agreement in November 2017 to improve relations and adapt Armenian legislation to EU norms. Many observers predicted that the democratization movement and the election of Nikol Pashinyan as prime minister in May 2018 would lead Armenia away from authoritarian Russia, but the new prime minister was quick to reassure Russia that the alliance remained sturdy (Armenia News 2018). However, in August, the South Caucasus Railway, the local subsidy of the Russian state-owned train company, came under investigation from Armenian authorities for financial wrongdoing. That same month, the Armenian military participated in a NATO exercise in Georgia, although it declined an invitation to participate in another NATO exercise in September. In November, Armenian tax authorities accused Russia's Gazprom of tax evasion.

Armenia went back to close relations with Russia in late 2020. Yerevan refused to participate in NATO exercises held in Georgia in September 2020. The same month (a few days before the war against Azerbaijan), Armenian justice dropped the charges against the South Caucasus Railway (Danielyan 2020). In November, Armenia accepted Russia's good offices to end the war with Azerbaijan and the subsequent presence of Russian peacekeepers in southern Armenia and Artsakh.

During the first months of 2021, Yerevan seemed to grow closer to the West. In March, the Armenia-EU Comprehensive and Enhanced Partnership Agreement entered into force. The Armenian military was scheduled to participate in the Defender-Europe exercises led by the U.S. Army in March 2021 but canceled only a few days before the beginning date (Radio Free Europe 2021). This rapprochement did not last, and in January 2022, Yerevan participated alongside Moscow in the CSTO's military operation to support the Kazakh government against a domestic uprising.

4.5. *Conclusion*

The period started with heightened tensions between Armenia and Azerbaijan, as well as poor relations with the United States. Yerevan pursued close relations with Moscow. Relations with Azerbaijan stabilized, U.S. support increased, and the Armenians chose a more pro-Western path. Violent clashes with Azerbaijan sent Armenia back into Russia's embrace. When tensions with Baku receded in 2011, Yerevan veered away from Moscow. However, Armenia inexplicably returned to alignment with Russia up to 2016. Better relations with Azerbaijan led to a distancing from the Kremlin despite lowering U.S. support. The Armenian-Azeri tensions and the all-out war of 2020 increased Yerevan's reliance on Moscow, but normalizing relations in 2021 stopped this trend. However, renewed hostility from mid-2021 once again sent Armenia into Russia's arms (*Table 3.4*).

Table 3.4. Summary

Hostility w/ Azerbaijan	e. 2008	m.-2008–9	2010	2011–m.-4	m.-2014–5	e. 2016	m.-2016–m.-20	l. 2020	e. 2021	m.-2021–2
	high	med.	high	med.-high	high	very high	med.-high	very high	med.	high

U.S. assistance	2008	2009–16				2017–20		2021–2		
	low	med.				low		low-med.		

Bandwagoning	e. 2008	m.-2008–m.-10	m.-2010–m.-1	m.-2011–2	2013–6 increase	2017–m.-20	l. 2020	e. 2021	m.-2021–2
	incr.	decr.	incr.	decr.		decr.	incr.	decr.	incr.

* e.: early, m.: mid, l.: late, med.: medium
*incr.: increase, decr.: decrease

Yerevan accommodated Moscow but never fully bandwagoned with it. Armenia's relative safety from Russian power has allowed it to maintain its foreign policy independence. However, this comes at a cost, as "it is viewed as too pro-Russian in Washington and Brussels, it is viewed as too pro-Western in Moscow" (Shirinyan 2019, 22). There is also no trace of internal balancing directed against Russia. Because the Kremlin is not an immediate threat, Armenian alignment choices are informed mainly by its violent relations with Azerbaijan, its archenemy.

5. Belarus

Belarus is a state of around nine million people located in Eastern Europe. It gained independence in 1991 when the Soviet Union collapsed and borders Lithuania, Latvia, Russia, Ukraine, and Poland. During most of its existence, Minsk maintained a balanced stance between Russia, its overpowering neighbor, and the West. However, 2020 marked a turning point, and Belarus appears to have thrown in its lot with Moscow. Much to the West's dismay, the Belarusians facilitated the 2022 Russian campaign in Ukraine by allowing Russian troops to use their soil.

This should be a hard case for this book's theory. Russia and Belarus are close in history, culture, and economy, and Russia inherited the Soviet Union's military bases on Belarusian territory. Few states in the world share such a thick relationship, and the imbalance of power is extreme. Therefore, one could expect Belarus to naturally gravitate toward Moscow and my theoretical claims to weigh little. Nevertheless, as demonstrated in this part, Minsk eschewed full alignment with Moscow up to 2020, only accommodating it. But when the United States became hostile toward Minsk during the 2020–2021 crisis, the Belarusians were left with no choice other than to fully bandwagon with Moscow.

5.1. *Threat Severity*

Russia represents an imminent threat to Belarus. It shares with Belarus a border of nearly 500 kilometers in a straight line. Terrain and natural elements offer no relief to Minsk. Belarus is a flat country with no significant natural barrier to protect it from the East. The forested, swampy areas dominating southern Belarus (called *polesye*) can hinder an incoming army and favor guerilla warfare, but the northern part of the border remains an ideal tank country. Most Belarusians live in medium and small towns or on farms, and there are few large urban centers to slow down an invader. Winters are less of an impediment than in Russia or Northern European states, and winter temperatures are on par with those of the U.S. upper Midwest (Blinnikov 2021, 456–457). However, landlocked Belarus does not need to bother defending a coastline.

As of 2021, the total of active Belarusian military personnel is less than 50,000, and Minsk has only a handful of small army brigades to defend itself. Contrary to Russia, most Belarusian combat units continue to rely on conscripts. Although the Belarusian military has large stocks of heavy weaponry compared to the European average, it primarily relies on Soviet-era platforms that lack the level of recapitalization enjoyed by the Russian military. Belarus has a large number of reservists, but its unpardoning geography and feeble active force offer only a poor buffer and little time to mobilize properly (IISS 2022, 185–186;

Muzyka 2021; Vanaga 2017, 62). During the relevant period, the Russian threat to Belarus is thus best characterized as high and increasing.

Did the Belarusians perceive the Russian threat that way? In 2009, Belarusian president Alexander Lukashenko warned that a Russian takeover of Belarus would be akin to "another Chechnya"; in that case, Belarusians would "wage a national liberation war" (Interfax-Ukraine 2009). It shows that Lukashenko does not consider its military likely to survive a Russian invasion and that he expects Russia to conquer Belarus. Hence, liberating the country from Russian occupation would fall on the citizenry. Indeed, the Belarusian president expressed on several occasions his fear of a Russian takeover (for example, President 2022c). Belarus's leadership thus clearly has a heightened perception of the Russian military threat.

5.2. *Third Conflict*

Lithuania

Belarus has rocky relations with Lithuania and Poland. During the early 2000s, Minsk feared Lithuania's imminent integration into NATO would threaten Belarus's security. Lukashenko worried that, on Lithuanian soil, "there are support bases that were created in order to exert influence on Belarus: these include the media, control measures, and spying on the part of Lithuania and Poland. They are also attempting to involve Ukraine." He also wondered, "what are the United States doing in Lithuania prior to the elections, together with the Lithuanian troops; incidentally, how many of those are remaining — five or six thousand? They are concentrating armed forces at our borders — just think, they want to hold some training exercises there" (quoted in Melyantsou and Kazakevich 2008, 49–50). Relations with Vilnius degraded further when the Lithuanians decided to build a depository of spent nuclear materials next to the Belarusian border, an endeavor the Belarusians labeled an "environmental war" (Melyantsou and Kazakevich 2008, 52–53).

After 2006, relations between Belarus and its western neighbors improved temporarily. In 2006, Russia's Gazprom increased gas prices following Belarus's refusal to let Russian capital enter important Belarusian companies. EU states and Lithuania saw this as an opportunity to improve ties and thus decrease Moscow's sway over Minsk. Vilnius rescinded its plan to build the nuclear waste depository in 2006. Belarusian leaders even envisioned a political alliance of Belarus, the Baltic states, Poland, and Ukraine, but that would not include Russia (Melyantsou and Kazakevich 2008, 53–59). In late 2008, Minsk announced it would build a new nuclear power plant in Astravyets, a few kilometers away from the Lithuanian border and close to Vilnius. The Lithuanians were displeased, but this project did not immediately degrade bilateral relations.

Lithuania became a strong advocate of the EU's Eastern Partnership launched in 2009, which also targeted Belarus. Lukashenko visited Vilnius in 2009 after a 12-year hiatus. In 2010, a Lithuanian president visited Minsk for the first time, marking a high point in bilateral relations. However, two months later, the contested presidential election in Belarus sunk bilateral relations to new lows, and Lukashenko was not even invited to the 2013 Eastern Partnership Summit in Vilnius. Vilnius's growing role as a hub for Lukashenko's political opponents also caused alarm in Minsk. Belarus threatened Lithuania to redirect Belarusian export goods toward Russia in case of further EU sanctions, thus potentially harming the Lithuanian port industry (Kłysiński 2013; Potjomkina and Šukytė 2017, 140–141).

Although the 2014 Ukrainian crisis encouraged many European states to try to pull Belarus away from Russia's orbit, Lithuania remained wary of Minsk and its nuclear power plant. An accident at the construction site in 2016 that the Belarusians tried to hide did nothing to reassure the Lithuanians. Also, the annexation of Crimea awoke in Lithuania diffuse fears that Minsk could use historical roots common to both states to lay claims to Lithuanian territory (Kesylytė-Alliks 2017). The Belarusian government's repression of a protest movement in 2017 and the large 2017 *Zapad* military maneuvers with Russia simulating an attack on Lithuania entrenched Vilnius in its hostility (Potjomkina and Šukytė 2017, 141, 151–153). Relations remained cold during the next couple of years. The rigged elections of August 2020 led to a definitive breakdown. The starting of the first reactor of the Astravyets nuclear power plant in November 2020 amid the Belarusian domestic crisis only hardened Lithuanian resolve to mobilize Western states against Minsk (Tsarik 2021, 1–2).

Poland

Belarus experienced tensions with Poland, in no small part due to a dispute over the Union of the Poles in Belarus, an association representing Poles living in the country. The association came to be seen as a hostile foreign agent and was growingly repressed after 2005. Subsequently, Poland increased efforts to promote democracy in Belarus and helped establish and fund Belsat TV to air in Belarus. It also funded other anti-Lukashenko media and NGOs. However, Warsaw reverted in 2008 to engagement with Minsk. It supported Belarus's membership in the European Union's Eastern Partnership Program, the Polish Foreign Minister visited Belarus, and Poland cooled down the dispute concerning the Union of Poles (Yeliseyeu 2017, 160–164).

Nevertheless, the honeymoon soon broke down, and Poland–Belarus relations reached a nadir during the 2011–2013 period. Warsaw condemned the repression of political opponents that followed Belarus's December 2010 presidential election and joined EU sanctions. In reaction, Minsk expelled both the EU and the Polish ambassadors in February 2012. The Belarusians accused Poland of trying to destabilize and overthrow the Lukashenko regime (Yeliseyeu 2017, 160–161).

The 2014 Ukrainian Crisis incentivized both sides to review their relations to hedge against Moscow's growing assertiveness. Soon came a flurry of meetings and forums. In 2015, the Belarusian government complied with an EU demand to release political prisoners. Furthermore, the Belarusian KGB provided Poland with documents concerning World War II Polish prisoners. Poland even started cutting its funding for anti-Lukashenko activities (Yeliseyeu 2017, 169–172). In 2016, Belarus's minister of foreign affairs saw Belarusian-Polish relations at "a historic moment in the transition to a new phase of bilateral relations, in which there will be no room for mistrust, confrontation, intrigue, outdated stereotypes and any ideological prejudices" (quoted in Polovyi 2021, 99). Lukashenko noticed in 2016 that "nobody is as much interested in independent and stable Belarus as Poland is. I think you do not need yet another unstable state in addition to Ukraine" (quoted in Yeliseyeu 2017, 170). Belarusian-Polish relations kept improving up to 2019 (Dyner 2020).

However, the contested elections of 2020 ruined bilateral relations. Poland offered large and multi-faced support to the Belarusian opposition and cut contacts with Lukashenko. In response, he decreased the number of Polish diplomats in the country. In 2021, the expulsion of diplomats and the arrest of members of the Union of Poles by Minsk worsened relations even more. The Belarusians saw a growing Polish threat against Belarusian territorial integrity. Finally, the Middle Eastern refugee influx towards the Polish border organized by Minsk sank relations to the bottom (Polovyi 2021).[1]

5.3. *U.S. Assistance*

Belarus-U.S. relations started from a low point. The Belarus Democracy Act of 2004 offered American support to opposition forces in Belarus. In 2006, the United States imposed sanctions on Belarusian entities and individuals, including Lukashenko, to punish Belarus's lack of democracy. The sanctions were strengthened in 2008, leading Belarus to expel most U.S. diplomats (only five remained in Minsk) and the U.S. ambassador (Mrachek 2019, 2; Woehrel 2010). Relations stayed poor for years.

However, the 2014 crisis in Ukraine changed the American outlook on Belarus, putting democracy promotion on the back burner. The Americans sought better relations. After Belarus released all its political prisoners in 2015,

---

[1] One can read the migrant crisis as a way for Lukashenko "to force the EU into political negotiations to legitimize his regime and break Belarus out of international isolation" (Estonian Foreign Intelligence Service 2022, 32), and thus gain breathing space from Moscow.

Washington offered partial sanctions relief (Mrachek 2019, 2). Lukashenko saw in April 2016 "a new stage in relations with the West, which I would still call empty talking [...] If we do not develop our relations, we will lose interest in each other after some time. In its relations with the West, Belarus's primary interest is investments and joint ventures" (quoted in Yeliseyeu 2017, 170).

Relations reached new heights after late 2018. In October 2018, Assistant Secretary Wess Mitchell became the first senior U.S. diplomat to travel to Minsk and meet Lukashenko in over a decade. 2019 saw a flurry of high-level contacts between American and Belarusian officials. In a gesture of goodwill, Belarus lifted the long-standing cap on the number of American diplomats present in the country. Washington extended a sanction moratorium on several Belarusian companies and signed a bilateral 'Open Skies' agreement with Minsk. Relations kept improving when U.S. National Security Advisor John Bolton visited Belarus in late August, obviously to discuss Russia (Fyodorov 2020, 97). After the visit of another senior official, Lukashenko rejoiced that "the United States has finally paid attention not only to Europe as a whole, but also to Belarus individually," and assured "to spare no efforts to continue building relations with the United States of America" (quoted in Fyodorov 2020, 98). After Minsk complained about U.S.-led military exercises near its borders, the U.S. embassy in Minsk moved swiftly to offer additional information about the maneuvers and allay Belarusian fears (Fyodorov 2020, 99). Lukashenko declared in December that if "Russia [...] tried to violate our sovereignty [...] the West and NATO will by no means accept that, because they will consider it a threat to them" (quoted in Fyodorov 2020, 99).

Finally, U.S. Secretary of State Michael Pompeo visited Belarus in February 2020, marking the heyday of Belarus-U.S. relations. The United States started to sell oil to Belarus in May 2020, while Belarus was in the midst of an oil price dispute with Russia (Nizhnikau and Moshes 2020, 49). According to Pompeo, "this competitive deal [...] strengthens Belarusian sovereignty and independence" and "demonstrates that the United States is ready to deliver trade opportunities for American companies interested in entering the Belarusian market" (quoted in Chiacu and Lambert 2020).

However, the American reaction to the 2020 contested presidential election sank the relations to the bottom. The United States not only sanctioned Belarus for the rigged election but also announced it would not recognize Lukashenko as Belarus's legitimate president (Mrachek 2021). In May 2021, Belarus created an air incident to divert a passenger jet and arrest an opposition journalist. In reaction, the United States imposed a new set of sanctions (Macias 2021).

5.4. *Belarusian Behavior Toward Russia*

Due to the Soviet legacy, the Belarusian and Russian militaries are similar in training, doctrine, and equipment. Belarusian officers generally received part of their education in Russia. Also, Belarus has been part of the CSTO, a Russian-led military alliance, since its inception. Furthermore, the two militaries formed in the late 1990s the 'Regional Grouping of Forces of Belarus and Russia,' which entails that Belarus's military would pass under Russian control in case of a major war, *à la* NATO. Since the fall of the Soviet Union, Russia has maintained two military facilities on Belarusian soil: the Hantsavichy Radar Station (an early warning radar) and the 43rd Communications Centre of the Russian Navy (a very low-frequency communications transmitter; Golts 2017, 87–89; Muzyka 2021). Despite this inherited proximity, Belarus's level of bandwagoning varied along this book's theoretical claims. Indeed, after 2008, relations between Belarusians and Russians have a mixed record.

After the 2008 Russo-Georgian War, Belarus refused to follow Russia and recognize the independence of Abkhazia and South Ossetia. Already irritated by that, Russia pushed Belarus to privatize its dairy industry. Instead, the Belarusians attempted to certify their milk for the European market. In June 2009, Moscow instituted a ban on Belarusian milk for a few days to punish Minsk (the so-called 'Milk War'). Minsk accused Moscow of supporting opponents to the regime and stopped several ongoing military cooperation programs. Following a string of Russian economic reprisals, Lukashenko stopped attending bilateral summits. In April 2010, he expressed his satisfaction with the Western financial support he received to counteract Russian pressure (Nizhnikau and Moshes 2020, 54–55). Lukashenko's frequent complaints about Russia eventually led Moscow to air TV programs presenting him as a backward tyrant in 2010 (Cepurītis 2017, 74).

But relations with Russia remained mostly cordial. On 1 June 2009, Lukashenko affirmed that Belarus would support Russian security interests unconditionally, and after years of foot-dragging, Minsk finally accepted Russia's request to create a joint air defense system, implemented only in 2012 due to Belarusian ill will (Golts 2017, 92, 94). Belarus agreed for the first time to hold Russia's *Zapad* military exercises on its soil in 2009 (Vanaga 2017, 65). Belarus's foreign minister explained this tension quite well:

> When it comes to our key partners, we are not going to break away from Russia, we realize that Belarus is overly dependent on it economically. But we want to get rid of this heavy dependence, we want to be less dependent on one state, because this is very disadvantageous during the financial crisis, which we have recently been witness to. (Quoted in Yeliseyeu 2017, 171)

Belarus appeared to align growingly with Russia after 2010. Indeed, following the feud with the West over the 2010 election, Belarus was left with few other choices than asking Russia for money. Between 2011 and 2015, Minsk borrowed an overall $8 billion, but Moscow asked the Belarusians to sell them state assets in return (they notably sold their pipeline system to Russia's Gazprom in June 2011). In 2011–12, Minsk dismantled the Belarusian Ground Forces Command; the Belarusian ground forces were now dependent on the Regional Forces Group — and thus Russia — for wartime command (Muzyka 2021, 17–18).

During the 2009 rough period, Minsk boycotted CSTO meetings, but in 2011, it showed itself as a proud member of the alliance, even boasting that Belarus "does not have a single CSTO document that is still not ratified" (Bohdan 2014, 29). In October 2011, Lukashenko expressed in the Russian newspaper Izvestia his enthusiasm toward greater integration with Russia and the post-Soviet space at large (President 2022b). In November 2011, Belarus committed alongside Kazakhstan and Russia to create the Eurasian Economic Union, which would closely align Belarus's economy with Russia (Nizhnikau and Moshes 2020, 55). In November 2012, Lukashenko announced that cargoes going from Belarus toward ports in Baltic states would be partly redirected toward Russian ports in the Leningrad Oblast, thus hurting their economy and benefiting Russia's (Kłysiński 2013, 5–6). Plans to establish a Russian air base in the Belarusian town of Lida were confirmed in 2013 (Golts 2017, 96–97). In July 2013, Lukashenko took a stance against Western foreign policy, stating that "new countries under seemingly nice pretexts [...] become the subjects of open aggression. Such complicated circumstances oblige us to be concerned about our security" (quoted in Bohdan 2014, 6).

The 2014 Ukrainian Crisis reshuffled Belarus's cards. Belarus felt pulled apart between the still coldness of Western powers and the Russian threat. However, a heightened sense of Russian aggression encouraged NATO states to warm up to Belarus. After 2014, Belarus tried hard to reduce Russia's influence on its military, and the number of cadets sent to study in Russia decreased after years of increase (Cepurītis 2017, 78–79; Golts 2017, 89). In response to Western sanctions, Russia banned imports of many types of foodstuff from states joining the sanctions. But Belarus used its free-trade agreements with Russia to sell on the Russian market reconditioned European foodstuff. This displeased Moscow and showed Belarus's defiant attitude towards the Kremlin (Cepurītis 2017, 80–82).

In April 2014, Lukashenko exclaimed: "we are not pro-Russian, not pro-Ukrainian, and not pro-Polish. We are not Russians, we are Belarusians!" (President 2022a). Lukashenko clarified in March 2014 that he "does not define NATO as a potential aggressor and will not do so" (quoted in Bohdan 2014, 30). In late 2014, Lukashenko expressed his fear of being "dictated and maltreated. We will take care of our land, our national identity and independence" but also knew that breaking with Russia was too dangerous; indeed, he had to "assess the situation realistically and to offer solutions taking into account the existing capacities" (quoted in Vanaga 2017, 57–58). In January 2015, Lukashenko declared that those "believing that the land of Belarus is, as they say, a part of the Russian world or nearly of Russia itself — forget it! We welcome everyone, but we will also teach everyone to respect our sovereignty and independence," a clear warning to Russia. However, only four months later, he threatened the West that "if, for God's sake something will go wrong — we'll stand side by side with Russia. This is our ally!" (quoted in Kudors 2017, 1).

In September 2015, when Putin ordered to sign the official agreement to establish a Russian air base, the Belarusians played ignorance, and Lukashenko denied he ever accepted a Russian base, thus killing the project (Golts 2017, 97). The 2016 iteration of the Belarusian military doctrine discussed the threat posed by private military companies and irregular formations acting against the government from neighboring countries, a veiled reference to Russia and its preferred strategies (Vanaga 2017, 59). Contrary to Russia, the Belarusian military doctrine adopted in 2016 did not identify NATO or the United States as threats. Also, the doctrine emphasizes that Belarusian troops cannot be used outside of Belarus except for peacekeeping operations. This is a direct blow to Russia to ensure that Belarus's troops cannot be deployed outside under CSTO's (and thus Russia's) command (Golts 2017, 93). A new energy conflict flared up in 2016 after Belarus refused to pay its gas at the preestablished price and requested lower prices. The Kremlin answered with a flurry of economic retaliations, and Minsk ultimately caved in, gaining only a small discount in 2017. It was also forced to sign the Customs Code of the Eurasian Economic Union, which it had used as a bargaining chip (Nizhnikau and Moshes 2020, 56).

During that period, Minsk also attempted leash-slipping by reinterpreting the agreements for forming a unified military command with Russia in times of crisis. The joint command was supposed to enter into effect if both states faced a "period of threat"; in March 2017, the Belarusians replaced this with "period of direct threat of aggression." In other words, the Russian military could take over Belarusian defense only if a foreign attack was imminent (Golts 2017, 95). Tensions further escalated in early 2017 when Minsk established a visa-free travel regime for short-term visits to citizens of numerous countries while maintaining its open-border, visa-free travel regime with Russia. This unilateral move displeased the Russians and forced them to reinforce controls on the border (Cepurītis 2017, 84). Also, Lukashenko was afraid that the 2017 *Zapad* military maneuvers would degrade relations with the West and thus invited NATO observers to attend the exercise (Potjomkina and Šukytė 2017, 153).

Starting in December 2018, Russia pressured Minsk to make political concessions and integrate more closely with Russia if it wanted Russian economic support to continue flowing in. But the Belarusians resisted, and the integration process remained stalled during 2019 (Nizhnikau and Moshes 2020, 57; Pankovski 2020). Lukashenko threatened to exit Moscow's embrace if the Russians kept requesting higher prices for crude supplies. He warned in January 2019, "if the Russian leadership opts for such course and the loss of its only ally in the West, it would be their choice" (Associated Press 2019). Belarus introduced a visa-free regime for short-term travel for EU and U.S. citizens in 2019 and launched a policy of 'soft Belarusianisation' to reduce Russian influence within Belarusian society (Nizhnikau and Moshes 2020, 49). While agreeing on paper to merge Belarus and Russia's military-industrial complexes, Lukashenko refused in practice to sell Belarussian companies to Russians (Golts 2017, 93).

Lukashenko adopted in December 2019 a plan to increase defense spending to 1.5% of the gross domestic product, modernize his military, and toughen draft rules to bolster the number of conscripts. The plan emphasized preventing aggression by 'strategic deterrence.' Belarus also expressed its willingness to improve military cooperation with Lithuania, Poland, and Ukraine in February 2019, all at odds with Moscow. In August, John Bolton and the heads of the Security Councils of Belarus, Poland, and Ukraine met in Warsaw. On this occasion, the Belarusian side signaled that it wanted to expand its contacts with NATO and Ukraine. Meanwhile, a Latvian military delegation visited a Belarusian military base, a rare occurrence for a NATO member. In December, an Italian delegation discussed a possible joint peacekeeping deployment in Lebanon (Muzyka 2021, 15; Porotnikov 2020, 30–32). As noticed by two observers, "by the end of 2019 [...] Belarus–Russia relations had descended into open crisis" (Nizhnikau and Moshes 2020, 48). The same month, Lukashenko lashed out at Russia: "I am not going to put [Belarus's sovereignty] in a box with a cross on top and throw it away or pass it on over to someone else. [...] This is our country. We are sovereign and independent" (President 2022c). An obscure affair of Russian mercenaries arrested near Minsk two weeks before Belarus's 2020 presidential election sent Belarus-Russian relations to a new low (Chance and Ullah 2021).

Despite that, Russia remained Belarus's first security provider even if relations with rivals and the United States generally bettered. It was torn between the Russian threat and the poor options to balance it: "the recent actions of our eastern brother cannot but raise concern. However, we are not drawing any conclusions yet, including me" (quoted in President 2014). Belarus's air force was so decrepit that Russian fighters had to ensure air security missions from 2013 to 2016, and the joint air defense system became operational that last year. Additional technical cooperation agreements were also signed in 2016 (Muzyka 2021, 19). Lukashenko stated in October 2016 that the Belarusians "together with the Russian people, the Russians, will defend our common Fatherland [...]

In the Western direction, we will die in defense of Belarus and Russia" (quoted in Golts 2017, 91). Lukashenko is also wary that NATO's growing military capabilities on its border may one day take aim at him; in November 2016, he "noticed for a while now, how new NATO forces are being deployed by our Belarusian borders. Belarus is reacting to this in an adequate and clear manner, but without unnecessary hubbub and noise" (quoted in Potjomkina and Šukytė 2017, 156–157). Also, Belarus continued to import most of its weaponry from Russia (IISS 2022, 179). Accommodation bent but did not break.

After the 2020 presidential election, alignment with Russia increased quickly. In March 2021, Belarus and Russia agreed on a five-year military partnership program, the first of this type. In April, air defense units from both countries started joint combat duties, and the Belarusian air base in Bobruysk was offered to host Russian combat and logistics aircraft (Muzyka 2021, 18). Lukashenko and Putin met in September 2021 and agreed to accelerate the integration process in exchange for Russian economic and financial rewards. Numerous phone conversations and meetings followed. In November, Lukashenko made substantial concessions to the Kremlin by promising to intervene in a potential war for the Donbas and declaring that "Crimea is *de facto* Russian and after the [2014] referendum, Crimea became *de jure* Russia" (quoted in Hedenskog 2022). In late 2021, Belarus started the process of amending its constitution to enable hosting Russian nuclear weapons on its soil. The constitutional referendum also aimed for Russia to weaken Lukashenko's grip on power and increase its own influence within Belarusian political institutions. On December 29, Minsk invited the Russians to build military-training centers and increase the number of joint exercises (Alberque 2022; Hedenskog 2022).

Before 2021, Russian troops entered Belarus only for prearranged exercises, and the joint regional grouping remained solely a formal arrangement (Golts 2017, 93). Nevertheless, under cover of military maneuvers, Russia deployed a large military contingent in late 2021 to Belarus for the first time, accompanied by *Iskander* ballistic missile and S-400 anti-aircraft systems (Estonian Foreign Intelligence Service 2022, 9). This growing alignment of Belarus with Russia continued until 24 February 2022, when Russia used Belarusian territory to attack Ukraine.

5.5. *Conclusion*

Initially, Belarus had poor relations with the United States but improved ties with Lithuania and Poland. This period saw Minsk take its distance from Moscow. As American support remained low and tensions with its neighbors increased, Belarus came back toward Russia. However, relations with Vilnius and Warsaw improved in 2014, and those with the United States did the same after 2015. This encouraged the Belarusians to turn away from the Russians again. However, the 2020 election crisis sent Belarus on the path of full alignment with Russia, as its neighbors and the United States became hostile toward Minsk. As expected, there has been no large effort from Belarus to reorient its defense posture against Russia, as it mostly accommodated Moscow. However, a beginning of internal balancing can be seen in the 2019 defense plan after U.S. support markedly improved. Belarus made some concessions to Poland and agreed to improvements in human rights to please the United States. Minsk tried hard to escape the Kremlin's grasp but ultimately failed due to a hostile environment (*Table 3.5*).

Table 3.5. Summary

Hostility w/ third rivals	2008–10	2011–3	2014–early 20	late 2020–2
	low	medium	low-medium	high
U.S. assistance	2008–13	2014–8	late 2018–mid-20	late 2020–2
	none	low	low-medium	none
Bandwagoning	2008–10	2011–3	2014–early 20	late 2020–2
	decrease	increase	decrease	increase

6. Serbia

Serbia is a small landlocked country located in Southeastern Europe. Its population is around seven million, and it borders Bosnia, Bulgaria, Croatia, Hungary, Kosovo, Montenegro, North Macedonia, and Romania. Until the 1990s, Serbia represented the heart of Yugoslavia, a multiethnic state. Yugoslavia disintegrated one piece after the other, and Serbia formally took existence in 2006. During most of the Cold War, relations between the Soviet Union and Yugoslavia were frosty. The collapse of the two states reset relations between Moscow and Belgrade. Serbia now finds in Russia its strongest ally and the Serbians generally support Russian positions on the international scene. This shift provides an interesting testing ground for this book's theory since Serbia is a liberal democracy while Russia is an authoritarian regime. Thus, the Serbian case appears to contradict liberal beliefs that states ally with similar regimes.

6.1. *Threat Severity*

Serbia's territory is relatively small (almost 90,000 square kilometers) and lacks strategic depth. Northern Serbia is made of the Pannonian Plain, thus offering few defensible features. However, the capital, Belgrade, is located south of the

Danube River, protecting it against an attack from the north or Romania. Save for Belgrade, Serbia has no large city to block the path of an invader. The southern borders are covered by mountains, offering some security. The temperate climate does not hinder offensive military operations (Manić, Nikitović, and Djurović 2022).

The Serbian military is small, with less than 30,000 active troops. The entire ground forces represent the equivalent of an army division. The air force relies on only a handful of combat-capable aircraft. Although Serbia still relies on numerous aging Soviet and local platforms and has a shortage of specialists to operate its most sophisticated weapon systems, it started acquiring more modern weaponry in recent years, notably from Russia (IISS 2022, 142–144). Overall, Belgrade appears to lack the combat power to push back a great power onslaught, and its geography helps little.

Nevertheless, the Russian threat level to Serbia is low due to sheer geographic distance. The Russian military has no readily available route to attack Serbian territory. The shortest way goes through Ukraine, hostile to Russia, and Romania, a NATO member state. Since Serbia is landlocked, an amphibious attack is a nonstarter. Although sporadic missile and air strikes may still occur, Russia has no pathway to swiftly conquering Serbia. A former Serbian diplomat joked that the only way for Russia to reach Serbia "is if they dig up a deep tunnel from the Urals to Avala (the mountain overlooking Belgrade) or from outer space" (Vuksanovic 2021, 216). Serbian leaders often portray Russia as a formidable but benevolent great power, and there is little trace of Belgrade perceiving Moscow as an imminent threat (Samorukov 2022; Vuksanovic 2021, 140–141).

6.2. *Third Conflict*

Kosovo is a breakaway state of Serbia and has been functionally independent since the end of the Kosovo War in 1999. Serbia never recognized the independence of Kosovo and hoped to restore control over the region. The period started poorly, as Pristina formally declared independence in February 2008. The declaration provoked popular uprisings in Serb-populated regions. Gunfire between Serbian militants and international troops present in the region occurred. In June, Kosovo Serbs formed an organization to resist the Pristina government. Serbia vowed to support its Kosovar compatriots and excited resistance against the government. Meanwhile, Kosovo saw the protest movement as coordinated by Belgrade (Radovanovic 2008). Protests dialed down by the summer, but relations remained frozen.

Relations somehow bettered in early 2011. During EU-mediated talks, Kosovo and Serbia began to negotiate directly for the first time in March. However, relations suddenly worsened in late July 2011 when the Kosovar police entered Serb-dominated North Kosovo to take control of border crossings. In October, NATO troops moved to establish control over border crossings in rebellious northern Kosovo on behalf of the Kosovar government, eliciting more Serbian resentment (Krstic 2011). In March 2012, a number of Kosovo Serbs were arrested on the charge of fomenting instability. In retaliation, Serbia arrested Kosovar citizens for alleged spying activities.

Nonetheless, in October 2012, talks for normalization resumed, and an agreement to solve several contentious issues was signed in December. In February 2013, the Kosovar and Serbian presidents met in Brussels. In April, both states agreed through the Brussels Agreement to integrate parallel Serbian institutions of Northern Kosovo into the Kosovar state and not to block each other's bid to join the EU. The agreements were implemented throughout 2013. In September 2014, a Kosovar hardline party took the reins of negotiations with Serbia, thus worsening relations (Zogiani 2014). In December, the Serbian president declared that any new agreement with Kosovo would need to go through referendums, complicating negotiations with Pristina (Nikolic 2014). But relations made a significant leap in August 2015, when Belgrade and Pristina signed several agreements, solving several lingering disputes (BBC 2015a). Little happened throughout 2016.

In January 2017, a train donated by Russia painted in Serbian colors and proclaiming "Kosovo is Serbia" departed Serbia toward Kosovo without the approval of Kosovar authorities. The Kosovars stopped the train at the border. The Kosovar president feared "Serbia's intention is to use this train, which was donated by Russia, first to help carve away the northern part of Kosovo and then [...] attach it to Serbia. It is the Crimea model." The Serbians saw Kosovo's response as hostile, and Serbia's president, Tomislav Nikolic, threatened that "if [the Kosovars] are killing Serbs, we will send the army, all of us will go, I will go as well, it would not be my first time" (Bytyci 2017). Both states mobilized their army at their border, raising fears of war.

The murder of a North Kosovo Serbian politician in January 2018 increased mutual defiance. Shortly after, a Serbian politician crossed the border into Kosovo illegally and was arrested. This event enraged Belgrade. In April, the Serbian president declared that he was ready to concede Kosovar independence if Serbia received appropriate compensation (Walker 2018), and in August, the two states' presidents suggested a land swap to improve bilateral relations, but this led nowhere (Conley and Saric 2021, 7). In November 2018, Kosovo imposed customs tariffs on Serbia to punish Belgrade's hostility (Zivanovic and Morina 2018). A few days later, it raised the tariffs to 100%. In December, Kosovo upgraded its paramilitary force into a fully-fledged military. This move angered Serbia, which warned that military action was "one of the options on the table" (Baynes 2018). In July 2019, Pristina forbade the Serbian defense minister from entering its territory (Bami 2020).

Under American mediation, relations improved after late 2019. In early October, Donald Trump appointed a special envoy that energized Kosovar-Serbian normalization talks. In January 2020, Kosovo and Serbia agreed to restore direct flights between the two states' capitals, which had been suspended for many years. In April, Kosovo announced it lifted its punishing tariffs on Serbian products (Radio Free Europe 2020). In September, Belgrade and Pristina signed several agreements, including a project to build a new transborder highway (Conley and Saric 2021, 8).

But the reprieve was short-lived, and the period ended with renewed conflict. That same September, Kosovo forbade a Serbian minister from entering the country. Soon after, it also forbade the Serbian president to do the same (Bami 2020). In December 2020, Serbia sent the COVID-19 vaccine across the border to North Kosovo without Kosovar's consent, thus enraging Pristina (Bami and Ahmeti 2020). In May 2021, Pristina threatened to sue Belgrade for genocide during the 1998–1999 war in an international court. Bilateral relations worsened again when Kosovar authorities stopped accepting vehicles passing the border with Serbian license plates. In September, Belgrade threatened to intervene militarily in northern Kosovo. The Serbian military also deployed near the border for a show of strength (AFP 2021; Kraemer 2022, 7).

6.3. *U.S. Assistance*

Serbian-U.S. relations started on a poor basis, with the memories of the 1999 NATO bombing still fresh. During the unrest following the February 2008 events, a mob torched the U.S. embassy in Belgrade. Serbia recalled its ambassador to Washington. The United States strongly criticized Serbia for failing to protect the U.S. embassy and encouraging nationalist sentiments (VOA 2009). In March, the Serbian prime minister condemned the American military presence in Kosovo (B92 2008a).

Yet, the United States tried to mend fences, and U.S. Vice President Joseph Biden visited Serbia in May 2009, pledging to maintain good relations with Serbia despite the different over Kosovo. But, in July 2010, the United States expressed support for the International Court of Justice's (ICJ) ruling supporting Kosovo's declaration of independence. Although Secretary of State Hillary Clinton visited Belgrade in October 2010 to round out the angles, Serbian-U.S. relations remained in limbo for several years.

The 2014 Ukrainian crisis increased U.S. interest in the Balkan region. A flurry of high-level meetings between Americans and Serbians occurred from mid-2015 to mid-2016 (Vuksanovic 2021, 199–200). Also, Serbia signed an Individual Partnership Action Plan with NATO in January 2015. A senior U.S. diplomat noticed in June 2016 that "Serbia has demonstrated great enthusiasm for the partnership with NATO, relations between NATO and Serbia will be developing, benefits for Serbia will increase" (Vasovic 2016). The Serbian president met U.S. Vice President Mike Pence in July 2017, and the two promised to bolster links.

However, Washington resented Serbia's proximity to Russia. An American official warned the Serbians in October 2017 that they had to choose between Russia and the West since "you cannot sit on two chairs at the same time, especially if they are so far apart" (Sherwin 2017). This comment highly displeased Belgrade (Rudic 2017b). The United States supported Kosovo's decision to create a regular military in December 2018, which further alienated the Serbians (Baynes 2018). Nevertheless, the Trump administration soon returned to engaging Belgrade. Although cautious, the Serbian president indeed perceived a more sympathetic American approach toward Belgrade, stating in June 2020 that "I do not believe in big changes in American policy, but I do believe in small changes in the US policy, which would be of great importance for Serbia" (quoted in Vuksanovic 2021, 204). In September, Serbia agreed with the Trump administration to open an embassy in Jerusalem, declare Hezbollah a terrorist group, and receive support from American financial organizations (Conley and Saric 2021, 8).

U.S. support for Serbia decreased with the coming of the Biden administration in 2021. For example, in April, the Serbian interior minister vehemently criticized the United States after Washington published a report denouncing human rights violations in the country (EURACTIV 2021). However, despite low points throughout the period, relations never broke, unlike in Belarus's case. The Serbian armed forces maintained military exchanges with the American military, notably through the U.S. International Military Education and Training program and a partnership with the Ohio National Guard. Numerous exercises also occurred either bilaterally or through NATO.

6.4. *Serbian Behavior Toward Russia*

Although relations between Russia and Serbia remained cordial during the 2000s, they did not reach the closeness they had before the Slobodan Milošević regime's fall in 2000. The Kosovar declaration of independence in February 2008 rekindled the relationship. Indeed, Belgrade reached out to Moscow for support to protect Kosovo Serbs (Reuters 2008). Reacting to European support for Kosovo's independence, the Serbian prime minister declared in March 2008 that EU membership should be "left aside" (B92 2008b). In May 2009, Serbia agreed to the construction of South Stream, a Russian project of gas pipeline. The Serbian president justified the move by saying that "one should not forget the political context, as Russia has advocated Serbian interests over Kosovo in the UN Security Council" (quoted in Vuksanovic 2021, 138–139). Yet, this alignment was far from total. A few days later, when Biden was visiting Serbia, president Boris Tadic assured that "notwithstanding our different positions on the Kosovo question, Serbia wishes for the best possible relations with the United States, as partners" (Al Jazeera 2009).

Dmitry Medvedev visited Serbia in October 2009, the first visit ever to the country by a Russian president, and the Serbian president thanked him "for his strong support in defending Serbia's territorial integrity and sovereignty over Kosovo" (Radio Free Europe 2009). In early 2010, a conference set to discuss Serbia's potential NATO membership was postponed at the insistence of the Russian ambassador (Konitzer 2011, 116). Yet, despite its friendship with Russia, Serbia accepted in September 2010 an EU proposal to mediate between Belgrade and Pristina (Economides and Ker-Lindsay 2015, 1033).

The Serbian foreign minister went to Moscow in March 2012, where he acknowledged Russia as Serbia's closest ally and partner (Vuksanovic 2021, 144). In April, Belgrade allowed Moscow to create a humanitarian center in the southern city of Nis to increase Russia's ability to respond to humanitarian and natural crises throughout the Balkans. The United States and others were opposed to the center, which was seen as a potential security hazard for the region. However, despite Moscow's outcry, Serbia refused to give this center's employees diplomatic status.

Belgrade acquired observer status in the Russian-led Collective Security Treaty Organization in April 2013. In May, the Serbian president visited Russia and elevated the bilateral relationship to a 'strategic partnership.' He declared on that occasion that "Serbia is grateful to the Russian Federation for being on the right side, on the side of international law, concerning our Kosovo problem" (B92 2013). In November, Russia and Serbia signed a 15-year military cooperation agreement to conduct military exchanges and joint exercises and share strategic intelligence. Russian Defense Minister Sergei Shoigu was awarded at this occasion the Serbian Flag First Degree medal for "developing friendship" between Belgrade and Moscow (Radio Free Europe 2013).

Vladimir Putin visited Serbia in October 2014 and received a warm welcome. He received from the Serbian president the country's new highest honor, the Order of the Republic of Serbia, specially created for Putin's visit. The Serbians also organized for him the biggest military parade the country had seen since 1985 (Borger 2014). Furthermore, Serbia did not join the Western sanctions against Russia that followed the 2014 Ukrainian crisis. Indeed, President Nikolić assured Putin that "Serbia will not endanger its morality by any hostility towards Russia" (Borger 2014). The Russian and Serbian militaries started to train together regularly after November 2014 on both states' soil (Bechev 2021, 197).

A shift appeared in 2015 as Belgrade distanced itself from Moscow. In January 2015, Serbia signed an Individual Partnership Agreement with NATO. Since 2015, Serbia has participated in the annual Slavic Brotherhood military exercises alongside Belarus and Russia. Also, since October 2015, the two states have conducted annual aerial exercises called Brotherhood of Aviators of Russia and Serbia. Yet, Serbia denied prioritizing cooperation with Russia to the detriment of the West, promising that "when it comes to activities with the Russian Armed Forces, the Ministry of Defence pays equal attention to all other key partners" (Jovanovic 2015). In November, NATO secretary-general Jens Stoltenberg visited Serbia, which granted NATO freedom of movement in Serbia and allowed the use of its military infrastructure (Vuksanovic 2021, 199).

In February 2016, Serbia granted NATO staff diplomatic immunity, a status that had been refused by the Russian personnel of the Russian-Serbian Humanitarian Center in Nis (Beta 2016). The Serbian prime minister stated that Belgrade "remains militarily neutral, but needs NATO as an ally to protect the Serb people in Kosovo and Metohija" (Tanjug 2016). A Serbian defense official then explained that "Russia remains a partner, we will not join NATO, but our road heads to the West" (Vasovic 2016). Serbia deported a group of Russians suspected of plotting the October 2016 coup attempt in neighboring Montenegro, although it did not publicize the affair (Borger, MacDowall, and Walker 2016). In late November 2017, Serbian paratroops exercised alongside American troops, with the Serbian president attending (Vuksanovic 2021, 202).

After that, alignment with Moscow increased. In December 2017, the Serbian president visited Moscow. He invited Russia to take part in Kosovo-Serbia peace talks in response to Kosovo's willingness to invite the United States to join negotiations (Rudic 2017a). Vladimir Putin was given a grandiose welcome for his January 2019 visit to Serbia and was told by the Serbian president that "although Serbia is not a very large country geographically, you can rely on us" (Walker 2019a). Milovan Drecun, a member of the ruling Serbian Progressive Party and chair of the Serbian Assembly's Committee on Kosovo and Metohija, explained needing "Russia to strengthen us with the Americans because when Russia puts its weight behind us, the Americans know that no solution can pass without its consent" (Vuksanovic 2019). Russian Prime Minister Dmitry Medvedev visited Belgrade in October. A few days later, the Russian military deployed for the first time for exercises abroad its S-400 and Pantsir air defense system during the joint maneuvers Slavic Shield 2019 in Serbia (Vuksanovic 2019). At the same time, after three years of negotiation, Serbia signed a free-trade agreement with the Russian-led Eurasian Economic Union, despite European warnings not to (Radio Free Europe 2019b).

Relations degraded in late 2019. In November 2019, the Serbians caught a former Russian diplomat spying for Moscow. The Serbian president summoned the Russian ambassador over the incident, although he quickly assured that "we will not change our policy towards Russia, which we see as a brotherly and friendly country [...] but we will strengthen our own intelligence defences" (Walker 2019b). In December, the Serbian president announced that Serbia would stop buying weapons from Russia for fear of American financial sanctions (Vuksanovic 2021, 202). In September 2020, the Serbians canceled their annual exercise with the Belarusians and the Russians, blaming Western pressure (Vuksanovic 2021, 218).

For the remainder of the period, Serbian alignment increased. In October 2020, Belgrade agreed to a Russian proposal to open a military office in the country to facilitate military and technical exchanges (Vuksanovic 2021, 219). The Russian Foreign Minister visited Belgrade in December 2020, and the two states promised to increase cooperation. In December, Serbia opposed a UN General Assembly resolution requesting Russia to withdraw its troops based in Crimea. During the September 2021 Kosovar crisis, the Serbian defense minister invited Russian diplomats to inspect troops a few kilometers away from the Kosovar border.

6.5. *Conclusion*

Serbia behaved in line with this book's expectations. The period started for Serbia with both U.S. hostility and heightened conflict with Kosovo. This led to Belgrade aligning with Moscow. After a thaw in Kosovar-Serbian relations in early 2011, tensions flared up again, and alignment with Russia continued increasing despite somewhat better relations with Washington. After mid-2012, relations with Kosovo slowly improved until a breakthrough in 2015. Similarly, the United States became more sympathetic toward Belgrade in 2015. Therefore, Serbia distanced itself from Russia.

Hostility with Kosovo returned in 2017, and American policy hardened in mid-2017. The Serbians returned to alignment with the Russians. The United States opened up to Serbia in 2019, and relations with Pristina improved in late 2019. Following that, Belgrade grew distant from Moscow. But in late 2020, relations started to degrade again. U.S. support also decreased soon after. Unsurprisingly, from late 2020 to 2022, Serbia again aligned with Russia (*see Table 3.6*).

Table 3.6. Summary

Hostility w/ Kosovo

2008–10	e. 2011	m.-2011–m.-2	m.-2012–4	2015–6	2017–l. 9	l. 2019–m.-21	m.-2021–2
high	med.	high	med.	low	high	low	high

U.S. assistance

2008	2009–14	2015–m.-7	m.-2017–8	2019–20	2021–2
low	low-med.	med.	low-med.	med.	low-med.

Bandwagoning

2008–11	2012–4	2015–l. 7	l. 2017–l. 9	l. 2019–l. 20	l. 2020–2
increase	increase	decrease	increase	decrease	increase

* e.: early, m.: mid, l.: late, med.: medium

To sum up, Serbia accommodated Russia overall but never fully aligned with it. There is little trace of internal balancing. Serbia did increase military spending and acquisitions in the late 2010s, but new weapons often came from Russia (Kraemer 2022, 5–6). The Serbians made several concessions to Kosovo and the United States under the Trump administration. Since Serbia remains far away from Russian power, Belgrade has little to fear from Moscow and thus enjoys ample freedom of action. It has thus fewer incentives to react to the level of U.S. support and instead reacted more strongly to Kosovar hostility. The Serbians resent the lack of American sympathy. As put by a former Serbian official, "the Americans are not present enough" (Vuksanovic 2021, 123). For another, "everybody was aware of the importance of the US, but unfortunately, everybody also knew that we could not expect a friendly relationship with them" (Vuksanovic 2021, 126). However, Moscow is not enough of a threat to compel Belgrade to change course to please Washington. As the Serbian proverb goes, "God is high above and Russia is far away" (Konitzer 2011, 103).

Chapter IV

Cases in Asia

1. Background

This chapter treats Asia as a single coherent region whose dynamics are distinct from the other regions of the world. 'Asia' here corresponds to what is commonly referred to as the Indo-Pacific region. It comprises all the landmass east of Iran, south of the former Soviet Union, and the adjacent islands (including Australasia). Although Britain, France, and the United States have territories in the Pacific Ocean, they are not considered Asian states since their heartland is not in the region. Also, as explained in the preceding chapter, Russia is treated as a European power. This does not distort the analysis since Chinese decision-makers treat Moscow so too. As Ross remarks,

> The decline of Russian capabilities in Northeast Asia diminishes the necessity for Beijing to allocate significant resources to defend its northern border. Chinese analysts have minimal concern that Russia will reemerge as an East Asian great power that can challenge Chinese security. Thus, in terms of the domestic security of the great power, the Sino-Russian border increasingly resembles the U.S.-Canadian border. (Ross 2018, 35)

2. Balance of Power

This part justifies that China was the strongest power, and ultimately a potential hegemon, in Asia between 2008 and 2022. It first describes its military capabilities in numbers before discussing them in qualitative terms.

2.1. *Quantitative Discussion of Power*

This section argues that China had, for the period, the strongest military force in the region, at least in numbers. Data from the 2011 and 2021 editions of *The Military Balance* are used to count the total military personnel, the ground troops, the main battle tanks, the combat aircraft, the capital ships, and the attack submarines of the leading Asian powers — China, India, Japan, North Korea, Pakistan, South Korea, and Taiwan (*Tables 4.1* and *4.2*).

For Mearsheimer (2014, 45), a potential hegemon is a great power markedly stronger than any other great power and potentially stronger enough to defeat two opponents in tandem. Although there was no great power in Asia except China for most of the period, we can try to apply that standard to regional powers. Between 2008 and 2022, China was the strongest state in Asia. Save for ground forces personnel, Beijing enjoyed a large lead in most categories during the relevant period. China also maintained a clear lead in military spending for the entire period (*Figure 4.1*).

Table 4.1. Balance of conventional forces in Asia, 2010

	Total personnel	Ground forces*	Main battle tanks**	Combat aircraft***	Capital ships	Attack submarines
China	2,285,000	1,610,000	7,050	1,701	78	67
India	1,325,000	1,131,100	4,117 (1,133)	646	23	16
Japan	247,746	151,641	850	374	49	18
N. Korea	1,190,000	1,020,000	3,500	540	3	22
Pakistan	617,000	551,400	2,386 (270)	443	9	5
S. Korea	655,000	549,000	2,514 (400)	489	47	12
Taiwan	290,000	215,000	926	427	26	4
Chinese percentage	35	31	33 (30)	37	33	47

Source: International Institute for Strategic Studies. 2011. *The Military Balance, 2011.* Abingdon: Routledge.
Note: Weapons in store are indicated within parentheses. Percentages have been rounded.
* Including special forces, naval infantry, and airborne forces, excluding paramilitary forces.
** Including naval infantry and airborne forces, excluding paramilitary forces.
*** Including naval aviation, excluding training aircraft and strategic bombers.

Table 4.2. Balance of conventional forces in Asia, 2020

	Total personnel	Ground forces*	Main battle tanks**	Combat aircraft***	Capital ships	Attack submarines
China	2,035,000	1,000,000	5,650	1,868	80	52
India	1,458,500	1,238,200	3,640 (1,100)	710	28	15
Japan	247,150	150,700	580	335	51	22
N. Korea	1,280,000	1,100,000	3,500	465 (18)	2	20
Pakistan	651,800	563,200	2,467	375	8	5
S. Korea	599,000	493,000	2,321	499	23	18
Taiwan	163,000	98,000	565	418	26	4
Chinese percentage	32	22	30 (29)	40 (40)	37	38

Source: International Institute for Strategic Studies. 2021. *The Military Balance, 2021*. Abingdon: Routledge.
Note: Weapons in store are indicated within parentheses. Percentages have been rounded.
* Including special forces, naval infantry, and airborne forces, excluding paramilitary forces.
** Including naval infantry and airborne forces, excluding paramilitary forces.
*** Including naval aviation, excluding training aircraft and strategic bombers.

Figure 4.1. Military expenditures in Asia, 2008–2020, PPP (billion USD)

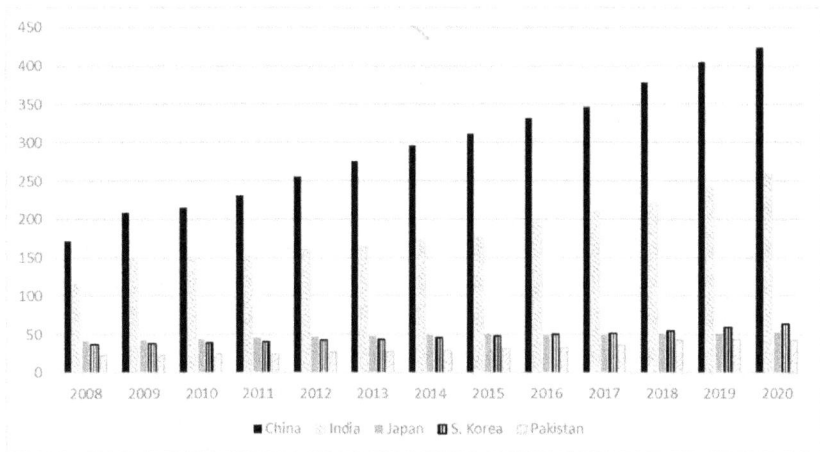

Source: The author's calculation, based on World Bank. https://data.worldbank.org/ (accessed 2022, January 22).
Note: No data for North Korea and Taiwan.

Beyond military power, China was also first in population numbers in the region (*Table 4.3*). The only Asian state boxing in the same category as China is India, and China's lead disappeared toward the end of the period. Yet, it remains that Beijing undoubtedly was the most potent military power in Asia between 2008 and 2022, at least in numbers. Do qualitative considerations support this assessment?

Table 4.3. Population of the main Asian states, 2010, 2020

	2010	2020
China	1,337,705,000	1,410,929,360
India	1,234,281,160	1,380,004,390
Japan	128,070,000	125,836,021
N. Korea	24,548,840	25,778,815
Pakistan	179,424,643	220,892,331
S. Korea	49,554,112	51,780,579
Taiwan	23,162,123	23,604,265
Chinese percentage	45	44

Source: National Statistics. https://eng.stat.gov.tw/point.asp?index=9 (accessed 2022, January 9); World Bank. https://data.worldbank.org/ (accessed 2022, January 5).

2.2. *Qualitative Discussion of Power*

During most of the Cold War, China's chronicle underdevelopment heavily constrained the resources available to modernize the People's Liberation Army (PLA). Furthermore, Mao Zedong's erratic leadership and political indoctrination left the military lacking in realistic training and operational capabilities. It is no surprise that Chinese forces made a poor showing during the 1979 Sino-Vietnamese war. Under the leadership of Deng Xiaoping, the 1980s saw increased efforts to increase the quality of the force. Efforts to modernize the military gathered steam during the 1990s and the 2000s.

During the period under study, the PLA kept modernizing its military at a fast pace. Large cuts in personnel (notably a 300,000-people reduction announced in 2015) have allowed focusing more on the quality of training and on weapon acquisitions and thus increased the warfighting capability of the military. The PLA Ground Force modernized by leaps and bounds. Jointness with other forces has improved. The former seven Military Regions were replaced by five joint Theater Commands in 2016. The structure of the army has been consolidated around combined arms brigades. Niche capabilities like special operations and electronic warfare gained in sophistication. Although legacy Soviet-era equipment remained in service, newer weapons have been introduced at a steady pace. The Ground Force also benefited from increasingly realistic training (Blasko 2021).

Modernization of the navy has been given priority due to the overwhelming importance given to the Taiwan issue. The PLA Navy is now the largest in the world numerically, and its ships are increasingly capable. Naval aviation has gained mass and sophistication, and China has invested significant resources in surface-to-ship ballistic and cruise missiles. Chinese shipyards' production capability is massive and growing in efficiency and complexity. The navy improved supporting capabilities and training and increased the frequency of exercises. The Marine Corps has also tripled in size to allow for expeditionary operations (Cole 2016, chap. 2; O'Rourke 2022; Wuthnow and Fravel 2022).

In late 2011 and throughout 2012, the PLA Air Force merged its surface-to-air missiles and anti-aircraft artillery branches into a single one, trimmed its organizational tree, and devoted more resources to training. 2016–2017 saw another massive effort at reforms. Personnel was cut. The regional architecture of the force was consolidated into five Theater Commands to match the Ground Force's, and the lower echelons' organization was rationalized. The training was modernized and standardized still more. Modern domestic and Russian designs have growingly replaced outdated Soviet-design aircraft. The PLAAF also gave increased attention to emerging technologies like uncrewed aerial vehicles, artificial intelligence, and hypersonics (Allen, Mulvaney, and Char 2021).

The logistical system has been upgraded to modern standards. The Joint Logistic Support Force was created in September 2016 to centralize the PLA's logistics efforts. The acquisition of new air and sea mobility assets has increased China's ability to support long-distance military operations. Civilian infrastructures have also been optimized to promote PLA's mobility (Wuthnow 2021). China has considerably expanded its fleet of navigation, communication, and earth-observation satellites and developed anti-space capabilities. Beijing formed in December 2015 the PLA Strategic Support Force to consolidate within a single structure its space, cyber, and information capabilities and create synergies among them (Kania and Costello 2021). While China still lacks actual combat experience, this is true of most Asian states.

China's enormous economy — the world's first or second, depending on how one counts — and its mastering of advanced industrial capabilities means that its military power is sustainable. Although China is not self-sufficient for numerous natural resource items — notably oil — it has sufficient reserves on its soil to keep its military machine functioning even during a major conflict

(Mirski 2013, 412–415). Despite lingering technological dependencies on Russia, Beijing is now largely able to procure advanced weapons from domestic producers in sufficient quantities. Many Asian states also developed and modernized their forces in the meanwhile. Yet, it is reasonable to assume that Beijing progressed at least as fast as most others. Therefore, qualitative factors, too, support qualifying China as the strongest power in Asia.

3. Case Selection

First, I scrutinize the existing literature to identify which Asian states are described as bandwagoning with China. Indeed, the literature agrees that Cambodia is aligned with China, yet observers notice that Cambodia maintains its margin of maneuver; it is not fully aligned with Beijing (Burgos and Ear 2010; Chheang 2021; Ciorciari 2015; Doung, Kang, and Kim 2022; Po and Primiano 2020). Most observers also see Myanmar as a limited bandwagoner, safe for an anti-Chinese shift during the early- to mid-2010s (Chen, Tsung-Yen, and Yang 2013; Chow and Easley 2019b; Egreteau and Chenyang 2018; Han 2018; Jones and Myo 2021; Malik 2018). Many experts agree that China is North Korea's closest ally, although the North Koreans are wary of fully aligning with Beijing (Chow and Easley 2019b; Kong 2018; Obe and Byrne 2021; Xiao 2015). Pakistan, too, is widely described as a Chinese ally, some even designating it "China's Israel" (Khan 2016; Khan 2020; Pande 2021; Paul 2019; Shah 2022; Small 2015; 2020). Only those four states out of 38 chose to bandwagon, and they also are the only four to suffer from a combination of both U.S. hostility and third conflicts throughout Asia (Appendix 1, *Table A1.3*).

4. Cambodia

Cambodia is a state of over 17 million located in Southeast Asia that gained independence from France in 1953. Cambodia borders Laos, Thailand, and Vietnam. During the 1980s, Phnom Penh was allied with the Soviet Union and Vietnam and had poor relations with China. Relations with Beijing warmed up during the 1990s but less so with the United States. Washington took a more sympathetic stance throughout the 2000s while Cambodia growingly aligned with Beijing.

There was no predestination in Cambodia working closely with China. Historically, relations with Beijing have been filled with resentment. Many Cambodians remember Chinese support for the genocidal Khmer Rouge regime that killed nearly two million people during the 1970s. Prime Minister Hun Sen, in power during the whole period under study, had strong anti-Chinese opinions during the 1980s and 1990s, even declaring that China was the "root of everything that is evil" (Kynge, Haddou, and Peel 2016; also, Ciorciari 2015,

266). Anti-China sentiments are also rising among the citizenry (Heng 2019, 129–131). Bandwagoning with China was far from preordained.

4.1. *Threat Severity*

Cambodia is relatively small, covering around 180,000 square kilometers. It is mostly flat plains, although the Mekong River can offer a degree of protection against attacks coming from the north or the east. Also, heavy forests often cover regions away from lacks and rivers. Phnom Penh, the capital, has over two million people and is the only major urban area in the country (CountryReports). Terrain does not overwhelmingly favor either attackers or defenders.

The Royal Cambodian Armed Forces can count on around 125,000 troops. The army represents, in theory, close to 20 brigades of combat forces. Both the air force and the navy have only negligible combat capabilities. Significant territorial and paramilitary forces can reinforce the regular army, but their combat readiness is unclear. Many of Cambodia's platforms are old Soviet designs, and the country struggles to purchase modern weaponry due to limited budgets (IISS 2022, 253–254).

The Cambodians know well that China is more powerful than them and growingly so. According to a Cambodian official, "the power of China is getting much bigger" (quoted in Kynge, Haddou, and Peel 2016). However, Cambodia has no direct border with China and Beijing has few means to threaten it directly. It would need to gain access to Laotian or Vietnamese territory to mount an invasion of Cambodia. An amphibious operation might be possible, but this would likely be a protracted affair. The Chinese would need time to gain air superiority over the country, secure a beachhead, and assemble enough combat power and supplies to conquer the whole country from the coast. The threat level is thus relatively low.

Indeed, although Cambodian officials have expressed unease and diffuse wariness about Chinese influence and power, there is little trace of the Cambodians feeling an imminent military threat (Po and Primiano 2020b). According to a Cambodian ministry of foreign affairs official, "as far as security is concerned, leaders in Phnom Penh do not see the rise of China as a threat but a useful offshore balancing potential against security threats from immediate neighbors" (Cheunboran 2017, 241).

4.2. *Third Conflict*

Cambodia faces complex relations with two larger neighbors: Thailand and Vietnam (Po and Primiano 2020a, 454–456). For a Cambodian official, "Cambodia's geography of being sandwiched by two powerful, historically antagonistic neighbors — Thailand and Vietnam — has been a persistent compelling factor shaping the country's strategic direction" (Cheunboran 2017, 235).

Thailand

The rivalry with Thailand is the prime engine orienting Cambodia's force posture. Specifically, Thailand disputes with Cambodia the ownership of a 4.6 square kilometers area surrounding the Preah Vihear Temple (Var 2017). At first, discussions regarding the Preah Vihear issue were smooth until 2007.

However, Cambodia chose to register the temple as a World Heritage Site without Thai participation, which irritated Bangkok (Rattanasengchanh 2017, 70). In June 2008, Thai troops moved to occupy areas close to the temple that the Cambodians considered theirs (Po and Primiano 2020a, 456). The temple entered the UN World Heritage List in July 2008, leading a group of Thai militants to trespass the border near the temple. Cambodian authorities stepped in, and the Thai army entered the fray, leading to a clash with Cambodian soldiers (Var 2017, 157). The Cambodians launched a campaign to strengthen their military and sent reinforcements to the border, and new fighting broke out in October (Rattanasengchanh 2017, 71). Thai troops returned in April 2009, leading to new clashes (Rattanasengchanh 2017, 75).

Bilateral relations sank still more, and diplomatic ties were cut when Hun Sen appointed in October 2009 the former Thai Prime Minister Thaksin Shinawatra, ousted by a coup, as an economic advisor and turned down Thailand's request to hand him over (Sothirak 2013, 91; Var 2017, 161). In November 2009, Thailand canceled a memorandum of understanding on the joint exploitation of the hydrocarbons present in the contested areas of the Gulf of Thailand. Thailand also stopped developmental aid (Var 2017, 162). These events represented a severe economic loss for Cambodia.

In February 2010, Hun Sen denounced a Thai invasion and threatened retaliation (Rattanasengchanh 2017, 71). He added in late 2010 that "Cambodia will have no happiness as long as this [Thai government] is in power" (quoted in Rattanasengchanh 2017, 76). In February 2011, clashes broke out after Thai troops entered the disputed territory around the temple, and in May, fighting occurred near another two temples 150 kilometers away (Rattanasengchanh 2017, 77). April–May 2011 saw intense border clashes, with artillery and rocket exchanges, also extending to the two other contested temples (Var 2017, 159). In April 2011, Hun Sen emphasized the Thai threat. According to him, the Thai prime minister "was cruel, ordered the attack on Cambodia and threatened to take control of Cambodia […] Cambodia is poor and small, but our weapons are not like a slingshot and don't forget that the ant can hurt the elephant" (Strangio 2011).

The new Thai government elected in July 2011 took a less confrontational stance. The Thai minister of defense visited Phnom Penh in September 2011. Cambodians and Thais agreed to comply with the International Court of Justice's demand for troop withdrawal and took further appeasement measures in December. Troops effectively withdrew in July 2012 (Sothirak 2013, 90, 96). In early 2013, the Cambodians were still wary of Thailand, and Hun Sen feared that if the ICJ ruled in favor of Cambodia, "the Thais will use armed forces" (quoted in Rattanasengchanh 2017, 79). In 2013, the ICJ ruled mostly in favor of Cambodia, and Thailand had to withdraw all its remaining troops from the area (Rattanasengchanh 2017, 81). The May 2014 coup in Bangkok brought a new Thai government better disposed toward Cambodia, and Hun Sen visited Thailand in December 2015. Both states soon agreed to improve bilateral relations further (Deth 2017, 39–40).

Tensions did not disappear. For example, on July 3, 2017, the Cambodians closed all their border checkpoints with Thailand except for their nationals after the Thais imposed harsh punishments on illegal immigrant workers, often Cambodians (Croissant 2018, 198). But relations remained cordial for the rest of the period. In March 2018, both countries agreed to get over the border dispute and reinforce military ties (VNA 2018). Relations kept bettering throughout 2021, and Thailand agreed to reopen talks concerning the demarcation of the maritime border in October (Khmer Times 2021; Sochan 2021).

Vietnam

Demarcating the border and handling Vietnamese people living in Cambodia remain contentious issues between Hanoi and Phnom Penh. Relations with Vietnam started amicably in 2008 (Thayer 2009, 96). But in 2009, villagers uprooted border markers in the Svay Rieng province. Clashes occurred when lawmakers visited the contested border in June (Subhan 2018). In December 2010, Cambodia accused Vietnamese military officials of violating their border (Um 2011, 67).

Bilateral relations then bettered for a while. In April 2011, the Vietnamese prime minister visited Cambodia and signed a memorandum of understanding on the demarcation of the border (Leng 2017, 341). In December 2013, Hun Sen visited Vietnam, notably agreeing to harmonize custom practices to facilitate border flows (Leng 2017, 337–338). Furthermore, Hanoi supported Cambodia's candidature for membership in the United Nations Security Council in 2013 (Leng 2017, 335).

While Cambodia-Thailand relations quickly improved, under the surface, tensions with Vietnam were on the rise. The Vietnamese threat figured prominently during the summer of 2013 elections in Cambodia; Phnom Penh hardened its position on border disputes and its treatment of ethnic

Vietnamese after that (Cheunboran 2017, 238–239). Vietnam disliked how Cambodia handled anti-Vietnamese demonstrations in front of the Vietnamese embassy in 2014 and even pressured the Cambodians to crack down on the demonstrators (Leng 2017, 339). Also, the Cambodians increased the expulsions of illegal Vietnamese immigrants in mid-2014, which the Vietnamese complained about (Leng 2017, 340).

Between 2013 and 2015, Cambodia protested many times against alleged Vietnamese incursions beyond the border but kept these protestations secret. However, starting in 2015, the Cambodian government made these official protestations public (Leng 2017, 340). Indeed, a border clash in June 2015 added to the tensions (Heder 2018, 120). After talks in July 2015, the Vietnamese appeased Cambodia by stopping the construction of a military post and a road in contested areas (Leng 2017, 341).

However, the demarcation of the border remains a source of conflict. Despite progress, the demarcation process stalled after 2016. Hanoi also remained displeased by Cambodia's poor treatment of ethnic Vietnamese living there (Nguyen 2017, 92–94). The Cambodians fear that Vietnamese immigrants acquiring lands in border regions are part of Vietnamese expansionist designs (Po and Primiano 2020a, 458; also, Frewer 2016). That same year, Hun Sen asked people living near the border to stop renting land to Vietnamese people. The Vietnamese grew warier of Cambodia after Phnom Penh decided to vocally back Chinese claims over the South China Sea throughout 2016 (Kry and Chy 2017, 69–70). During the first half of 2016, Vietnamese direct investments in Cambodia collapsed to almost zero. It is hard not to see this as a political decision from Hanoi, as the Cambodians have constantly been complaining about the Vietnamese constructions in non-demarcated areas of the border (Hunt 2016). Hun Sen warned in August 2016 that "Vietnam is neither my dad nor my King" and that "Vietnam is not my boss" (quoted in Nguyen 2017, 91). A Cambodian-Vietnamese joint commission met in August 2016 to work on the border issue but failed even to issue a joint statement, with both sides camping on their positions (Kry and Chy 2017, 72).

Relations improved after that. In April 2017, the Vietnamese Prime Minister visited Phnom Penh and declared that "especially in the recent years and months, Vietnam-Cambodia relations have been very much more familial, affectionate, trusting and intimate" (Heder 2018, 113). In October 2019, both states noticed progress in demarcating the border (Sokhean 2019). Hanoi and Phnom Penh inaugurated in December 2019 a border market (Murg 2022, 131). The border conflict, however, soon resurfaced. In April 2020, The Cambodians discovered Vietnamese military encampments in a non-demarcated area of the border, eliciting official protests from Phnom Penh. Vietnam justified this as an anti-COVID-19 measure and promised to withdraw the encampments after the end of the pandemic (Heng 2022). Pushed by a heightened sense of threat, Vietnam created in June 2021 a new maritime militia unit based near the Cambodian border (Chhengpor 2021). But relations are not solely marked by conflict. The Vietnamese President visited Cambodia in December 2021 and signed numerous cooperation agreements, and Phnom Penh proposed to build a new border market (Heng 2022; Murg 2022, 131).

4.3. U.S. Assistance

Relations between Cambodia and the United States started on a poor footing but slowly bettered throughout the 2000s. Military ties were established in 2004, and the United States offered direct foreign assistance in 2007. The United States increasingly committed to supporting Cambodia; Deputy Secretary of State John Negroponte visited Phnom Penh in 2008, and Cambodia's Minister of Defense visited Washington back in 2009 when the United States pledged to help enhance Cambodia's military by financing and training assistance. In 2008–09, the United States donated 31 trucks along with excess equipment, and joint exercises started in mid-2009. In 2009, Washington lifted financial restrictions and offered Cambodia economic support. However, relations degraded in late 2009 when the Cambodians extradited Uyghur asylum seekers to China against American will.

But military cooperation soon restarted and grew in mid-2010 (Thayer 2010, 449–455). Secretary of State Hillary Clinton justified to a Cambodian audience in November 2010 that "you don't want to get too dependent on any one country," targeting China (quoted in Ciorciari 2015, 256). In 2010, 2011, and 2012, U.S. Navy ships visited Cambodia. U.S. President Barack Obama visited Phnom Penh in November 2012, the first-ever presidential visit to the country. Defense Secretary Leon Panetta also visited Cambodia in November 2012, ahead of Obama's visit. House Democratic Minority Leader Nancy Pelosi and First Lady Michelle Obama visited Cambodia in 2015, and Secretary of State John Kerry did the same in 2016. A U.S. ship visited Cambodia in 2016 (Doung, Kang, and Kim 2022, 64, 73).

Relations degraded soon after Donald Trump arrived in office. In early 2017, Washington asked Cambodia to repay its old debt of 500 million dollars, which enraged the Cambodians (Heng 2019, 128). In September 2017, opposition leader Kem Sokha was arrested on suspicions of helping the United States organize a color revolution in Cambodia (Po and Primiano 2020a, 451). In response, the United States banned in December 2017 several individuals from getting American visas due to their non-democratic practices. In June 2018, the U.S. Treasury Department sanctioned three individuals from Hun Sen's close circle for human rights violations (Doung, Kang, and Kim 2022, 78).

The Cambodian government resented the increasing American pressure over human rights and democratization under the Trump administration and postponed several exercises and programs with the United States (Po and Primiano 2020a, 447). Reflecting on that situation, an official from the Ministry of Foreign

Affairs affirmed in 2018 that "Cambodia wants to have good relations with the U.S., but it depends on the U.S. Due to the current political situation in Cambodia, the U.S. doesn't want to be a good friend with Cambodia." Another lamented that "the U.S. doesn't have much interest in Cambodia. However, our government tries" (quoted in Po and Primiano 2020a, 457).

Relations kept worsening after that. Non-democratic behaviors encouraged the United States to pass the Cambodia Democracy Act in 2019, which banned several Cambodians from visiting the United States and froze their assets (Kimseng 2019). Also, the United States became wary of Cambodia over suspicions that China was building a naval base at Ream (Leng and Chheang 2021, 128–129). Between 2017 and 2019, U.S. aid to Cambodia drastically decreased, and in December 2020, Washington terminated its trade preference program toward Cambodia (Doung, Kang, and Kim 2022, 79). In September 2020, Washington imposed sanctions on a Chinese company working in the country, an event that displeased the Cambodians (Chheang 2022, 349). The United States canceled a program sending Cambodian students to top American military academies in July 2021 (Reuters 2021).

4.4. *Cambodian Behavior Toward China*

As underlined above, Cambodia enjoyed, at first, a level of U.S. support, and relations were improving. Cambodia was interested in more American involvement; for example, Phnom Penh joined the U.S.-led Lower Mekong Initiative launched in July 2009 (Doung, Kang, and Kim 2022, 65).

Meanwhile, relations with China were also developing. They deepened throughout 2008, and Cambodia created a special economic zone in the town of Sihanoukville in February, mainly to produce goods for China (Thayer 2009, 95–96). In 2010, Cambodia and China elevated their bilateral relations to a 'comprehensive strategic partnership of cooperation' during the visit of China's premier Hu Jintao (Doung, Kang, and Kim 2022, 67). Cambodia asked China for weapons and ammunition during the 2008–11 border conflict with Thailand (Chheang 2022, 352). In February 2012, Hun Sen trumpeted "the magnificent bond of relations between Cambodia and China" (quoted in Ciorciari 2015, 250–251). Indeed, in March 2012, Hun Sen and Hu Jintao agreed to reinforce their strategic partnership and coordinate their regional and international policies (Ciorciari 2015, 262–263). Cambodia torpedoed the Association of Southeast Asian Nations (ASEAN)'s efforts to issue a joint statement mentioning the South China Sea conflict in 2012 (Nguyen 2017, 91). At the November 2012 ASEAN summit, Cambodia warned against 'internationalizing' the South China Sea problem, thus aligning with Chinese views that territorial conflicts should be solved bilaterally (Ciorciari 2015, 265). When U.S. President Barack Obama visited Phnom Penh for that summit, the Cambodians displayed on his way two large banners indicating "Long Live the People's Republic of China" (Kynge, Haddou, and Peel 2016).

However, these good relations remained far from full alignment. Cambodia maintained high-level security relations with Washington and made clear it was not ready to bandwagon with Beijing. The Cambodian foreign minister assured in 2010 that "China has no influence on Cambodia at all. We accept all foreign aid if it is given without conditions" (quoted in Ciorciari 2015, 262). In April 2012, Hun Sen affirmed that Cambodia was not a Chinese satellite and "not going to be bought by anyone" (quoted in Ciorciari 2015, 263). In late 2013, Cambodia declared a 'strategic partnership' with Japan and agreed to a joint ASEAN-Japan statement underlining the importance of the freedom of navigation, a jibe at China. In May 2014, Cambodia also failed to block an ASEAN statement implicitly condemning Chinese behavior in the South China Sea (Ciorciari 2015, 266).

There was then an inflection of trajectory, and close alignment came back. In June 2015, Cambodia and China signed a defense cooperation agreement under which Beijing is to finance Cambodian soldiers' training and medical services — around 30% of all Cambodian officers have received training in China. The Chinese also helped in the intelligence domain and military facility construction (Nguyen 2017, 94). After the June 2015 clash at the Vietnamese border, Cambodia's defense minister went to Beijing. The Chinese pledged to defend Cambodian sovereignty, and the Cambodians did the same in return. It was the first time Cambodia promised total support for China's sovereignty (Leng 2017, 341–342). In October 2015, a Cambodian defense ministry secretary of state saw the threat of foreign powers using their "soft power" to intervene in the country's domestic affairs, obviously referring to the United States (quoted in Heder 2018, 116). Cambodia became a founding member of China's Asian Infrastructure Investment Bank, created in December 2015 (Doung, Kang, and Kim 2022, 76). The 2016 Cambodian People's Party (CPP) Congress affirmed prioritizing "big donors, big countries, and neighboring ones," obviously China (quoted in Nguyen 2017, 88). Cambodia's Council of Ministers' spokesman stated in 2016 that "without Chinese aid, we go nowhere" (Hutt 2016). In February 2016, China and Cambodia conducted their first naval exercise (Po and Primiano 2020a, 456). The two states also started to conduct an annual exercise named *Golden Dragon* that same year.

Cambodia also grew more critical of the U.S. strategy in the region. The January 2016 CPP congress found that some "prevent the People's Republic of China from rising in the region and the rest of the world" (quoted in Nguyen 2017, 89). While showing no enthusiasm for U.S. initiatives, Phnom Penh readily supported Chinese initiatives such as the One Belt One Road/Belt and Road Initiative, the Asian Infrastructure Investment Bank, and the Boao Forum for Asia (Nguyen 2017, 89; Reaksmey 2019). Phnom Penh also condemned U.S. Freedom of Navigation Operations in the South China Sea (Nguyen 2017, 91).

Cambodia condemned the July 2016 Permanent Court of Arbitration's ruling that supported the Philippines's territorial claim against China, claiming it to be "the worst political collusion in the framework of international politics" (Xinhua 2016). When the ASEAN states hoped to issue a communique defending the ruling contradicting China's claims, Cambodia refused and pushed the others to ignore the ruling, a move to support China's interests (Kynge, Haddou, and Peel 2016).

The Cambodian government suspended all military exchanges with the United States in early 2017. It canceled the annual *Angkor Sentinel* exercise with the United States in January 2017 and canceled a U.S. Navy's humanitarian program soon after (Doung, Kang, and Kim 2022, 75, 79). The Cambodians also cracked down on U.S.-owned or financed media (Croissant 2018, 194–197). In early 2017, Cambodia forbade the Taiwanese flag from being displayed on its soil (Po and Primiano 2020a, 447). In February 2018, Hun Sen said that "Chinese leaders respect me highly and treat me as an equal," and asked, addressing the United States, "what have you offered me besides cursing and disciplining me and threatening to put sanctions on me?" (quoted in Beech 2018).

In 2019, Cambodia strongly expressed its support for Beijing's repressive policy in Hong Kong, and Hun Sen called China an "ironclad friend" (quoted in Po and Primiano 2020a, 447). Cambodia granted China access to the Ream Naval Base, a significant development. In March, Cambodia and China conducted an enlarged version of their joint exercise *Golden Dragon* in Cambodia, near the Vietnamese border (Radio Free Asia 2020), and, in April 2019, Cambodia and China signed a so-called "Action Plan 2019-2023 on Building China-Cambodia Community of Shared Future" (Doung, Kang, and Kim 2022, 78). In February 2020, Hun Sen became the first foreign leader to visit Beijing since the outbreak of COVID-19 (Doung, Kang, and Kim 2022, 78). In October, Hun Sen appointed a Chinese national, Chen Zhi, as his advisor (Murg 2022, 127). Cambodia and China then signed a free trade agreement (Murg 2022, 129).

However, the Cambodians still hope to gain U.S. support. In February 2020, the Cambodians tried to allay U.S. worries about a potential Chinese base and underlined that Cambodia did not want to depend overly on Beijing (Leng and Chheang 2021, 129). In June 2021, when the Americans expressed concerns about the Ream Naval Base, the Cambodians allowed an American delegation to visit the base, although that did not suffice to convince Washington (Leng and Chheang 2021, 129–130). Cambodia has remained supportive of U.S. involvement in Southeast Asia and pushed for upgrading the Mekong-U.S. Partnership in 2020 (Leng and Chheang 2021, 132). Indeed, the Cambodian Ministry of Foreign Affairs (2021) believes it "crucial and necessary to build synergy and complementary among flagship regional initiatives such as the 'Belt and Road,' the 'Indo-Pacific Strategy,' and other policies of major regional countries toward Southeast Asia." Nevertheless, the Cambodians are clearly disappointed by the United States' lack of support. In May 2021, Hun Sen rhetorically asked: "If I don't rely on China, who will I rely on? If I don't ask China, who am I to ask?" (Nikkei 2021).

4.5. *Conclusion*

At first, Cambodia enjoyed improving relations with the United States. However, Phnom Penh almost went to war with Thailand between 2008 and 2011, and relations with Vietnam deteriorated in 2009–2010. This period of high tensions with neighbors witnessed increasing Cambodian alignment with China. After 2012, relations with both Thailand and Vietnam bettered quickly while Cambodia still enjoyed American support. The Cambodians appeared to distance themselves from the Chinese between 2013 and 2014. Tensions with Vietnam came back with force in 2014, and Cambodia soon got closer to China. These tensions eventually receded, but the arrival of the Trump administration in early 2017 marked a major shift in American policy toward democracy promotion in Cambodia. Cambodia continued to seek Chinese support. After 2019, the Americans started to target the Cambodian regime more intensely, and the Cambodians aligned closer than ever with Beijing (see *Table 4.4*).

Table 4.4. Summary

Hostility w/ Thailand	2008–11			2012–22		
	high			low		
Hostility w/ Vietnam	2008	2009–10	2011–3	2014–6	2017–9	2020–22
	low	medium	low	medium	low	low-medium
U.S. assistance	2008–16				2017–8	2019–22
	low-medium				low	none
Bandwagoning	2008–12	2013–4		2015–8		2019–22
	increase	decrease		increase		increase

This case study suggests a strong link between third conflicts, U.S. support, and alignment with China. Periods of heightened tensions with Thailand, Vietnam, or both, were followed by increased alignment with China. U.S. support was always limited. As Cheunboran (2017, 243) put it, "Phnom Penh is of the view that Cambodia has never been in American strategic interest in Asia and that the White House has always preferred Thailand and Vietnam to Cambodia." However, even this low level of support was enough to limit the Chinese allure, at least when third conflicts remained subdued. As expected, there is little trace of internal balancing toward China. Cambodia's defense posture mostly targets Bangkok and Hanoi. Phnom Penh boosted its military effort during the near war with Thailand, with its military spending increasing by 17% from 2010 to 2011 (Var 2017, 163).

However, as expected, Cambodian officials understand full well the risks of bandwagoning; they fear a loss of sovereignty to China and worsening relations with other states (Po and Primiano 2020a, 457). According to a ministry of foreign affairs insider, "the current leaders in Phnom Penh are very much aware of the risk arising from Cambodia's overdependence on China [but] Cambodia's alignment options are also limited" (Cheunboran 2017, 244). Thus, Cambodia never fully aligned with China and maintained a margin of maneuver.

5. Myanmar

Myanmar is a Southeast Asian state of close to 680,000 square kilometers inhabited by around 55 million. It gained independence from Britain in 1948 and borders Bangladesh, China, India, Laos, and Thailand. Despite a rocky beginning, China and Myanmar have enjoyed close relations throughout the last decades. The Burmese describe their relationship with China as *pauk-phaw*, or 'brotherhood.' Yet, this alignment with Beijing is ill-explained by traditional idealist theories. China remains unpopular in Burmese society, and the elites resent Myanmar's dependency on Beijing (Egreteau and Chenyang 2018, 313; Kobayashi and King 2022, 1023; Peng 2021, 196; Zin 2012). Furthermore, Myanmar is a peculiar case due to its frequent regime change. It went from military dictatorship to democratic governance and back. This allows testing the influence of domestic regime type on alignment with China.

5.1. *Threat Severity*

Myanmar is a large state, bigger than France or Ukraine. The Irrawaddy River flows north to south and roughly cuts Myanmar in two. It is the heart of the country, and its drainage basin is relatively flat. This heartland is surrounded by mountains, which make up most of the borderlands. The Hengduan Mountains form most of the border with China, with mountains of several thousand meters high. However, only a thin part of the mountain range is on Myanmar's side of the border. The easternmost part of the border is lower in elevation and presents more points of access. The climate allows for military operations all year round, although rural roads are impassable during the wet season (Hadden 2008). The largest city by far, Yangon, is in the southern part of the country, while the capital, Naypyidaw, is relatively close to the Chinese border.

The Burmese military is large, with around 350,000 troops, the immense majority of whom are in the army. However, the army is highly infantry-centric and lacks armor. It possesses overall close to 200 tanks, primarily old Chinese designs. The air force is small and has only a handful of modern combat aircraft. In addition, Myanmar's air defense is weak. The navy counts some large ships but would likely be inconsequential in a war with China due to geographic distance. The military is primarily geared toward domestic conflict and has limited capability for high-intensity modern warfare (IISS 2022, 292–294; Selth 2018, 25–27).

Therefore, the Burmese military would have a hard time resisting a Chinese onslaught. Although geography offers some advantages — the sheer size of the country and mountainous borderlands — these do not compensate for the weakness of the Burmese military. Furthermore, the presence of pro-Chinese rebel groups in borderlands means that the Burmese government lacks control over part of its border and thus faces an even dire situation (Kobayashi and King 2022, 1021). Hence, the level of Chinese threat is high — a swift and easy invasion of Myanmar is likely possible.

As an expert noticed, "the security risk of being invaded by the northern giant has always been a main concern for the Burmese leaders who harbored deep distrust with China" (Peng 2021, 183). Fear of China is widespread among the military (Zin 2012). The Burmese are also wary of China's links to several rebel groups (Chow and Easley 2019a; Peng 2021, 184, 194). They even accused retired Chinese soldiers of joining rebel forces fighting the government (Peng 2018, 237). Naypyidaw is afraid of building new infrastructure connecting Myanmar to China due to security motives (Peng 2021, 193).

Burmese officials perceive China as a malevolent influence over Myanmar's domestic politics. They are unhappy with China's clout but believe they must work with the Chinese due to their sheer power (Kobayashi and King 2022, 1026–1027). As Aung San Suu Kyi, a major political figure, said, "we have to get along with the neighbouring country whether we like it or not" (Buncombe 2013). While relations with the West were quickly improving, the Burmese president declared that "if we do not take national defence seriously, we will fall under the rule of neo-colonialists again [...] neo-colonialists are anxious to interfere in the internal affairs of our country because our country occupies a strategic position geographically and economically" (Online Burma/Myanmar

Library 2011). It is hard not to see "neo-colonialists" as a codename for China. Overall, Myanmar has a heightened sense of threat emanating from Beijing.

5.2. *Third Conflict*

Myanmar has been embroiled in ethnic civil wars since its inception. Numerous ethnic armed organizations (EAOs) fight the Burmese government. Some of these EAOs muster combat capabilities worthy of small states; non-state groups may represent overall 100,000 troops (Selth 2018, 30).[1] Therefore, unsurprisingly, "Myanmar's leaders perceived their chief security threat to be the numerous ethnic armed groups within the country" (Chow and Easley 2019a).

The Wa State effectively controls a northeastern part of Myanmar bordering China and a small enclave bordering Thailand, territories where the Wa people reside. Although it officially recognizes the authority of the Burmese government, it is de facto an independent state. The statelet extracts significant revenues from drug trafficking. The United Wa State Army possesses over twenty-thousand troops and musters significant weaponry, including modern Chinese designs. It is thus the most powerful of Myanmar's rebel groups (Lintner 2019). The Kachin Independence Organization maintains an armed force, the Kachin Independence Army, and operates in the northernmost part of Myanmar. It may maintain up to 10,000 active-duty troops (Myanmar Peace Monitor). The Karen National Union is active in southeastern Myanmar along the Thai border and maintains significant combat forces (Jolliffe 2016, 23–25). Other major EAOs include the Myanmar National Democratic Alliance Army, the Arakan Rohingya Salvation Army, the Shan State Army, the Arakan Army, and the Ta'ang National Liberation Army.

The period started with relatively stable relations between the Naypyidaw regime and EAOs. In 2009, the army launched a major attack against the Myanmar National Democratic Alliance Army in the region of Kokang. This marked the beginning of a period of renewed large-scale violence. Violent clashes with Karen militants occurred throughout 2010. In 2011, the longstanding ceasefire between the Kachin Independence Organization and the Burmese military collapsed, leading to heavy fighting in the Kachin region.

Relations between the government and EAOs bettered in January 2012 with the signature of a ceasefire between Naypyidaw and the Karen National Union. Although fighting against the Myanmar National Democratic Alliance Army intensified in early 2015, the Nationwide Cease-Fire Agreement signed that same year between the government and several EAOs led to a more stable situation. The elections in 2015 allowed a pacific transition of power from the

---

[1] This figure likely increased greatly since the 2021 coup.

military junta-aligned party to the National League for Democracy in April 2016, nurturing hopes of national reconciliation. However, several EAOs launched a large offensive against the military in late 2016. Also, the Arakan Rohingya Salvation Army increased its attacks. The military responded with extreme violence, often targeting civilians, and sent tens of thousands on the roads. Clashes remained recurrent throughout Myanmar after that.

The 2021 coup led to increased insurgent activities from existing EAOs and the formation of new armed factions. The opposition to the coup regime created a government in exile, which established its own armed branch in May. These armed forces may have reached around 50,000 troops as of 2022 (Jagan 2022).

5.3. *U.S. Assistance*

Relations between Myanmar and the United States started on a poor footing, as the country has long been the target of U.S. sanctions. Indeed, the Bush administration considered Myanmar an "outpost of tyranny." At the beginning of the period, the Burmese regime felt an existential threat coming from the United States (Selth 2018, 27). The commander-in-chief of the Burmese military visited North Korea in 2008, hoping to acquire North Korean weapons. Numerous exchanges between the two countries happened throughout the year. Unsurprisingly, this increased Washington's threat perception (Steinberg 2018, 296). Congress took additional sanctions in 2008.

In February 2009, Secretary of State Hillary Clinton signaled a willingness to engage with Myanmar, even if sanctions would remain (Peng 2018, 171). Washington engaged in a policy review in the spring of 2009 and announced a new approach to Myanmar in September (Steinberg 2018, 293). Clinton also declared that the United States could eventually sign a treaty of cooperation with the ASEAN that was on hold due to Myanmar's membership in the association (Steinberg 2015, 436). Virginia Senator Jim Webb visited Myanmar in August 2009 and promised increased American support if Naypyidaw distanced itself from Beijing (Han 2018, 97). Aung San Suu Kyi was released from house arrest in November 2010. But despite these openings, sanctions remained in place.

In March 2011, the new president, Thein Sein, announced extensive political reforms toward democratization (Steinberg 2015, 439). Free and fair elections took place in May 2011. These and the following liberalization pleased the United States. In 2011, President Obama saw "flickers of progress" in Myanmar and wanted "to explore whether the United States can empower a positive transition in Burma" (quoted in Haacke 2015, 60). Clinton visited Myanmar in December 2011, the first visit by a senior U.S. official in decades (Han 2018, 97–98).

The liberal National League for Democracy participated in and won the April 2012 by-elections, thus eliciting U.S. sympathy. In May 2012, Obama nominated the first U.S. ambassador to Myanmar since 1990. In September 2012, Secretary Clinton stated that Washington would ease restrictions on importing Burmese goods (Haacke 2015, 62). Obama then went to Myanmar in November 2012, the first time an American president had ever visited the country (Han 2018, 97–98). He hinted at possible defense ties during this visit, and low-level cooperation started in 2013 (Selth 2018, 32). The Burmese president visited the United States in May 2013. Most American sanctions were lifted, and Washington helped Myanmar participate in multilateral organizations. In May 2014, Obama noticed that bilateral relations greatly improved and visited Myanmar again in November 2014 (Steinberg 2018, 297). Aung San Suu Kyi visited the United States in September 2016, marking the high point of Myanmar-U.S. relations. Washington terminated the remaining sanctions on Naypyidaw and offered it trade benefits.

However, the escalating Rohingya crisis soon soured the relationship. In October 2017, the United States stopped military aid and limited cooperation programs. In November 2017, the U.S. Secretary of State declared that the violence in the Rakhine state constituted a case of ethnic cleansing against the Rohingya. Personal sanctions on Burmese officials soon followed in late 2017 and throughout 2018 and 2019. In January 2020, the Trump administration severely restricted Burmese immigration to the United States. Finally, the 2021 coup led to a total breakdown. Washington broke diplomatic relations with Naypyidaw and imposed extensive sanctions. Relations remained inexistent after that.

5.4. *Burmese Behavior Toward China*

At first, Myanmar was mostly aligned with China and had poor relations with Washington. Myanmar refused to let U.S. aid workers enter the country despite the humanitarian catastrophe caused by cyclone Nargis in May 2008 for fear of U.S. malevolence. Also, 2008 saw growing relations between the Burmese and North Koreans. In mid-2008, the Burmese signed agreements to sell and transport gas to China while refusing a similar Indian proposal (Goh and Steinberg 2016, 68). In 2009, Beijing and Naypyidaw decided to build oil and gas pipelines from the Burmese port of Kyaukphyu on the Indian Ocean to the Chinese city of Kunming, thus helping secure China's energy supply by bypassing the Malacca Strait (Han 2018, 97).

In August 2009, the junta allowed the American senator Webb to meet Aung San Suu Kyi and released an American citizen arrested a few days prior in a gesture of goodwill to the United States (Peng 2018, 183). Nevertheless, relations with Beijing remained good overall, with Naypyidaw agreeing to several large Chinese economic projects. In May 2011, Thein Sein visited Beijing and agreed to establish a comprehensive strategic partnership.

However, due to Burmese actions, Sino-Burmese relations started to deteriorate soon after that. In September 2011, Naypyidaw suspended the construction of the Myitsone Dam without prior notice to Beijing, which was meant to supply electricity to China (Egreteau and Li 2018, 313–314; Han 2018, 98). Myanmar released in January 2012 hundreds of political prisoners, in part to please the United States. Myanmar joined the American-led Lower Mekong initiative in 2012. In 2013, Myanmar sent observers to the American-led Cobra Gold military exercise in Thailand (Selth 2018, 32). Also, Thein Sein visited Washington in May 2013.

Meanwhile, economic cooperation with China stalled, and Burmese defiance increased. Both sides had agreed to build a deep-sea port at Kyaukphyu in 2013, but no progress was made for a long time (Jones and Khin 2021, 302). In 2014, the Burmese side abandoned a plan to build a railway going from China to the Burmese coast. The Burmese showed little hurry to complete other ongoing projects with Beijing (Han 2018, 98). An agreement to build a transborder railway signed in April 2011 collapsed that same year (Jones and Khin 2021, 302). In 2015, Myanmar ignored Chinese calls to tone down its attacks on the Myanmar National Democratic Alliance Army and remained undeterred by Beijing's massive military drills near the border (Peng 2021, 194). During that period, Myanmar also engaged with European states, Japan, and especially India (Peng 2018, 279–291).

However, although alignment decreased, it never totally stopped. Aung San Suu Kyi visited China in June 2015, before her victory during the incoming national elections, and several times after that (Han 2018, 98). Myanmar became a founding member of the Asian Infrastructure Investment Bank in June 2015 (Jones and Khin 2021, 302). Chinese Foreign Minister Wang Yi was one of the first to visit Myanmar after the new civilian president Htin Kyaw took office in April 2016 (Han 2018, 98). In July 2016, Naypyidaw refused to take a stance between China and the ASEAN states over the South China Sea dispute (Passeri 2020, 949). Aung San Suu Kyi reserved her first visit to a non-ASEAN state in China in August 2016, where she talked positively about the Belt and Road Initiative (Egreteau and Chenyang 2018, 314; Jones and Khin 2021, 302).

After 2017, greater alignment with China returned. Burmese President Htin Kyaw visited the country in April 2017, restarting several stalled projects (Jones and Khin 2021, 302). Aung San Suu Kyi participated in the Belt and Road Initiative Forum of May 2017 in Beijing, committed to Chinese initiatives, and established an economic cooperation zone at the border (Jones and Khin 2021, 302–303). In November 2017, Suu Kyi expressed her gratitude for China's support, stating that "China and Myanmar will be good neighbors forever with fraternal spirit" (quoted in Han 2018, 98–99). Senior General Min Aung Hlaing also met President Xi Jinping in Beijing. He thanked China for backing Myanmar against foreign pressure and expressed support for Beijing's Belt and Road Initiative. A senior Burmese politician declared the same month that Myanmar had no choice but to align with China due to international pressure (Frontier Myanmar 2017; Kobayashi and King 2022, 1029). Relations kept bettering. China's Xi Jinping visited Myanmar in January 2020 and signed numerous agreements.

Nevertheless, that period did not correspond to full alignment. Myanmar kept working with India and Japan (Peng 2018, 338–340). The Burmese were unsatisfied with the agreement with China to build the Kyaukphyu port. When they renegotiated this agreement from 2016 to 2018, they invited the United States to support their efforts to extract better terms (Kobayashi and King 2022, 1028). A deal to build an oil refinery was canceled in November 2017 (Jones and Khin 2021, 302). A memorandum of understanding to build a China-Myanmar Economic Corridor was signed in September 2018, but implementation was impeded by Myanmar's wariness of the ordeal (Kobayashi and King 2022, 1019).

However, these reserves disappeared after the February 2021 coup, and Naypyidaw aligned fully with Beijing. The coup regime quickly approached China for support and agreed to increase economic cooperation with Beijing. Implementation of existing projects accelerated, and the Burmese government finally started work on the stalled Kyaukphyu port (Dossi and Gabusi 2023; Kurlantzick 2022). Also, the new regime appointed Wunna Maung Lwin, a known pro-Chinese element, as foreign minister (Lintner 2021).

5.5. *Conclusion*

The Burmese case confirms this book's expectations. At first, Myanmar was closely aligned with China in the face of tensions with the EAOs and poor relations with the United States. Although conflicts with EAOs worsened, the United States opted for engaging Naypyidaw, which took its distance from China. As third conflicts withered and U.S. support increased, the Burmese growingly closed their door to China. However, local conflicts flared up again while the Rohingya crisis disheartened Washington. These events led to renewed Burmese engagement with China. The 2021 coup was the coup de grâce for U.S. support while the civil war intensified. This forced Myanmar to fully align with Beijing *(see Table 4.5)*.

Table 4.5. Summary

Hostility w/ EAOs	2008	2009–11	2012–6	late 2016–20	2021–2
	medium	high	low	medium	high
U.S. assistance	2008	2009–10	2011–6	2017–20	2021–2
	none	low	medium	low	none
Bandwagoning	2008–mid-9	mid-2009–mid-1	mid-2011–6	2017–20	2021–2
	increase	decrease	decrease	increase	increase

Myanmar long tried to avoid aligning fully with Beijing and worked hard to diversify its foreign partnerships. As noticed by two observers, "China's dominant political and economic influence in the country was becoming a serious concern for the government, and the need to diversify its international partners was undoubtedly among the external reasons that prompted Thein Sein to start the [2011] reforms" (Dossi and Gabusi 2023, 1313). Myanmar has regularly imported Chinese weapons and has important defense connections with China. Yet, Sino-Burmese defense relations have decreased since the 2000s. Naypyidaw developed close military cooperation with Russia to reduce its reliance on Chinese weaponry. Myanmar also tried hard to build defense relationships with India (Peng 2018, 203–207; 2021, 189–192).

Myanmar belongs to the accommodator category since traces of internal balancing are slim. Furthermore, as expected, this case demonstrates that accommodators for security are likely to make concessions to rivals and the United States since Myanmar offered ceasefires to EAOs and made human rights improvements to get U.S. support.

6. North Korea

North Korea is located in Northeast Asia and has around 25 million people. It is 120,000 square kilometers large and borders China, Russia, and South Korea. It gained independence in 1948, after three years of Soviet supervision following the end of World War II. China and North Korea have been officially allied since 1961 and are allegedly as close as 'lips and teeth.' For constructivists, historical bounds and shared ideology would suggest that North Korea should closely align with China. Yet, North Korea often appears as a free electron and tries hard to stay out of Beijing's grasp. Pyongyang is thus an interesting case to test the present theory since most of the existing literature would expect a strong alignment between Chinese and North Koreans.

6.1. *Threat Severity*

North Korea's northern half is mainly mountainous, notably close to the Chinese border. Said border runs for almost 1,400 kilometers. Most of the border is made by two rivers, the Yalu and the Tumen, the former being harder to cross than the latter. The climate is relatively favorable to military operations all year round. Save for the capital area, there is no major urban barrier to stop an invader. If the Chinese can cross the Yalu River, the terrain most favorable to offensive operation is the plain region that makes the western third of North Korea, along the Yellow Sea's coast. It runs from the Chinese border to the demilitarized zone with South Korea. It contains most of the country's economic potential and its capital city, Pyongyang. Nevertheless, a northerly invader would still want to secure the mountains east of the plain to avoid entrapment on this thin stretch of land between mountains and sea. To bypass the mountains, the Chinese army could also try to invade along the eastern coast, where the Chinese, North Korean, and Russian borders meet. However, the eastern coastal plain is even thinner than the western one, and there are few critical targets to seize. In balance, North Korean geography favors the defense against a northerly attacker (Salter 2007, chap. 2).

North Korea boasts a gigantic military apparatus of around 1.2 million personnel. The army alone has over one million troops and is equipped with a plethora of heavy weapons. But most weapons are of dated Chinese and Russian designs. The actual readiness of the force is in doubt, as training is unsophisticated. The air force's inventory appears large, but only a part of the fleet is serviceable. Pyongyang's navy is feeble. It musters an impressive number of submarines on paper, but they are mostly small and decrepit. North Korea possesses a massive number of reservists, but their readiness is likely low.

The North Koreans compensate for their deficiencies in conventional forces by investing in weapons of mass destruction. North Korea's first nuclear detonation occurred in 2006, and it is now able to deliver nuclear strikes with short and medium-range ballistic missiles. Its capability to launch a nuclear warhead at intercontinental ranges remains uncertain, but Pyongyang is without doubt able to strike China and its political, economic, and military centers (IISS 2022, 280–282; Motin 2023, 5).

In that light, the level of Chinese threat remains low. A concerted Chinese offensive would overwhelm North Korea in the end, but a costless, easy victory is improbable. A decided resistance making the best of North Korea's oversized military machine and its difficult terrain could prevent a Chinese blitzkrieg and force Beijing into a costly war of attrition. Essential in this case is North Korea's nuclear deterrent. Attacking nuclear power is always a risky bet. During a war, North Korean nuclear strikes could heavily harm China, although likely not enough to defeat it decisively.

The North Koreans do worry about Chinese power. They are aware of existing discussions within China about using military force against them and denounced Chinese "big-power chauvinism" (Brunnstrom 2017). Indeed, as a leading expert remarked, "any North Korean counter-intelligence officer would tell you that China is their biggest domestic security threat because of its potential to disrupt from the inside" (quoted in Davies 2021). Two others notice that "DPRK officials devote much time and attention to anticipating, forestalling, and responding to what they perceive as harmful decisions by Beijing" (Fingar and Straub, 170–171). Kim Jong-il stated bluntly in May 2009 that "China cannot be trusted" (Lee, Lee, and Moon 2021, 242–243). The North Koreans are also always on the lookout to limit and reduce their economic dependency on China (Garnaut 2013; Keck 2014). However, there is little trace that Pyongyang considers a quick Chinese invasion an immediate threat, and its military remains primarily oriented southward against South Korea.

6.2. *Third Conflict*

North Korea's principal third rival is South Korea. Both states went to war during the early 1950s, and relations have been poisonous since then. Both hope to reunify the Korean Peninsula under their banner and concentrate most of their military forces against each other.

The progressive Roh Moo-hyun administration (2003–2008) was committed to improving relations with the North. But the arrival of a conservative president in February 2008, Lee Myung-bak, cooled the relationship and ended the 'Sunshine Policy.' The May 2009 North Korean nuclear test sank the relationship some more. Although North Korea released a South Korean prisoner in late 2009 (Nanto and Manyin 2011, 96), relations hardly bettered. The year 2010 was probably the worst of the period. In March 2010, a North Korean submarine sank a South Korean ship, the *Cheonan*, killing 46 seamen. In November, North Korean artillery shelled the South Korean island of Yeonpyeong, leaving four dead. Seoul retaliated with artillery fire of its own. This plunged bilateral relations to a new low, and war appeared increasingly likely.

Relations remained poor after that and hardly improved during the Park Geun-hye administration (2013–2017). On March 31, the two sides exchanged artillery fire off their west coast (Reuters 2014). Inter-Korean tensions increased in the Spring of 2014 due to joint U.S.-South Korean exercises deemed provocative by the North Koreans. North Korea talked of war and temporarily closed the Kaesong Industrial Complex (Wertz 2018, 14). Throughout 2014, the South Koreans discovered crashed North Korean reconnaissance drones on their soil (Park 2017). In August 2015, two South Korean soldiers were gravely injured by a landmine explosion in the demilitarized zone. Seoul was upset by what it saw as Pyongyang deliberately planting new mines to kill South Korean personnel

(AFP 2015). A short artillery exchange occurred on August 20 (BBC 2015b). North Korea's fourth nuclear test in early January 2016 worsened bilateral relations. In February, Seoul stopped operating the Kaesong Industrial Complex.

The new progressive Moon Jae-in administration that took office in May 2017 decided to restart the Sunshine Policy. Kim Jong-un's 2018 new year's address announced North Korea's intention to join the upcoming Winter Olympics organized in South Korea in February. The two states soon agreed to form a joint female hockey team and that Kim Jong-un's sister, Kim Yo-jong, would attend the opening ceremony. During the Olympics, Kim Yo-jong handed the South Korean president an invitation to visit Pyongyang. By the historic Avril 2018 Panmunjom Declaration, Kim Jong-un and Moon Jae-in promised to seek peace and cooperation and decrease military tensions. In late May 2018, the two met again at Panmunjom. Moon Jae-in visited Pyongyang in September 2018, where he met Kim Jong-un for the third time, and they pledged to increase inter-Korean cooperation.

In June 2020, North Korea demolished the Inter-Korean Liaison Office in Kaesong, a blow to Moon Jae-in's peace efforts. Yet, relations remained more cordial than their historical average. North and South even restored a hotline left inactive in July 2021. The Moon administration maintained a conciliant approach toward North Korea up to the end of the period.

6.3. U.S. Assistance

After a war scare in 1994, U.S.-North Korea relations improved at the turn of the century. However, the Bush administration placed North Korea on its target list, and the relationship sank to a new low. But George W. Bush's second term brought a new interest in diplomacy.

Throughout 2008, the Bush administration decided to opt for diplomatic engagement and delisted North Korea as a state supporting terrorism after it accepted to sign a verification arrangement over its nuclear program in October. It even terminated a small number of sanctions, but disagreement over the verification issue stalemated diplomacy (Wertz 2018, 12). Relations sharply declined during the first half of 2009 — a period notably marked by the second North Korean nuclear test — but diplomacy returned in the second half of the year. Washington negotiated a visit by Bill Clinton to Pyongyang in August, where he discussed ways to improve relations with Kim Jong-il. In December, Secretary of State Hillary Clinton announced a new North Korean policy of "strategic patience" while an American official visited Pyongyang to test the waters for renewed diplomacy. However, North Korea's 2010 attacks against South Korea encouraged the United States to take a strong stand against Pyongyang. Washington, consequently, increased its military activities around North Korea and took additional sanctions (Jackson 2019, 60–64).

Washington engaged in exploratory talks with Pyongyang from July 2011 to February 2012. The two capitals announced an agreement on February 29 (the 'Leap Day Deal'), according to which the United States would provide food aid in exchange for North Korea freezing its nuclear and missile-related activities. But this soon collapsed due to new North Korean missile tests and the February 2013 nuclear test. Joint U.S.-ROK military exercises conducted in early 2014 involved strategic bombers, which irritated the North Koreans (Wertz 2018, 13–14). In 2014, Sony Pictures Entertainment released a comedy parodying Kim Jong-un. This movie highly displeased the North Korean regime, and Sony suffered in November a large cyberattack. The United States condemned North Korea before a cyberattack, likely American, temporarily brought down the entire North Korean internet infrastructure. After that, new sanctions were introduced throughout 2015 and 2016.

The January 2016 nuclear test led the Americans to broaden sanctions again. Kim Jong-un was personally targeted in July 2016, leading to a break in official contacts (Wertz 2018, 15). The newly-installed Trump administration committed to a 'maximum pressure' strategy. It enforced existing sanctions with an increased determination, pushed third states to cut their relations with North Korea, and appeared to consider military action. After North Korea launched two intercontinental ballistic missiles, Donald Trump warned in August 2017 that any North Korean threat would "be met with fire and fury like the world has never seen" (Wertz 2018, 16). A volley of heavy U.S.-led UN sanctions crippled North Korea in late 2017, strongly complicating Pyongyang's international dealings. In September 2017, President Trump threatened at the UN General Assembly to "totally destroy" North Korea (Kim 2022, 66–67).

Yet, after North Korean overtures, U.S. intelligence agencies contacted the North Koreans in early 2018. In March, Trump accepted North Korean offers for a summit, and the then CIA director Mike Pompeo secretly visited Pyongyang to meet Kim Jong-un. In May 2018, Pompeo, now Secretary of State, visited Pyongyang again. At the June 2018 Singapore summit, Trump pledged to suspend joint military exercises with South Korea, while Kim promised to dismantle a missile testing site. The American president also assured Kim Jong-un of his willingness to sign a formal peace agreement to end the Korean War. After that summit, Trump rejoiced that the North Korean nuclear problem was now "largely solved" (Wertz 2018, 17–18).

In February 2019, Donald Trump and Kim Jong-un met once more in Hanoi but failed to reach an agreement about denuclearization. In June 2019, Donald Trump expressed his satisfaction with his good relations with North Korea and assured "that something will happen that's going to be very positive" (quoted in Hwang 2019). On June 30, Donald Trump became the first American president to walk on North Korean soil and met with Kim Jong-un again. Discussions continued up to the Stockholm meeting of October but, despite conciliatory signals from the North Korean side, failed to break the stalemate (Kim 2022, 69). In November 2019, the United States even postponed military exercises with South Korea in an "act of goodwill" after North Korean complains (VOA 2019).

At a NATO meeting in December 2019, Donald Trump made a veiled military threat toward North Korea, irritating Pyongyang (Cummings 2019). Throughout 2020, U.S.-North Korean relations reverted to the pattern of threats and missile tests. The election of Joe Biden hardly changed anything, and relations remained poor up to the end of the period.

6.4. *North Korean Behavior Toward China*

In June 2008, North Korea responded to U.S. diplomatic overtures by destroying the cooling tower of the Yongbyon nuclear reactor. But, by September, it had already restarted its nuclear activities to their full. Missile tests in early 2009 irritated the Americans, and North Korea expelled the American and international monitors from the Yongbyon nuclear complex in April. The second nuclear test took place soon after, on May 25. However, North Korea soon signaled a willingness to reengage with Washington. In August, former president Bill Clinton visited Pyongyang, met with Kim Jong-il, and secured the liberation of two detained American journalists. Another American official visited in December to discuss potential further negotiations (Wertz 2018, 13). Chinese Prime Minister Wen Jiabao visited North Korea in October 2009, while Kim Jong-il visited China four times between 2010 and his death in 2011. China and North Korea agreed in November 2010 to create two special economic zones on their common border (Kong 2018, 81).

The first face-to-face visit between the newly-installed Kim Jong-un and a Chinese representative did not occur until July 2012 (Xiao 2015, 65). North Korea's nominal president, Kim Yong-nam, reserved his first visit abroad in May 2012 to Southeast Asia, avoiding China (Kong 2018, 89). Meanwhile, U.S.-North Korean bilateral discussions led in late February 2012 to a moratorium on missile launches, nuclear tests, and nuclear activities. Washington planned to deliver food aid as a reward. However, North Korea launched satellites in April and December, weakening the deal, and the nuclear test in February 2013 buried it for good (Panda 2016).

The third North Korean nuclear took place in February 2013, a few weeks before Xi Jinping became president. But in May, Kim Jong-un sent a delegation to China to make amends and improve strained relations (Xiao 2015, 70–71). Although in late March, the North Koreans had warned of an all-out war on the Peninsula and threatened to attack the United States (Kim 2022, 62), in June, they called for diplomacy with the United States without preconditions and expressed interest in denuclearization (Wertz 2018, 14).

A Japanese official visited North Korea in May 2013 to discuss the Japanese abductee issue. Jang Song-thaek, one of the main pro-Chinese voices in Pyongyang, was executed in December 2013, in no small part due to his role in supporting Chinese investments in the country (Williams 2013). In 2014, North Korea established a committee to work on the abductee issue, and talks eventually led in August 2015 to a foreign minister-level meeting. The North Koreans made additional concessions to the United States: they liberated American prisoners and closed an infamous gulag (Kim 2022, 64; Kong 2018, 89). Meanwhile, in early 2014, domestic propaganda became very belligerent toward China, even calling the country "the sworn enemy" (Zhu 2016, 578–579).

Relations hardly improved after that. The fifth nuclear test happened immediately after the September 2016 G20 summit hosted in China. North Korean agents assassinated Kim Jong-nam, Kim Jong-un's brother, in February 2017 while he was visiting Malaysia. He lived in China and was known as a pro-Chinese element in North Korean politics. North Korean propaganda violently criticized China throughout the first half of 2017 (Brunnstrom 2017). The North Koreans launched a ballistic missile the same day Xi Jinping inaugurated the Belt and Road Forum in May 2017. On May 21, 2017, only a few days later, another missile was launched with a mounted camera pointed westward, thus showing Chinese territory in the footage (Nakazawa 2017). If the message was not explicit enough, the propaganda clarified that "the recent successfully developed new rocket Hwasong-12 is a nuclear transportation vehicle that can conduct attacks on the whole of China" (quoted in Obe and Byrne 2021). The sixth nuclear test occurred in September 2017, during the opening of a BRICS (Brazil, Russia, India, China, and South Africa) summit in China. That same month, the North Koreans declined to host Wang Yi, the Chinese foreign minister. Relations sank to the extent that North Korean officials feared military clashes (Ford 2018, 16).

In early 2018, North Korea resumed contact with the United States, starting with a conciliatory new year's address (Kim 2022, 60). In February, a North Korean delegation attended the Pyeongchang Winter Olympics and laid the groundwork for diplomacy with the United States. Kim Jong-un proposed to Donald Trump to meet for a summit in March. In April 2018, the Workers' Party of Korea unveiled a plan for economic development based on improved relations with Washington. In May 2018, Mike Pompeo visited North Korea and secured the release of three Americans who were detained there. In a conciliatory gesture, North Korea destroyed one of its nuclear testing sites, and the first-ever North Korea-United States summit took place on June 12, 2018, in

Singapore. Meanwhile, the Panmunjom Declaration of Avril 2018 implied that Chinese involvement in Korean affairs was optional, a clear blow to China by North Korea (Ministry of Foreign Affairs 2018).

In fact, in April 2018, Kim Jong-un privately expressed to Moon Jae-in that North Korea did not insist on withdrawing U.S. troops from the Peninsula as a condition for diplomacy. The joint American-North Korean statement produced during the June 2018 Singapore summit did not mention U.S. troops in Korea (BBC 2018). During his 2019 new year's address, Kim Jong-un hoped for the "establishment of new North Korea–US relations" (quoted in Kim 2022, 69). In February 2019, Donald Trump and Kim Jong-un met in Hanoi but failed to secure an agreement. Diplomacy was stalemated after that, although discussions continued up to the end of the year.

The 2012–19 period saw poor Sino-North Korean relations and, at times, improving ties between Pyongyang and Washington. Yet, links to China never totally broke. For example, Jang Song-thaek, Kim Jong-un's uncle-by-marriage and a top official, went to China in August 2012 to oversee the last details of the special economic zones project (Kong 2018, 82). Numerous Chinese-North Korean meetings occurred throughout 2012 and early 2013 (Kim 2022, 62). In July 2016, North Korea agreed to open sea and land tourism routes with China and Russia (Kim 2022, 68). A number of high-level bilateral summits occurred in 2018.

After mid-2019, relations between China and North Korea quickly bettered. Xi Jinping finally made his first visit to Pyongyang in June 2019 (Kim 2022, 70). In August, Pyongyang offered verbal support to Chinese authorities' handling of Hong Kong (Park 2019). Throughout 2021, the North Koreans verbally backed Chinese positions on human rights problems and denounced the December 2021 Summit for Democracy organized by the United States as "a prelude to confrontation and division" (Kim 2022, 72).

6.5. *Conclusion*

Relations between Pyongyang and Seoul were generally very tense before 2017 and more amicable after that. North Korea started the period by improving its relations with Washington. Between mid-2008 and 2011, North Korea sometimes left the door open to the United States but worked closely with China. 2012 started with better relations between Americans and North Koreans, while relations between Beijing and Pyongyang sank. They remained poor for most of the decade until a thaw in mid-2019 when North Korea-U.S. relations stalemated. After that, North Korea growingly aligned with China (see *Table 4.6*). Alignment with China evolved according to this study's theoretical claims less than in other cases. My claims hold for 2008, mid-2011 to mid-2012, and 2018–22. However, for the remainder of the period, the theory poorly explains North Korean alignment with China.

Table 4.6. Summary

Hostility w/ South Korea	2008–16				2017–22		
	high				med.		
U.S. assistance	2008–9	2010–m.-1	m.-2011–m.-2	m.-2012–5	2016–7	2018–m.-9	m.-2019–22
	low	none	low	none	none	med.-low	low
Bandwagoning	2008–m.-8	m.-2008–11		2012–m.-9			m.-2019–22
	decrease	increase		decrease			increase

* e.: early, m.: mid, l.: late, med.: medium

Despite overall alignment with China, it is clear that the North Koreans feel unease about Beijing and would like better relations with the United States and its allies. This is what Kim Jong-il told Bill Clinton during his 2009 visit (Brown 2016). As Kim Jong-un put it, "after denuclearization, we hope to gain the help of the United States to develop our economy and become a normal state" (Lee, Lee, and Moon 2021, 243). Kim once confessed to Pompeo "that he needed the Americans in South Korea to protect him from the CCP, and that the CCP needs the Americans out so they can treat the peninsula like Tibet and Xinjiang" (Byun 2023). In 2007, a North Korean delegation to New York even proposed to help the United States contain China (Barannikova 2019, 18). Also, military provocations target not only South Korea or the United States but also China (Garnaut 2013). As a North Korean official said, "although Japan is a century-old enemy […], China is a thousand-year-old enemy" (quoted in Kim 2018).

7. Pakistan

Pakistan is a South Asian state of over 200 million. It was established in 1947 and shares borders with Afghanistan, China, India, and Iran. Although China-Pakistan relations have long been good, Pakistan has had close relations with the United States during most of its existence and received extensive American financial and military support. Also, numerous people in Pakistan are displeased with the growingly visible Chinese presence in the country (International Crisis Group 2018; Ullah, Khan, Rahman, and Ullah 2021). Explaining why Pakistan drifted toward China would thus be insightful.

7.1. *Threat Severity*

Pakistan is a large state of almost 900,000 square kilometers. Northern Pakistan, along the Chinese border, is covered by high mountains, with numerous ones well over 4,000 meters high. The main road leading to China goes through the Khunjerab Pass at an altitude of close to 4,700 meters (Garlick 2018, 524). South of these mountains, the North Indian River Plain offers a flat terrain less favorable to the defense. The Indus River system can help a defender, although less so as one moves southward (Spate and Learmonth 2017). Pakistan also possesses numerous large cities likely to impede enemy movements.

The Pakistani military musters around 650,000 troops. The troops are overall well-trained and competent. With close to 560,000 personnel, Pakistan's ground forces are larger than even the Russian or the U.S. army. It also has ample heavy equipment, although often relying on old American and Chinese platforms. The Pakistani navy has several capital ships and submarines. As of 2021, Islamabad's air force could count on over 400 combat-capable aircraft, most fairly modern. Large paramilitary forces offer an immediately available reserve force. Pakistan is a nuclear power, possesses land-launched and air-launched nuclear weapons, and is capable of striking deep within China (IISS 2022, 296–300). The material threat level appears thus low.

Unsurprisingly, "some Pakistani officials are growing concerned about losing sovereignty to their deep-pocketed Asian ally" (quoted in Abi-Habib 2018). After interviewing Pakistani military officers, an observer reports "a clear reluctance to allow Pakistan to fall too far under China's sway" (Markey 2016, 154). However, Islamabad appears to fear little China's growing military capabilities. Indeed, there are few traces that the Pakistanis perceive an imminent military threat emanating from Beijing.

7.2. *Third Conflict*

India is Pakistan's main rival, and the Indian threat informs Pakistan's foreign and defense policies (Einhorn and Sidhu 2017, 7–9). Relations between Pakistan and

India, its gigantic eastern neighbor, have been poisonous since the two states' independence in 1947. The two fought wars in 1947, 1965, 1971, and 1999 and engaged in numerous skirmishes directly and attacks through proxies (Hiro 2015).

The relations were already strained at the beginning of the period, with a background of clashes blamed on the other (Mukherjee 2009). A series of terrorist attacks struck Mumbai from 26 to 29 November 2008. The Indians suspected a Pakistani plot, and India seemingly prepared to retaliate. U.S. Senator John McCain warned Pakistan that India was ready to launch air strikes on the country (Subramanian 2008). Both sides increased readiness levels and deployed their forces for a potential conflagration throughout December (NDTV 2008). Relations remained poor throughout 2009. In February 2010, nine Indians — including two military and the assistant consul general from the local consulate — were killed in an attack in Kandahar. The Indians interpreted this as a Pakistani plot. The month after that, large terrorist attacks occurred in Lahore, and the Pakistanis denounced Indian involvement (Zaman 2015, 233).

In February 2011, Delhi and Islamabad resumed peace discussions, suspended after the 2008 Mumbai attacks, and foreign ministers met in July. However, in July and August 2011, transborder attacks killed personnel on both sides (Hindu 2016). Relations improved in 2012, as India allowed foreign direct investment from Pakistan, and the two states opened a border trading post in April (Banerji 2012). The Foreign Minister of Pakistan signaled in July 2012 his intention to solve disputes with India (Indian Express 2012), and in September 2012, the Indian minister of foreign affairs visited Pakistan. However, heavy skirmishes occurred throughout 2013 (Dawn 2013).

New prime minister Narendra Modi invited his Pakistani counterpart, Nawaz Sharif, to his swearing-in ceremony in late May 2014, showing a willingness to reset relations on a more positive footing (Grare 2014, 101). But from July 2014 and throughout 2015, renewed clashes across the border killed numerous military and civilians (DNA 2015). Indian and Pakistani Prime Ministers Narendra Modi and Nawaz Sharif met in Paris at a UN climate summit in November 2015 and agreed to peace talks (Haidar 2015). In a rare feat, Modi visited Pakistan in December 2015. This marked a high point in bilateral relations, which steadily worsened thereafter.

In April 2016, the Pakistanis arrested a former Indian Navy officer in Balochistan, and the Pakistani Chief of Army Staff accused Indian secret services of working to sabotage the China-Pakistan Economic Corridor (CPEC; Shah 2016). In September 2016, terrorists from Pakistan attacked Uri in Kashmir and killed numerous Indian soldiers. India responded by striking terrorist bases inside Pakistan. Recurring cross-border clashes between 2016 and 2018 killed dozens on both sides (Khajuria 2018).

In mid-February 2019, a suicide attack blamed on Pakistan killed 40 Indian police officers (Masood 2021). In response, on February 26, 2019, an Indian plane stroke an alleged terrorist camp in Pakistan. Islamabad retaliated the next day and shot down an Indian aircraft. Exchanges of artillery fire followed (Gettleman, Kumar, and Yasir 2019). In August 2019, Delhi abrogated Kashmir's autonomy and placed the region under its direct control, a decision that worsened relations with Pakistan still more.

Between November 2020 and February 2021, border skirmishes left many dead on both sides. 2020 was actually the bloodiest year for India since 2003, with nearly 5,000 skirmishes. This series of clashes ended with a ceasefire on February 25, which marked a breakthrough in the bilateral relationship (Fareed 2021). Although violence receded, this led to little improvement despite low-level attempts at dialogue (Amir 2022).

7.3. *U.S. Assistance*

The Americans started the period with discontent about Pakistan's protection and support for terrorist groups. The November 2008 Mumbai attack, which has been linked to Pakistani agents and killed six Americans, irritated Washington, and the incoming Obama administration promised a tougher approach to Islamabad (Zaman 2015, 217–221).

Nevertheless, relations remain overall cordial. The Congress passed the Enhanced Partnership with Pakistan Act in October 2009. U.S. aid to Pakistan kept increasing — the 2010 total reached $4.3 billion, putting Pakistan ahead of Israel (Zaman 2015, 222–226). In 2009, Obama wrote to Pakistani president Asif Ali Zardari a letter praising the bilateral relationship and assuring him to pursue "new patterns of cooperation between and among India, Afghanistan, and Pakistan to counter those who seek to create permanent tension and conflict on the subcontinent" (quoted in Zaman 2015, 225).

In 2011, bilateral relations entered a crisis. In January 2011, a CIA contractor killed two Pakistani nationals in Lahore. Washington succeeded in having him released from custody, but the Pakistanis were displeased by the scale of the CIA's clandestine operations on their soil. The day after the contractor left the country, a CIA drone strike killed 38 people, enraging Pakistani leaders even more. Pakistan asked for the departure of numerous CIA and other American forces active there (Zaman 2015, 234–236).

The next quarrel broke out on May 2, 2011, when U.S. special forces infiltrated Pakistan and killed the infamous terrorist Osama bin Laden. This violation of Pakistani borders plunged the relationship to a new low. Washington decided to suspend military aid programs in July. In November, a NATO airstrike along the Afghan-Pakistani border killed 24 soldiers. In reaction, Islamabad closed down NATO's supply roads to Afghanistan, complicating NATO's logistics. Pakistan asked for apologies and threatened to downgrade relations. The Americans responded by withholding their military assistance (Zaman 2015, 237–241). However, both sides wanted to mend fences, and the United States apologized for the killing. Pakistan reopened NATO's supply roads in July 2012, and U.S. military aid restarted. The peaceful power transfer to Nawaz Sharif in June 2013 encouraged the United States to resume strategic dialogue, stalled since 2011 (241–243).

Relations remained stable during the next few years. In October 2015, Sharif visited Washington and, despite lingering contentious issues, "expressed satisfaction with the cooperation achieved in defense relations" (quoted in Brunnstrom and Ali 2015). In February 2016, the Obama administration announced considerable aid to Pakistan — $860 million in total, including $265 million to purchase military equipment. This aimed at "ensuring the safety of Pakistani nuclear installations, working with Pakistan to facilitate the peace process in Afghanistan, and promoting improved relations with India" (Economic Times 2018). Washington agreed to sell eight F-16 fighter jets to Islamabad at the risk of irritating India (Singh 2016).

Relations degraded in 2017 and 2018, as the Americans pressured Pakistan by stopping security assistance and drastically reducing economic assistance. The Trump administration also increased drone strikes in Pakistan and threatened its status as a non-NATO alliance partner. Furthermore, Washington pushed to put Pakistan on the anti-terrorist Financial Action Task Force blacklist, complicating the country's financial dealings (Mistry 2020, 258). Donald Trump tweeted on January 1, 2018, that Pakistan has "given us nothing but lies & deceit" (quoted in Mistry 2020, 243). In October 2018, Washington expressed little interest in granting IMF loans to Pakistan because of Islamabad's financial dependency on China. Obviously, the Pakistanis did not like these criticisms much (Mistry 2020, 255; Rabbi, Munawar, and Bukhari 2022, 196–198).

Pakistani Prime Minister Imran Khan visited the United States in July 2019. Donald Trump thanked Pakistan for its help in the Afghan peace process and offered his mediation to solve the Kashmir issue. The United States also helped Pakistan secure loans from international organizations. Relations remained cordial throughout the year (Rabbi, Munawar, and Bukhari 2022, 204). Trump remarked that "we have a better relationship with Pakistan right now" (quoted in Mistry 2020, 243). Trump and Khan met again at the World Economic Forum in early 2020, having developed a good personal relationship (Afzal 2020).

Washington lost interest in Pakistan after Trump left office. On January 28, 2021, Pakistani justice acquitted Omar Saeed Sheikh, who was convicted of kidnapping American journalist Daniel Pearl in 2002. The newly-installed Biden administration strongly condemned that decision (Afzal 2021b). After

Secretary of State Anthony Blinken denounced the shadowy role of Pakistan during the Afghan war, Khan complained that the relationship was "lopsided" and asked for more equal relations (Mir 2021). Biden avoided talking to Khan for many months, which displeased the Pakistanis. U.S. Deputy Secretary of State Wendy Sherman visited India and Pakistan in October 2021. While in India, she undiplomatically stated that her visit to Pakistan had "a very specific and narrow purpose, we don't see ourselves building a broad relationship with Pakistan. And we have no interest in returning to the days of hyphenated India-Pakistan" (quoted in Afzal 2021a).

7.4. *Pakistani Behavior Toward China*

Bilateral relations between China and Pakistan started on a good, albeit limited footing. In October 2008, Pakistani president Asif Ali Zardari paid his first visit abroad to China (Hussain, Hussain, and Qambari 2020, 152–153). A joint military exercise named 'Friendship' occurred in 2010, four years after the last iteration (Hussain, Hussain, and Qambari 2020, 162–163).

Alignment with China increased in 2011. Prime minister Raza Gilani visited China in May 2011, a few weeks after the killing of bin Laden, and the two states launched efforts to develop space technologies jointly in August 2011. Both the Pakistani president and prime minister visited China again in December 2011 to discuss economic cooperation and defense (Calabrese 2015, 4; Hussain, Hussain, and Qambari 2020, 153). In 2012, the Chinese agreed to build nuclear power plants in Pakistan (Calabrese 2015, 4).

In February 2013, the Pakistani government leased the Gwadar Port to China Overseas Ports Holding Company-Pakistan (International Crisis Group 2018, 17). Prime Minister Sharif chose China for his first visit abroad in 2013, which was noticed in Beijing. Beijing and Islamabad signed a treaty in 2013, enabling trade in their respective currencies instead of using the U.S. dollar (Hussain, Hussain, and Qambari 2020, 153, 159). In April 2014, Sharif visited China and expressed his wish to deepen cooperation with Beijing, said to be the "cornerstone" of Pakistani foreign policy. In November, Sharif went again to China and met Xi Jinping. He promised to help Beijing fight Uighur militants and to work closely with China on the Afghan issue (Munir 2018, 30–31). In November 2014, Sharif visited China again and told Xi that "Pakistan will, as always, firmly support China on all major issues, especially on those involving China's core interests since the enhancement of the strategic cooperation with China is a cornerstone for Pakistan's diplomatic policies," and that he will "continue cracking down on terrorist forces such as the East Turkistan Islamic Movement," a Uighur separatist movement (quoted in Embassy 2014).

While President Obama visited India in January 2015, the Pakistani chief of army staff went on a high-profile visit to China (Reeves 2015). Chinese Foreign

Minister Wang Yi visited Pakistan in February, and the two states announced their intention to build the 'China-Pakistan Economic Corridor,' a network of roads, railways, pipelines, and other infrastructures to connect western China to the Gwadar Port in Baluchistan (Calabrese 2015, 7–8; Garlick 2018). When Xi Jinping visited Pakistan in April, Islamabad said it considered "friendship with China as the cornerstone of its foreign policy," and the two "agreed to elevate the Pakistan-China relationship to the All-Weather Strategic Cooperative Partnership, enriching the Pakistan-China Community of Shared Destiny, to ensure the perpetual continuity in Pakistan-China friendship from generation to generation" (Ministry of Foreign Affairs 2015).

Furthermore, in 2015, the Pakistani military mounted an operation against Uighur militants in North Waziristan to please China. In November, China Overseas Ports Holding Company-Pakistan was granted control over Gwadar's free trade zone. People willing to invest in that zone now have to deal with Chinese and not Pakistani managers. Since late 2016, disappearances of local personalities critical of Chinese influence in the country have become common occurrences (International Crisis Group 2018, 6, 18, 25–26).

2017 marks a turn toward even deeper Sino-Pakistani relations. In April, Pakistan's foreign minister expressed his willingness to pivot away from the United States and move closer to China and Russia, justifying that "China lives next to us, and we have a common wall" (quoted in Ballesteros 2018). In September, the Pakistani minister of defense complained of the growing American support for India and linked this to deepening relations with China (Jabri 2017). In October, the Pakistani government announced its intention to send an astronaut into space with Chinese help; a minister noticed that "we are close to China, and we are getting more close [...] It's time for the West to wake up and recognise our importance" (quoted in Abi-Habib 2018). In November, China requested Pakistan to legalize the use of the Chinese renminbi in Gwadar's free trade zone, which was nonetheless rejected (International Crisis Group 2018, 18). A business leader with inside knowledge explained that same month that "as Pakistan gets more isolated internationally, we're hoping that China will give us a veto [exercise a veto on Pakistan's behalf] in the UN Security Council, diplomatic and moral support, as well as put pressure on India" (quoted in International Crisis Group 2018, 4).

A few days after Washington cut all military aid to Pakistan in January 2018, the Pakistani defense minister declared that Islamabad was going through a "regional recalibration [...] towards better relations with Russia, deepening our relationship with China, [...] a response to what the Americans have been doing" (quoted in Ballesteros 2018). Indeed, two weeks after the United States suspended its military aid, the Pakistanis and the Chinese secretly agreed to expand their military cooperation in many spheres, including space. Islamabad was also granted access to China's Beidou satellite navigation system for military applications, making it the first country ever to do so (Abi-Habib 2018). In February, China and Pakistan conducted joint naval exercises called *Ribat-2018* in the Arabian Sea (Shah 2022, 40).

Relations remained excellent thereafter. In January 2020, the two states conducted another joint naval exercise, *Sea Guardians 2020* (Shah 2022, 40). In May, the Pakistani government banned a political party hostile to China's growing influence in the country (Rehman 2020). Prime Minister Khan visited Beijing in early February 2022 to attend the Winter Olympic Games opening ceremony. The two were enthused over their bilateral relationship and "expressed their strong determination to safeguard CPEC from all threats and negative propaganda" (Embassy 2022).

7.5. *Conclusion*

Overall, the Pakistani case confirms this work's theoretical claims. First, Pakistan faced intense tensions with India but cordial relations with the United States. Alignment with China increased, albeit in an unimpressive manner. Relations with India came back from the edge of the precipice, but violent encounters remained frequent. Meanwhile, relations with the United States reached a historical low. Islamabad quickly bolstered its relations with Beijing. After 2016, relations with India were once again mired in conflict. The arrival of the Trump administration in 2017 dealt a blow to the relationship, as Washington drastically reduced its support for Pakistan. This situation propelled Sino-Pakistani relations to a new high (see *Table 4.7*).

Table 4.7. Summary

Hostility w/ India	2008–10	2011–5	2016–20			2021–2
	high	medium-high	high			medium-high
U.S. assistance	2008–10	2011–2	2013–6	2017–8	2019–20	2021–2
	medium	low	medium	low	medium	low
Bandwagoning	2008–10	2011–6	2017–22			
	increase	increase	increase			

This does not mean that Pakistan fully aligned with China; Islamabad left the door open to other relationships. Pakistan's Foreign Minister Shah Mehmood Qureshi, talking in January 2021, remained keen on cooperating with the United States. For him, the Americans "have to understand that our relationship with China is not a zero-sum game," and "they should come, compete and invest" (quoted in Hashim 2021). Indeed, China was Pakistan's leading arms provider during the period, but Islamabad kept buying weapons from other states, including the United States (Mistry 2020, 254–255). Pakistani military officers confessed that their preference "is less to be the junior partner in a tighter Sino-Pakistani alliance than to enjoy the generous affections of both Beijing and Washington for as long as possible" (Markey 2016, 154).

Chapter V

Conclusion

1. Summary

This chapter summarizes the case studies' findings, discards rival hypotheses, checks whether the theory can travel to other historical cases, and discusses further avenues for research and policy implications. This book argued that bandwagoning to China or Russia was a rare strategy found only when a minor power faces a third conflict and receives little great power assistance. Bandwagoning can take three forms: survival accommodation, profit accommodation, and full alignment.

Survival accommodation occurs when a minor power is under direct threat of invasion from the potential hegemon. This imminent threat pushes survival accommodators to try to alleviate third conflicts and make concessions to available great powers to gain support against the potential hegemon. Profit accommodation occurs when the potential hegemon is less imminent a threat. More secure, the profit accommodator can use the potential hegemon's support to defend its interests against third rivals and a third great power's pressure and thus is less inclined to make concessions. Full alignment occurs when the bandwagoner quits mere accommodation and loyally bandwagons with the potential hegemon. Since it is an extremely dangerous choice, only states facing an overwhelming threat from the potential hegemon, a third conflict, and that totally lacks great power assistance will make such a radical decision.

Armenia, Belarus, Cambodia, Myanmar, North Korea, Pakistan, and Serbia were the only states in Asia and in Europe to face both third conflicts and poor relations with the United States, and also the only states to choose bandwagoning with either China or Russia. The empirical part demonstrated that within-case variations of my two causal variables are usually correlated with alignment shifts toward Beijing and Moscow.

Belarus and Myanmar initially belonged to the security accommodation category. Both faced a high threat severity, and both appeared eager to find ways to escape bandwagoning by offering concessions to third rivals or the United States. These two security accommodators are, as expected, the only two states to have shifted to full alignment. They are the only two that faced a high threat severity and totally lost U.S. assistance. Washington refused to acknowledge Lukashenko as Belarusian president after the rigged elections of Summer 2020 and broke all bridges with Minsk. The United States also stopped all contact with Myanmar after the military coup of January 2021 and pushed for the new government's ousting. Belarus and Myanmar are thus the only two bandwagoners to have fully thrown in their lot with China and Russia.

Armenia, Cambodia, North Korea, Pakistan, and Serbia all belong in the profit accommodation category. All these states were spared from the threat of immediate military conquest by China or Russia. Therefore, they had more margin for maneuver and felt less urge to make concessions to adversaries or Washington. Also, they could avoid full alignment with the regional potential hegemon thanks to their relative security. To summarize, this book's theory explains five cases well (Armenia, Belarus, Cambodia, Myanmar, and Pakistan), one relatively well (Serbia), and another poorly (North Korea). Overall, it is clear that my argument's success rate is better than random. The evidence supports this book's theoretical claims (*Table 5.1*). The six hypotheses extracted from the theory found support.

Table 5.1. Case study summary

	Threat severity	Number of shifts explained	Shifts explained by third conflicts when threat low	Unilateral concessions?
Armenia	low	8/9	8/9	no
Belarus	high	4/4	N/A	yes
Cambodia	low	4/4	3/4	no
Myanmar	high	5/5	N/A	yes
North Korea	low	1/4	0/4	no
Pakistan	low	3/3	2/3	no
Serbia	low	4/6	4/6	yes
Cases explained	N/A	29/35 (83%)	17/26 (65%)	6/7 (86%)

Note: Percentages have been rounded up.

H1. Bandwagoning and accommodation should be a minority choice among regional states.

Neorealists expect bandwagoning to be rare because it places a state at the mercy of its powerful neighbor. States bordering a potential hegemon should favor balancing, buck-passing, or any alternative strategy eschewing bandwagoning. If a majority of Asian and European states chose to ally with China and Russia, it would be a significant challenge for neorealism. Out of 52 European states, only nine (17%) bandwagoned with Russia. Out of the nine, six are captive states; thus, only three chose bandwagoning willingly (6%). Out of 38 Asian states, only four (11%) bandwagoned with China. In both Asia and Europe, bandwagoning with the potential regional hegemon was clearly a minority choice during the studied period.

H2. The best predictor of bandwagoning to a potential hegemon is the combination of a conflict with a third and the absence of great power assistance.

Since bandwagoning is a dangerous choice, only states experiencing especially unfavorable conditions will bandwagon. I argued that only those in conflict with a third and deprived of U.S. support, the sole available balancing great power, are likely to bandwagon. The seven states that chose to bandwagon with Beijing or Moscow were the only states in their respective region to experience both severe conflicts with third states and poor relations with the United States. Therefore, conflicts with thirds and shifts in great power support do a good job of predicting bandwagoning.

H3. Changes in the severity of third conflicts and the level of great power assistance should correlate with alignment shifts.

When conflicts with thirds wind down, or U.S. support increases, a bandwagoner will have less incentive to accommodate the potential hegemon. Conversely, when third conflicts worsen, or U.S. support decreases, the bandwagoner should be more willing to appease its powerful neighbor. Hence, if my theoretical framework is valid, variations in these two factors should be followed by variations in the level of bandwagoning. As shown in *Table 5.1*, changes in the severity of third conflicts and the level of great power support generally explain alignment shifts.

H4. When threat severity is high, third conflicts are intense, and great power assistance is nonexistent, the minor power should choose full alignment.

Full alignment is the strongest form of bandwagoning an independent state can choose. Fully aligned states wholeheartedly support the potential hegemons' endeavors and maintain limited relations with the balancing coalitions. It is also the most dangerous option since it leaves no leverage to resist the stronger partner. As shown in the cases of Belarus and Myanmar, the combination of a high threat from the potential hegemon, intense third conflicts, and a total lack of U.S. support led Minsk and Naypyidaw to fully align with Moscow and Beijing, respectively. The two are the sole of the seven cases where the three variables were found and the only two to shift from accommodation toward full alignment.

H5. Survival accommodators should be more willing than profit accommodators to make concessions to rivals and the United States.

Survival accommodators have limited military capabilities to deter or defeat the potential hegemon. Therefore, the latter could easily subjugate its weak neighbor. In order to escape this threatening condition, the survival accommodator should be more willing than profit accommodators to appease rivals and the United States. As shown in *Table 5.1*, the two survival accommodators (Belarus and Myanmar) made concessions to allay third conflicts and gain U.S. support. Except for Serbia, no profit accommodator did the same.

H6. For profit accommodators, shifts in alignment should correlate closely with the severity of third conflicts.

The potential hegemon is less able to defeat profit accommodators easily. Because they are less directly threatened, these are less in a hurry to secure U.S. assistance. They should also be less interested in concessions and more willing to benefit from the aspiring hegemon's support to push their interests against rivals. Hence, for these states, American behavior matters relatively less, while the third conflict variable will be more essential. As shown in *Table 5.1*, most alignment shifts of profit accommodators can be explained by changes in the severity of third conflicts.

2. Rival Hypotheses

One can extract and test five rival hypotheses grounded in bandwagoning realism and non-realist approaches from the literature review in Chapter One, in addition to three context-specific counter-explanations. No alternative explanation appears to explain bandwagoning well in contemporary Asia or Europe.

Hegemonic realism. Hegemonic realists expect military power to force bandwagoning and the lack thereof to elicit resistance. The stronger the potential hegemon, the more regional states will be willing to align with it. Balancing should be rare, mostly chosen by those less threatened. Accordingly, regional states should generally bandwagon when faced with a high threat severity.

The hypothesis that high threat severity forces alignment can be readily discarded. Only two bandwagoners (Belarus and Myanmar) out of the seven studied faced a high threat from the potential hegemon. The five others bandwagoned despite the potential hegemon's threat being more distant. In addition, numerous Asian and European states face a severe threat from the potential hegemon but eschewed bandwagoning. The most obvious cases are Azerbaijan, the three Baltic states, Finland, Georgia, and Ukraine in Europe, and Bhutan, Laos, Mongolia, and Nepal in Asia. Consider also the numerous microstates without military capabilities (like the small Pacific islands or Monaco). Military capabilities alone are unlikely to compel alignment. However, hegemonic realism provides an interesting insight regarding the *intensity* of bandwagoning: a high threat severity appears necessary to force full alignment, the strongest type of bandwagoning discussed in this book.

There is an implicit fourth variable at play in this book. I treat the potential hegemon's behavior as a constant. I assumed that the potential hegemon would readily accept the bandwagoner as an ally. If it is unremittingly hostile towards the minor power, bandwagoning is obviously not an option. Yet, this book explains well alignment choices by looking only at the minor powers' behavior. There is no known case where China or Russia totally rejected a state willing to follow them in the perimeter of this study; as lone great powers, both states would likely rejoice at making new allies. This study took the liberty of ignoring the potential hegemon's strategy to focus solely on the bandwagoners, and the theory worked well except for the North Korean case. This point suggests that minor powers have more agency than hegemonic realists believe.

Liberalism. Contrary to realism, liberalism does not see the balance of power as an independent variable. According to liberals, political leaders are foremost interested in contenting their domestic constituencies, notably by maximizing economic growth. They expect economic benefits to influence alignment decisions. Therefore, lucrative economic intercourse with the potential hegemon should push towards bandwagoning. Economic interest should explain bandwagoning and its intensity. The volume of exports is used here as a proxy for economic interest. Data on the exports of each bandwagoner toward the potential hegemon are taken from the United Nations Comtrade database (2022). However, no data exist for North Korea. I check whether alignment correlates with the export volume toward Beijing and Moscow.

Export volume provides a better explanation than random in only three cases out of six. Among them, only the case of Cambodia could show a strong correlation between export volume and alignment. In the Armenian and Burmese cases, export volumes seem actually negatively correlated with alignment. Therefore, this book supports prior scholarship suggesting that economic intercourse has only a limited impact on alignment and the possibility of conflict (Ripsman and Blanchard 1996; Rowe 2005).

Innenpolitik. One could imagine political leaders feeling sympathy toward regimes resembling their own while disliking dissimilar states. *Innenpolitik* theorists expect states to ally with those possessing similar domestic political regimes. Typically, democracies should ally with democracies and autocracies with autocracies. Therefore, alignment should correlate with the domestic regime. The *Polity5* dataset (Center for Systemic Peace 2019) is used to test this theory. I compare regime type and alignment choices by employing Polity data for the year 2018. Although data are missing for several Asian and European states, data for all the case study's states are available.

According to the Polity classification, China is an autocracy. Yet, only a minority of Asia's autocracies bandwagoned with Beijing. Conversely, two democracies bandwagoned with it. If Asian states are divided between only democracies and non-democracies, no correlation exists either. Bandwagon remains a minority choice, whatever the regime type. Russia is classified as an open anocracy. No open anocracy in Europe bandwagoned with Russia. European bandwagoners were either more or less democratic than Moscow; Armenia and Serbia are classified as democracies, and Belarus as an autocracy. Out of the three European non-democracies, only Belarus bandwagoned. Hence, in the European case, too, regime type plays no clear role in alignment with the potential hegemon. Overall, it is hard to see a correlation between regime type and bandwagoning.

Furthermore, the intensity of a bandwagoner's alignment with China and Russia could correlate with both states' level of democracy. I use the *V-Dem* dataset (2022) to check whether democracy scores correlate with alignment. Trends in V-Dem scores predict alignment well in one case (Myanmar), slightly better than random in two cases (Belarus and Serbia), as well as random in two cases (North Korea and Pakistan), and worse than random in two cases (Armenia and Cambodia). Overall, V-Dem scores predict alignment better than random in three cases only. Relative levels of democratization appear thus unrelated to bandwagoning intensity.

Benevolent hegemon theory. According to constructivists, ideas and perceptions about other states inform alignment decisions. For some, China is, by nature, a benevolent great power, and neighboring states know that. Therefore, most East Asian states should have chosen to bandwagon with China. East Asia traditionally comprises Mongolia, Japan, Taiwan, and the two Koreas. Out of these five states, only North Korea bandwagoned with China. Contrary to constructivist beliefs, there is no trace that East Asian states eagerly followed China's benevolent hegemony. More broadly, accommodating China has been a minority choice throughout Asia.

Russian world theory. Constructivists correlate alignment with identity. Therefore, states culturally close to Russia should tend to bandwagon with it, while unrelated states less so. Are states of the 'Russian world' more likely to bandwagon with Russia? The proportion of the population speaking Russian as their mother tongue is used as a proxy here. Out of the ten states counting over 2% of Russian speakers, only Belarus and Armenia chose to bandwagon. Furthermore, relations between Russia and Latvia, Ukraine, and Estonia, states with an important proportion of Russian speakers, are especially venomous. One could still argue that states belonging to the 'Russian world' are slightly more likely to bandwagon with Russia than the European average, but it is hard to see a strong causal relationship.

Neighbor of Germany. Several scholars expected reunified Germany to become a great power in post-Cold War Europe (Mearsheimer 1990; Waltz 1993). Although this never materialized, and Germany remained a weak military power, it still maintained significant latent capabilities. Therefore, states that allied with Russia could do so out of fear of German power. Logically, states bordering Germany — Austria, Belgium, Czechia, Denmark, France, Luxembourg, the Netherlands, Poland, and Switzerland — should be the most afraid of German power. Yet, none of these states bandwagoned with Russia. It stretches the imagination that Armenia, Belarus, and Serbia are the only states in Europe afraid of Germany, and there is little trace of the German threat in their decision to align with Moscow.

Southern Europe. European states bordering the Mediterranean Sea, Iran, and Turkey also need to compute state and non-state threats from the Middle East and North Africa. These additional threats may prevent balancing and compel them to ally with Russia. Said states are Albania, Armenia, Azerbaijan, Bosnia, Bulgaria, Croatia, France, Georgia, Greece, Italy, Malta, Monaco, Montenegro, Slovenia, and Spain. Among them, only Armenia chose alignment with Russia. Although extra-regional threats may add to the comprehension of the Armenian case, this explanation is overall unconvincing.

Former Japanese colony. Historical resentments against past Japanese imperialism could push Asian states to accommodate China. Former Japanese colonies are Cambodia, Timor-Leste, Indonesia, Kiribati, Laos, Malaysia, the Marshall Islands, Myanmar, Nauru, North Korea, Papua New Guinea, the Philippines, Singapore, the Solomon Islands, South Korea, Taiwan, Thailand, and Vietnam. Of these 18 states, only Cambodia, Myanmar, and North Korea aligned with Beijing (17%). Therefore, being a former Japanese colony is unlikely to elicit much bandwagoning.

3. Additional Cold War Cases

This part briefly describes several Cold War cases of minor powers that chose to bandwagon with a potential regional hegemon, the Soviet Union. Scholars generally agree that the Soviet Union and the United States were the two sole great powers during the Cold War. The Soviet Union was a potential hegemon in Asia and Europe between 1945 and 1991 because it maintained by far the strongest military in both regions (Mearsheimer 2014, 322–329; Motin 2022a, 191; Rosato 2011). Asia and Europe counted five non-captive states that bandwagoned with Moscow: Albania, China, North Korea, Vietnam, and Yugoslavia. These additional cases show that this book's theory has explanatory power beyond the contemporary era, thus reinforcing the confidence in the argument (*Table 5.2*).

3.1. *Albania*

Albania was a small Balkan country neighboring Greece and Yugoslavia. At the end of World War II, it was liberated from Axis occupation without the Soviet army, thus avoiding captivity, unlike most Eastern European states. It nevertheless chose to maintain close relations with Moscow until the mid-1950s.

Threat severity. Although Albania had only a feeble military, it was shielded from the Soviet block by Greece and Yugoslavia. Therefore, Moscow had little means to conquer the country easily.

Third conflict. Albania supported the Greek communists in their civil war against the monarchical regime. In return, the Greek military repeatedly violated the Albanian border. The Albanians feared that Greece would invade the country. However, relations smoothed during the early 1950s, and Athens and Tirana established diplomatic relations in 1953.

U.S. assistance. Albanian-U.S. relations were almost none existent for most of the Cold War.

Alignment. The Albanians maintained close relations with both the Soviet Union and Yugoslavia until 1948. However, Albania chose to fully align with Moscow after that. Contrary to the Yugoslavs, the Albanians made little effort to distance themselves from the Soviet Union. During the mid-1950s, Khrushchev's destalinization and rapprochement with Yugoslavia antagonized Albania, which rebelled against Soviet rule.

As expected, Albania faced a third-party conflict and enjoyed no assistance from the United States. It distanced itself from the Soviet Union after having solved its conflict with Greece. Nevertheless, the theory would have expected Albania to be a profit accommodator and not a full bandwagoner since it was not under direct Soviet threat. Instead, it fully bandwagoned with Moscow from 1948 to 1955 (Naimark 2019, chap. 2; Perović 2007, 57).

3.2. *China*

Despite its formidable potential, China remained a minor power between the late nineteenth and the late twentieth century. From the end of World War II until 1949, the country was embroiled in a civil war between nationalists and communists. The communists triumphed and soon allied with the Soviet Union.

Threat severity. Although the Soviets had a sizeable military superiority, China's sheer size (both in population and territory) rendered an invasion a gargantuan task. Even if it were decrepit, the multi-million Chinese army would likely have seriously hampered any Soviet attempt at blitzkrieg. Indeed, Chinese planners believed that the Soviets lacked the means to wage an all-out war against China because their army was focused on Europe. Moscow would require mass mobilization to even envisage an invasion (Jian 2001, 246–249). The threat severity was thus low.

Third conflict. China conflicted with many neighbors. It frequently clashed with Taiwan until relations appeased somehow during the 1970s. It waged war against India in 1962 and Vietnam in 1979.

U.S. assistance. China-U.S. relations were tense until 1969. The Chinese long feared that the United States would attack them (Jian 2001, 50), and the two even fought over Korea from 1950 to 1953.

Alignment. China and the Soviet Union enjoyed cordial relations from 1949 to the mid-1950s, but Beijing always maintained an independent foreign policy. The Chinese growingly criticized the Soviet government after the death of Stalin in 1953. After 1965, both states increased their military deployment at their border (Jian 2001, 240). Armed clashes even occurred during the Spring and Summer of 1969.

This book's theory explains why China aligned with the Soviet Union. It faced third conflicts and U.S. hostility. Also, as predicted, Beijing was a profit accommodator since it made little effort to solve third-party conflicts or gain U.S. assistance. Nevertheless, the theory cannot sufficiently explain the Sino-Soviet split because it happened despite third conflicts and the lack of U.S. assistance.

3.3. *North Korea*

The Japanese defeat in World War II led the Soviet army to occupy the northern half of the Korean Peninsula. It created an allied communist regime there before withdrawing in 1948. This new state bordered China, South Korea, and the USSR.

Threat severity. North Korea shared with the Soviet Union a border of only a few kilometers long. A large river formed this border. In addition, North Korea was shielded from Soviet power by Chinese territory, thus making a large-scale Soviet invasion hard to imagine.

Third conflict. Since its inception, North Korea has confronted South Korea to reunify the Peninsula on its own terms. This rivalry devolved into an all-out war between 1950 and 1953. Relations remained highly hostile during the remainder of the Cold War.

U.S. assistance. Relations between North Korea and the United States were catastrophic from the start and remained so until the end of the Cold War.

Alignment. Pyongyang maintained friendly relations with Moscow until the end of the Cold War and usually followed its leadership. However, it never fully bandwagoned with the Soviet Union and even maintained close relations with China, a rival of the USSR.

North Korea faced a low threat severity, a third-party conflict, and hostile relations with the United States. It aligned with the Soviet Union but always maintained its foreign policy freedom of maneuver. Also, it made little concessions to third rivals and Washington to gain their support. Therefore, it belongs to the profit accommodator category.

3.4. *Vietnam*

Vietnam gained independence from France in 1954 and soon aligned with the Soviet Union until its collapse in 1991. Hanoi controlled at first only the northern part of the country, bordering China, Laos, and South Vietnam. After conquering the latter in 1975, Vietnam gained a border with Cambodia.

Threat severity. The Soviet Union had no realistic path to invade Vietnam due to the sheer geographic distance and China being a formidable buffer between the two.

Third conflict. North Vietnam confronted South Vietnam from its inception until the fall of Saigon in 1975. During the 1970s, relations between Vietnam, Cambodia, and China quickly worsened. Vietnam invaded Cambodia in 1978 and pushed back a Chinese attack in 1979. Hanoi occupied Cambodia until 1989 and skirmished with China until 1991.

U.S. assistance. For most of the Cold War, relations between Vietnam and the United States were highly conflictual. The two even fought directly from 1964 to 1973.

Alignment. During the entire Cold War, Vietnam maintained close relations with the Soviet Union. However, Hanoi maintained an independent foreign policy, for example, escalating the Vietnam War against Soviet opinion and maintaining good relations with China despite the Sino-Soviet split until the mid-1970s.

During the Cold War, Vietnam confronted several third rivals and poisonous relations with Washington. Vietnam was a profit accommodator, which readily aligned with Moscow but never fully bandwagoned (Khoo 2011). Bandwagoning only stopped with the collapse of the Soviet Union, which forced Hanoi to adopt a status quoist foreign policy.

3.5. *Yugoslavia*

Yugoslavia, a defunct Balkan country, shared borders with Italy, Austria, Hungary, Romania, Bulgaria, Greece, and Albania. It freed itself from Axis occupation and thus avoided the fate of Eastern European states liberated by the Red Army, which lost their sovereignty. Belgrade maintained an independent foreign policy. Its willingness to annex neighboring Albania, seize parts of Greece and Italy, support Greek communists, and build an independent military against Stalin's will displeased the Kremlin.

Threat severity. After 1945, the Soviet army occupied Bulgaria, Hungary, and Romania, Yugoslavia's eastern neighbors. Moscow and its newfound Eastern European satellites could easily attack Yugoslavia if they wished. The Yugoslav military was sizeable but outmatched by the Soviet bloc's unrivaled firepower.

Third conflict. At the end of World War II, Yugoslavia intended to seize the Italian city of Trieste, risking war with Rome and the Western Allies. However, in early 1947, the peace treaty between the victors and Italy created the Free Territory of Trieste, thus ending the threat of war between Italians and Yugoslavs and appeasing bilateral relations.

U.S. assistance. Relations between the United States and Yugoslavia were catastrophic. The Yugoslavs even shot down a U.S. military aircraft in 1946, killing five personnel.

Alignment. Although the Yugoslavs disagreed with the Soviet policy of territorial status quo, they had little choice other than to maintain alignment with Moscow. Yugoslavia angered the Soviet Union by signing an alliance with Bulgaria in August 1947 without warning the Soviets first. Although the Yugoslavs assured Stalin of their support, their decision to merge the militaries of Albania and Yugoslavia led to an open dispute in March 1948. Relations worsened during the spring to the point that Belgrade believed a Soviet invasion was imminent (Kramer 2017; Perović 2007).

Yugoslavia faced a third conflict, poor relations with Washington, and bandwagoned with Moscow. It corresponds to a survival accommodator since it was under imminent Soviet threat. It was eager to solve conflicts with neighbors. The Yugoslavs openly broke with Moscow in mid-1947 and mid-1948, a few months after the risk of war with Italy receded.

Table 5.2. Summary of Cold War cases

	Does the theory explain…		
Case	bandwagoning?	the end of bandwagoning?	bandwagoning type?
Albania	yes	yes	no
China	yes	no	yes
North Korea	yes	yes	yes
Vietnam	yes	N/A	yes
Yugoslavia	yes	yes	yes

4. Avenues for Further Research

Far from exhausting the topic, this book left much to discover. Further research on earlier cases of minor power bandwagoning to test and refine this book's argument is warranted. During the early twentieth century, Imperial Germany was a potential hegemon in Europe, and Nazi Germany and Japan were potential hegemons in Europe and Asia, respectively, between 1939 and 1945 (Mearsheimer 2014; Motin 2022a). Bulgaria and Turkey bandwagoned with Imperial Germany, and Bulgaria, Finland, Hungary, and Romania bandwagoned with Nazi Germany. A cursory overview suggests that these states had preexisting conflicts with neighbors and little opportunity to receive third-great power support.

Conversely, Thailand resisted the Japanese request to base troops on Thai territory despite Japan's growing power and a territorial dispute with France. Thailand had cordial relations with the United States and especially Britain, and the Japanese had to attack the country in December 1941 to compel bandwagoning. Great power support seemingly prevented bandwagoning. Similarly, British involvement managed to keep Spain away from Germany throughout World War II (Crawford 2008). In the same vein, the presence of a great power supporter "may explain why Belgium and Poland chose to fight in 1914 and 1939, respectively, and why Czechoslovakia in 1938 did not. The former had strong alliances and security guarantees; the latter had been abandoned by the Great Powers" (Labs 1992, 399–400).

Another related puzzle is why some states stop bandwagoning with an actual hegemon. The only regional hegemon in modern history is the United States, which established hegemony over the Western Hemisphere in the late nineteenth century. The realist expectation that states quit balancing once a great power obtains a dominant share of a region's power holds overall (Fiammenghi 2011). Canada is representative; since Washington reached hegemony, the Canadians assimilated that balancing was futile and have accommodated the Americans ever since (Barry and Bratt 2008). However, one cannot but notice that a handful of weak Hemispheric states chose to confront U.S. hegemony head-on. Consider Cuba, Nicaragua, and Venezuela for the contemporary era. Minor powers defying an actual hegemon are an intriguing topic to explore.[1]

A social science theory is always a simplification of reality that can account for only so many variables. This book did not investigate China and Russia's behavior toward the bandwagoners. Notably, in the case of North Korea, Beijing has sometimes adopted a confrontational attitude toward Pyongyang,

---

[1] A promising first cut is Mares (1988).

mechanically rendering close alignment unlikely. Further studies incorporating the potential hegemon's behavior and explaining when and how it tries to elicit alignment (or not) would thus be valuable. A few, like Crawford (2011; 2021) and Izumikawa (2018), have discussed wedge strategies in depth. Additional studies of wedge strategies in the context of states' natural tendency to balance and the rarity of bandwagoning are warranted.

Relatedly, how alliance politics differ in balancing and bandwagoning coalitions deserves attention. A potential hegemon will generally have few major power allies and mainly small allies. Thus, the power differential will be greater among the states of the bandwagoning coalition than among the balancing coalition. Today's United States must articulate coalitions counting heavyweights like Britain, France, Germany, India, and Japan. Meanwhile, most of China and Russia's bandwagoners are relatively unimpressive. Similarly, during the Cold War, the Soviet Union had only allies of little significance (except Mao's China for a decade) while balancing coalitions in Asia and Europe counted several major states. Therefore, bandwagoning coalitions are more hierarchic than balancing ones. They should tend to be more cohesive and unitary because the potential hegemon can orchestrate everything (Gheorghe 2022). Members will be highly committed to the task and support the aspirant with their resources as Warsaw Pact states did during the Cold War (Herf 2014; Liberman 1996, chap. 7; Yordanov 2021). Paradoxically, however, bandwagoning coalitions remain more fragile. The balancing instinct always remains: Moscow had to keep its allies at arm's length during the Cold War, while Washington had less to worry about. The potential hegemon will also be reluctant to provide large economic support and advanced military technologies because it does not trust the bandwagoners to stay loyal in the long run.

Going one step further, one may want to know whether China, Russia, and potential hegemons in general are aware of the natural tendency of their neighbors to balance. For instance, there are clues that the Russian government is aware of that tendency. Ministry of Foreign Affairs spokeswoman Maria Zakharova talked of those "who are preoccupied about us, and those who are somehow trying to halt our development: through the containment policy and through isolation attempts" (Jonassen 2021). Vladimir Putin remarked that "no matter what we do, no matter how we try to satisfy the appetites of those who are attempting to contain us, still, the containment will continue, because to many of our opponents, […] a country like Russia is simply not needed. Yet […] we will do everything not only in order to preserve [it] but also to reinforce it, make it stronger" (TASS 2021; also, Feinstein and Pirro 2021). Although the degree of China's self-awareness is unclear, Chinese analysts seem to understand that neighbors tend to balance (Wuthnow 2022). Interestingly, the late Soviets also expected balancing when they made headways (Hopf 1991).

Finally, although this book did not touch upon the issue of great power bandwagoning, its theoretical framework may be adapted to discuss it. World War I Austria-Hungary exemplifies the dilemmas of a great power neighboring a potential hegemon, embroiled in disputes with thirds, and lacking great power support. The Austrians lamented that if Germany won the war, Austria would, at best, turn into a German protectorate and, at worst, be directly annexed by Germany. Conversely, an Allied victory would mean the empire's dismemberment; the only exit ramp was maintaining a balance between Germans and Allies (Sondhaus 2009). Yet, Austria-Hungary had poor relations with all the balancing great powers, and its only ally was the potential hegemon, Germany. During the conflict, "Austria would fight a war on three fronts, allied with Europe's most revisionist power, without […] meaningful alliance options among the other Great Powers" (Mitchell 2018, 302) and ultimately disappear. Furthermore, Fascist Italy engaged in armed expansion in Africa and the Balkans, had poor relations with Britain and France, and ultimately chose to bandwagon with Germany, too.

5. Policy Implications

This discussion has clear policy implications. States are reluctant to bandwagon with China and Russia and do so only if they face both a third-rival conflict and lack U.S. assistance. First, balancing states should want to allay regional conflicts to make bandwagoning less alluring. Some conflicts are more entrenched than others. Among the cases of this study, Cambodia's tensions with Vietnam and Thailand appear the most readily solvable. The United States, Australia, India, Japan, and others should accentuate their efforts to mediate these border disputes. Western states could also promote better relations between Kosovo and Serbia. Since Serbia is a profit accommodator, they should encourage the Kosovars to make concessions first.

Other rivalries like the Indo-Pakistani and Korean conflicts are more intractable, but opportunities still exist. One thinks of the 2018–2019 peace attempts on the Korean Peninsula (Min 2023; Motin 2022c). U.S. military support to India cannot but scare Pakistan, which will then be tempted to entice China to its side to compensate. In other words, Washington will have a hard time maintaining friendly relations with Islamabad as long as the Indo-Pakistani conflict goes unabated. The United States, under Obama and Trump, did try to assuage the Indo-Pakistani conflict but with little success. Washington is unlikely to bring Islamabad back from China's grasp without solving that conflict first, and that will be no easy task.

At the time of writing, it is still unclear what awaits Armenian-Azeri relations after Azerbaijan's conquest of Nagorno-Karabakh in September 2023. Following this book's argument, if the resolution of the Nagorno dispute leads to an appeased relationship, then Armenia will have less incentive to bandwagon with Russia. Without the threat of war with Baku, it will be freer to pursue closer relations with NATO states. Furthermore, the United States seems now more open to security engagement with Armenia (Kucera 2023). If these trends continue, Armenia will likely abandon bandwagoning altogether in favor of some form of hedging or buck-passing.

The Ukraine War could profoundly reshuffle the European security landscape and neighboring states' incentives to either contain or accommodate Moscow. It is hard to divine what the war's issue will be. If Russia scores a decisive victory, it may annex large chunks of Ukraine up to Odesa. In that case, it would obtain a border with Moldova and Romania. Moldova already has a third conflict with the pro-Russian and separatist proto-state of Transnistria. It possesses an especially weak military, and if relations with the United States were to worsen for any reason, Chisinau could quickly be forced into bandwagoning.

Although it may look like out-of-reach goals, one should remember that Washington succeeded in allaying third conflicts to close the door to potential hegemons in the past. For example, after World War II, the 'American pacifier' (Joffe 1984) worked hard to better France-Germany (Choi and Alexandrova 2020) and Japan-Korea relations (Yoo 2022) so rivals could not easily drive wedges between them. U.S. commitment does not necessarily end all disputes and rancor overnight (Cha 2000), but it drastically reduces the chance that these escalate to cold or even hot wars.

Second, the United States must refocus its foreign policy away from ideology if it wants to counteract bandwagoning tendencies. Despite a clumsily more realist approach under the Trump administration (Chung 2017), old habits still have a hold over the Beltway. Criticizing Cambodia, Myanmar, and North Korea for their poor track record in democracy and human rights is understandable, but American pressure only pushes them toward China. Although distasteful, Washington should thus debate whether pressuring these states, with limited results, is worth growing China's sphere of influence. Greater engagement with Armenia and Serbia is also needed. The United States cut all bridges with Belarus in 2020. Now that Minsk has thrown in its lot with Moscow and has a massive Russian military presence on its soil, it may already be too late. America could still send some rapprochement feelers to check the mood in Minsk, but the Russians are likely here to stay. Relations with India are essential to maintain the balance of power in the Indo-Pacific region (Montgomery 2013); Washington is thus walking on thin ice regarding Pakistan. It should try to befriend Islamabad but cannot afford to antagonize Delhi in the process.[2]

---

[2] Assuming that the United States would want to roll back Chinese and Russian power and influence. O'Rourke and Shifrinson (2022) make a good case that not challenging

The main goal of U.S. foreign policy since America's rise as a great power during the late nineteenth century has been to ensure that no rival power dominates Asia, Europe, or both. To accomplish that, Washington needs to keep most Asian and European states away from any potential hegemon, be it Germany, Japan, the Soviet Union, Russia, or China (Colby 2021; Green 2017; Mearsheimer 2014; Ross 2013; Spykman 1942). The United States enjoys the great advantage of not scaring away Asian and European states because it is too distant to threaten their survival. Illustrating that, a high-level European diplomat once confessed that "among Europeans, it is not acceptable that the lead nation be European. A European power broker is a hegemonic power. We can agree on U.S. leadership, but not on one of our own" (quoted in Art 1996, 36). Washington must not artificially push states toward Beijing and Moscow for vain ideological pursuits and, instead, fully accept its role as the cornerstone of Asian and European balancing coalitions.

That the United States must refocus its military efforts on containing China, its prime competitor, is now a relative consensus. Beijing's power potential is superior to Russia's, and the disposition of forces is significantly more worrisome in Asia than in Europe. Krepinevich (2017, vi) explains that "the United States lacks strategic depth in the Western Pacific. This […] requires the United States to adopt a forward defense posture in that theater" while, conversely, "the United States enjoys great strategic depth in Europe, providing a greater opportunity to recover from initial setbacks. The United States can deploy reinforcements in the alliance's large 'rear area' in relative safety." This book's results strongly suggest that Washington can safely maintain only a minimal military footprint in Europe without its allies defecting to Moscow.

IR scholars have debated since at least the Cold War how much American commitment is necessary to avoid allies defecting to the other side and maintain the balance of power. In that light, this book entails both an optimistic and pessimistic conclusion. On the optimistic side, China and Russia are unlikely to attract many of their neighbors and form large bandwagoning coalitions. Washington should find it relatively easy to block attempts at luring allies away from balancing coalitions. For instance, it can take a relaxed approach toward China's economic endeavors like the One Belt One Road initiative because Chinese economic incentives will not push regional states to bandwagon. Allies and partners will not abandon the United States even if Washington does not always show unconditional loyalty at every corner and sometimes defends its own interests. On the pessimistic side, this implies that China and Russia will have to fight their way toward regional hegemony

---

Beijing and Moscow everywhere and letting them keep a small sphere of influence could stabilize relations.

because nonviolent revisionism will not work. The only realistic path to regional hegemony is at the point of the bayonet. This bodes ill for peace in both Asia and Europe.

Appendix 1. Case Selection

Table A1.1. List of cases

	Europe		Asia	
	State	**Bandwagoning?**	**State**	**Bandwagoning?**
1	Abkhazia	.	Afghanistan	.
2	Albania	.	Australia	.
3	Andorra	.	Bangladesh	.
4	Armenia	yes	Bhutan	.
5	Artsakh	.	Brunei	.
6	Austria	.	Cambodia	yes
7	Azerbaijan	.	Fiji	.
8	Belarus	yes	India	.
9	Belgium	.	Indonesia	.
10	Bosnia	.	Japan	.
11	Bulgaria	.	Kiribati	.
12	Croatia	.	Laos	.
13	Czechia	.	Malaysia	.
14	Denmark	.	Maldives	.
15	Donetsk (2014–22)	.	Marshall Islands	.
16	Estonia	.	Micronesia	.
17	Finland	.	Mongolia	.
18	France	.	Myanmar	yes
19	Georgia	.	Nauru	.
20	Germany	.	Nepal	.
21	Greece	.	New Zealand	.
22	Hungary	.	North Korea	yes
23	Iceland	.	Pakistan	yes
24	Ireland	.	Palau	.
25	Italy	.	Papua New Guinea	.

26	Kosovo	.	Philippines	.
27	Latvia	.	Samoa	.
28	Liechtenstein	.	Singapore	.
29	Lithuania	.	Solomon Islands	.
30	Luhansk (2014–22)	.	South Korea	.
31	Luxembourg	.	Sri Lanka	.
32	Malta	.	Taiwan	.
33	Moldova	.	Thailand	.
34	Monaco	.	Timor-Leste	.
35	Montenegro	.	Tonga	.
36	Netherlands	.	Tuvalu	.
37	North Macedonia	.	Vanuatu	.
38	Norway	.	Vietnam	.
39	Poland	.		
40	Portugal	.		
41	Romania	.		
42	San Marino	.		
43	Serbia	yes		
44	Slovakia	.		
45	Slovenia	.		
46	Spain	.		
47	South Ossetia	.		
48	Sweden	.		
49	Switzerland	.		
50	Transnistria	.		
51	Ukraine	.		
52	United Kingdom	.		

Note: Asia encompasses the 'Australia and Oceania,' 'East and Southeast Asia,' and 'South Asia' regions of the CIA's *World Factbook*. 'Europe' encompasses the *World Factbook*'s 'Europe' in addition to the six recognized and unrecognized states of the Caucasus (CIA 2022).

Table A1.2. Summary of European cases

	State	Third conflict	U.S. hostility	Bandwagoning?
1	Abkhazia	yes	yes	captive
2	Albania	no	no	.
3	Andorra	no	no	.
4	Armenia	yes	yes	yes
5	Artsakh	yes	yes	captive
6	Austria	no	no	.
7	Azerbaijan	yes	no	.
8	Belarus	yes	yes	yes
9	Belgium	no	no	.
10	Bosnia	no	no	.
11	Bulgaria	no	no	.
12	Croatia	no	no	.
13	Czechia	no	no	.
14	Denmark	no	no	.
15	Donetsk (2014–22)	yes	yes	captive
16	Estonia	no	no	.
17	Finland	no	no	.
18	France	no	no	.
19	Georgia	yes	no	.
20	Germany	no	no	.
21	Greece	yes	no	.
22	Hungary	no	no	.
23	Iceland	no	no	.
24	Ireland	no	no	.
25	Italy	no	no	.
26	Kosovo	yes	no	.
27	Latvia	no	no	.

28	Liechtenstein	no	no	.
29	Lithuania	no	no	.
30	Luhansk (2014–22)	yes	yes	captive
31	Luxembourg	no	no	.
32	Malta	no	no	.
33	Moldova	yes	no	.
34	Monaco	no	no	.
35	Montenegro	no	no	.
36	Netherlands	no	no	.
37	North Macedonia	no	no	.
38	Norway	no	no	.
39	Poland	no	no	.
40	Portugal	no	no	.
41	Romania	no	no	.
42	San Marino	no	no	.
43	Serbia	yes	yes	yes
44	Slovakia	no	no	.
45	Slovenia	no	no	.
46	Spain	no	no	.
47	South Ossetia	yes	yes	captive
48	Sweden	no	no	.
49	Switzerland	no	no	.
50	Transnistria	yes	yes	captive
51	Ukraine	yes	no	.
52	United Kingdom	no	no	.

Table A1.3. Summary of Asian cases

	State	Third conflict	U.S. hostility	Bandwagoning?
1	Afghanistan	yes (before 2021)	no (before 2021)	.
2	Australia	no	no	.
3	Bangladesh	no	no	.
4	Bhutan	no	no	.
5	Brunei	no	no	.
6	Cambodia	yes	yes	yes
7	Fiji	no	no	.
8	India	yes	no	.
9	Indonesia	no	no	.
10	Japan	yes	no	.
11	Kiribati	no	no	.
12	Laos	no	no	.
13	Malaysia	no	no	.
14	Maldives	no	no	.
15	Marshall Islands	no	no	.
16	Micronesia	no	no	.
17	Mongolia	no	no	.
18	Myanmar	yes	yes	yes
19	Nauru	no	no	.
20	Nepal	no	no	.
21	New Zealand	no	no	.
22	North Korea	yes	yes	yes
23	Pakistan	yes	yes	yes
24	Palau	no	no	.
25	Papua New Guinea	no	no	.
26	Philippines	partly	no	.
27	Samoa	no	no	.

28	Singapore	no	no	.
29	Solomon Islands	no	no	.
30	South Korea	yes	no	.
31	Sri Lanka	partly	no	.
32	Taiwan	no	no	.
33	Thailand	yes	no	.
34	Timor-Leste	no	no	.
35	Tonga	no	no	.
36	Tuvalu	no	no	.
37	Vanuatu	no	no	.
38	Vietnam	yes	no	.

Appendix 2. Calculations of Military Expenditures

No clear-cut indicator for economic power exists (Rauch 2017). Although gross domestic product (GDP) is probably the most used indicator for comparing economies, it is deeply flawed. For instance, many observers underline that Russia's nominal GDP approaches Italy or Spain's, hardly the earmark of a great power. While data in dollars would suggest an economic collapse of Russia after 2014, data expressed in ruble show that the Russian economy kept growing at a steady rate up to the coronavirus crisis (Statista 2021). Such a discrepancy is due to the changing dollar-ruble exchange rate and has nothing to do with the actual shape of the Russian economy. The 2020 Russian GDP expressed in the 2013 exchange rate (around 1 dollar for 32 rubles) comes out at 3,332 billion dollars, which would place the Russian economy as the fifth most powerful in the world, behind Germany. If the exchange rate were to reach tomorrow 1 dollar for 10 rubles, the Russian GDP would become number three (around 10.7 trillion dollars), behind China but before Japan.

Following the same logic, data in the current dollar exchange rate tend to make Russian military expenditures look smaller than they are because the dollar-ruble exchange rate felt after 2014. According to SIPRI (2021), China's 2020 figure in local currency was 1,741 billion yuan. At the 2020 exchange rate, this represents around 250 billion dollars, but at 2013's rate, it represents 283 billion. The difference is more impressive for Russia. At the 2020 rate, its military expenditures represent only around 62 billion dollars, but at the 2013 rate, it represents around 140 billion.

To circumvent that issue, this book used purchasing power parity (PPP) exchange rate, a methodology that aims to adjust gross domestic product figures to account for price differences among countries (for instance, a pizza will typically be cheaper in China than in the United States). The military expenditure data used here comes from the World Bank's compilation of the SIPRI's data. However, data are ultimately based on what governments self-report; data about Chinese and Russian military spending publicly available are notoriously smaller than the actual ones (Kofman 2018; Kofman and Connolly 2019; Nouwens and Béraud-Sudreau 2020).

Figure A2.1. Military expenditures in Europe, 2008–2020, PPP (billion USD)

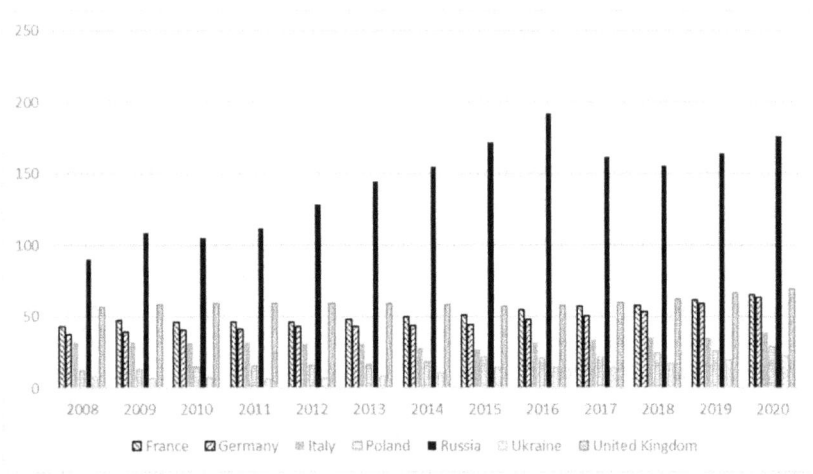

Source: The author's calculation, based on World Bank. https://data.worldbank.org/ (accessed 2022, January 22).

Figure A2.2. Military expenditures in Asia, 2008–2020, PPP (billion USD)

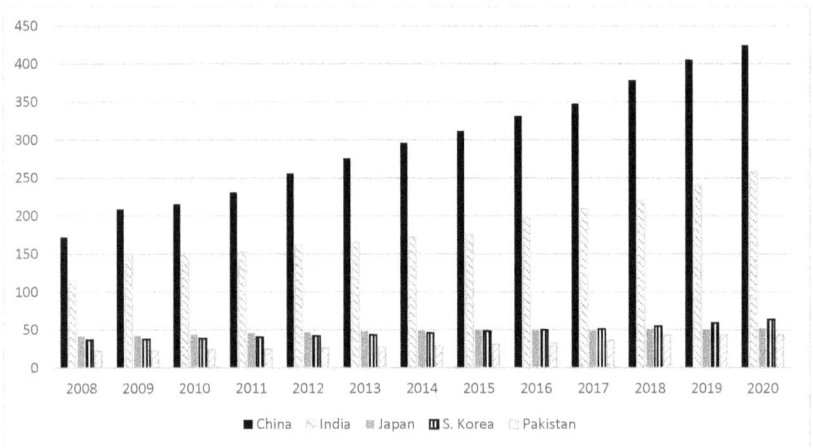

Source: The author's calculation, based on World Bank. https://data.worldbank.org/ (accessed 2022, January 22).
Note: No data for North Korea and Taiwan.

I recalculated here Chinese and Russian expenditures accordingly. To simplify, I assumed that the SIPRI's data are accurate for the other states. They probably are not, but it seems likely that China and Russia would tend to dissimulate their total military expenditures more often and systematically than the others (see *Figures A2.1* and *A2.2*).

A Heritage Foundation report adjusted Chinese military spending for 2017 to account for labor costs and established it at 467.4 billion (Bartels 2020). Kofman and Connolly (2019; also, Connolly 2019) gave the number of 200 billion for the Russian budget in 2019. The U.S. Joint Chiefs Chairman Mark Milley concurs with both figures (Babb 2021; also, Inhofe 2021). Hence, the Heritage Foundation's 2017 figure for China is close to 35% larger, and Kofman and Connolly's 2019 Russian figure is around 22% larger than my figures.

Figure A2.3. Adjusted military expenditures in Europe, 2000–2020, PPP (billion USD)

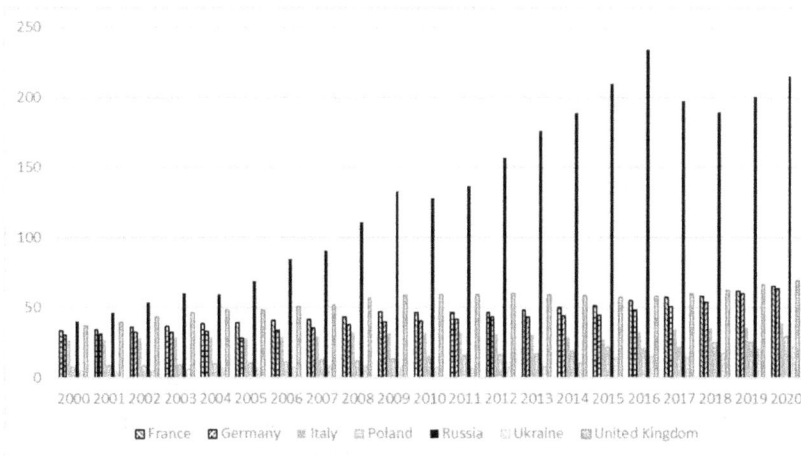

Source: The author's calculation based on Kofman, Michael, and Richard Connolly. 2019. "Why Russian Military Expenditure Is Much Higher Than Commonly Understood (as Is China's)." *War on the Rocks*, December 16, https://warontherocks.com/2019/12/why-russian-military-expenditure-is-much-higher-than-commonly-understood-as-is-china s/ (accessed 2022, January 21); and World Bank. https://data.worldbank.org/ (accessed 2022, January 22).

Figure A2.4. Adjusted military expenditures in Asia, 2000–2020, PPP (billion USD)

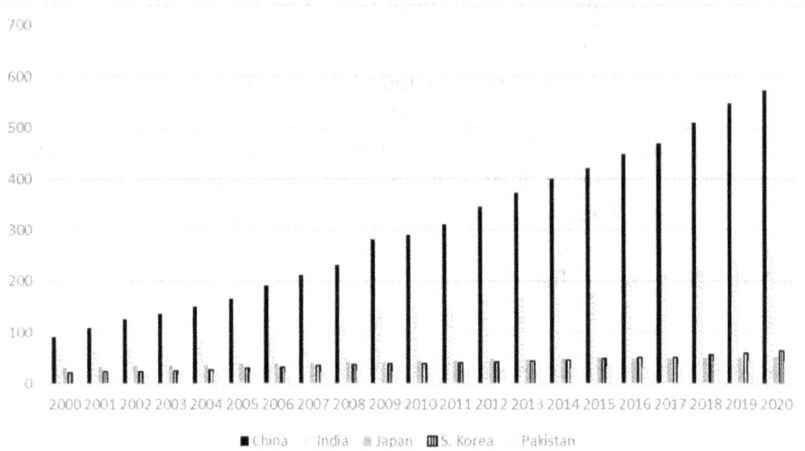

Source: The author's calculation based on Bartels, Frederico. 2020. *China's Defense Budget in Context: How Under-Reporting and Differing Standards and Economies Distort the Picture.* Washington, D.C.: Heritage Foundation; and World Bank. https://data.worldbank. org/ (accessed 2022, January 22).
Note: No data for North Korea and Taiwan.

For the sake of conservatism, this book does not use figures adjusted to follow the abovementioned sources (*Figures A2.3* and *A2.4*). Furthermore, if significant expenditures by neighboring states were underreported, it might bias the data by showing China and Russia as more dominant than they are. As a final point, no methodology for counting military spending is perfect. Using PPP figures overestimates the purchasing power of states that rely on imported weapons — notably India. Also, available PPP data are based on prices for civilian goods, which are not necessarily representative of military-related prices (Robertson 2022). Relatedly, others like Anders, Fariss, and Markowitz (2020; also, Heim and Miller 2020), and Berkley (2018) make strong cases for their own indicators of wealth. All these approaches have their strengths and flaws, and the debate cannot find a conclusion there. Suffice to say that there is no universally accepted way of counting wealth and military spending.

References

Abi-Habib, Maria. 2018. "China's 'Belt and Road' Plan in Pakistan Takes a Military Turn." *New York Times*, December 19, https://www.nytimes.com/ 2018/12/1 9/world/asia/pakistan-china-belt-road-military.html (accessed 2022, July 1).

Acheson, Dean. 1969. *Present at the Creation.* New York: W.W. Norton.

AFP. 2015. "South Korea Blames North for Mine Blasts, Vows 'Harsh' Response." *ABC News*, August 10, https://www.abc.net.au/news/2015-08-10/skorea-blam es-north-for-mine-blasts/6685710 (accessed 2022, July 15).

AFP. 2021. "Tensions High as Serbia Deploys Armoured Vehicles at Kosovo Border." *Barron's*, September 27, https://www.barrons.com/news/tensions-high-as-serbia-deploys-armoured-vehicles-at-kosovo-border-01632746107 (accessed 2022, September 4).

Afzal, Madiha. 2020. "Evaluating the Trump Administration's Pakistan Reset." *Brookings*, October 26, https://www.brookings.edu/blog/order-from-chaos/ 2020/10/26/evaluating-the-trump-administrations-pakistan-reset/ (accessed 2022, June 30).

Afzal, Madiha. 2021a. "Post Afghanistan, US-Pakistan Relations Stand on the Edge of a Precipice." *Brookings*, October 13, https://www.brookings.edu/ blog/order-from-chaos/2021/10/13/post-afghanistan-us-pakistan-relations -stand-on-the-edge-of-a-precipice/ (accessed 2022, June 30).

Afzal, Madiha. 2021b. "Under Biden, Pakistan and the US Face a Dilemma about the Breadth of Their Relationship." *Brookings*, April 12, https://www. brookings.edu/blog/order-from-chaos/2021/04/12/under-biden-pakistan-a nd-the-us-face-a-dilemma-about-the-breadth-of-their-relationship (accessed 2022, June 30).

Agayev, Zulfugar, and Sara Khojoyan. 2014. "Azerbaijan Risks New Armenia Conflict as Chopper Downed." *Bloomberg*, November 12, https://www.bloom berg.com/news/articles/2014-11-12/azerbaijan-says-armenian-helicopter-s hot-down-in-conflict-zone (accessed 2022, September 8).

Al Jazeera. 2009. "Biden Visit Sparks Anger in Serbia." May 20, https://www.alja zeera.com/news/2009/5/20/biden-visit-sparks-anger-in-serbia (accessed 2022, August 23).

Alberque, William. 2022. "Belarus Seeks to Amend Its Constitution to Host Russian Nuclear Weapons." February 4, https://www.iiss.org/blogs/analysis/ 2022/02/belarus-seeks-to-amend-its-constitution-to-host-russian-nuclear-w eapons (accessed 2022, June 2).

Allen, Kenneth W., Brendan S. Mulvaney, and James Char. 2021. "Ongoing Organizational Reforms of the People's Liberation Army Air Force." *Journal of Strategic Studies* 44(2): 184–217.

Allen, Michael A. 2018. "The Influence of Regional Power Distributions on Interdependence." *Journal of Conflict Resolution* 62(5): 1072–1099.

Allison, Graham. 2018. "The Myth of the Liberal Order: From Historical Accident to Conventional Widsom." *Foreign Affairs* 97(4): 124–133.

Allison, Graham. 2020. "The New Spheres of Influence: Sharing the Globe with Other Great Powers." *Foreign Affairs* 99(2): 30–40.

Amir, Hamza. 2022. "India, Pakistan Engage in 'Back Channel' Talks to Revive Relations." *ABP Live*, May 31, https://news.abplive.com/news/india/india-pa kistan-engage-in-back-channel-talks-to-revive-relations-1534803 (accessed 2022, June 30).

Anders, Therese, Christopher J. Fariss, and Jonathan N. Markowitz. 2020. "Bread Before Guns or Butter: Introducing Surplus Domestic Product (SDP)." *International Studies Quarterly* 64(2): 392–405.

Andersen, Morten S. 2011. *How Empires Emerge*. Oslo: Norwegian Institute of International Affairs.

Armenia News. 2018. "Armenia's Pashinyan: We Hope Russia Has Done Nothing Against Us." July 27, https://news.am/eng/news/463782.html (accessed 2022, September 6).

Armenian Weekly. 2017. "ANCA: 'We Are Troubled by Trump's Ill-Advised and Misguided Proposal to Cut Aid to Armenia'." May 25, https://armenianweek ly.com/2017/05/25/anca-we-are-troubled-by-trumps-ill-advised-and-misgu ided-proposal-to-cut-aid-to-armenia/ (accessed 2022, September 9).

ARMENPRESS. 2019. "Armenian Company Baffled After Getting Included in United States BIS Entity List." August 14, https://armenpress.am/eng/news/ 9 84888.html (accessed 2022, September 8).

Aron, Raymond. 2004. *Paix et guerre entre les nations* [Peace and War among Nations]. Paris: Calmann-Lévy.

Art, Robert J. 1980. "To What Ends Military Power?" *International Security* 4(4): 3–35.

Art, Robert J. 1996. "Why Western Europe Needs the United States and NATO." *Political Science Quarterly* 111(1): 1–39.

Associated Press. 2019. "Belarus Issues Tough Warning to Russia over Energy Dispute." *Seattle Times*, January 10, https://www.seattletimes.com/business/ belarus-issues-tough-warning-to-russia-over-energy-dispute (accessed 2022, May 29).

Axelrod, Robert, and Robert O. Keohane. 1985. "Achieving Cooperation Under Anarchy: Strategies and Institutions." *World Politics* 38(1): 226–254.

B92. 2008a. "Koštunica: NATO Bombed to Create Own State." March 24, https: //www.b92.net/eng/news/politics.php?yyyy=2008&mm=03&dd=24&nav_id =48748 (accessed 2022, September 2).

B92. 2008b. "PM: Serbia not Choosing Between Russia and West." March 25, https://web.archive.org/web/20110607012855/http://www.b92.net/eng/news/ politics-article.php?yyyy=2008&mm=03&dd=25&nav_id=48766 (accessed 2022, August 29).

B92. 2013. "Nikolić, Putin Sign Strategic Partnership Declaration." May 24, https ://www.b92.net/eng/news/politics.php?yyyy=2013&mm=05&dd=24&nav_id =86333 (accessed 2022, September 2).

Babb, Carla. 2021. "China, Russia Military Budgets Combined Exceed US Spending, Top General Says." *Voice of America*, June 10, https://www.voanew s.com/a/usa_us-politics_china-russia-military-budgets-combined-exceed-u s-spending-top-general-says/6206876.html (accessed 2022, January 21).

Bailey, Colin. 2018. "Rome, Carthage, and Numidia: Diplomatic Favouritism Before the Third Punic War." *Antichthon* 52: 43–71.

Ballesteros, Carlos. 2018. "Pakistan Wants to Buy Military Supplies from Russia and China After U.S. Funding Freeze." *Newsweek*, January 28, https://www.newsweek.com/pakistan-russia-china-military-supplies-us-funding-793258 (accessed 2022, June 30).

Bami, Xhorxhina. 2020. "EU Envoy Criticises Kosovo for Blocking Serbian President's Visit." *Balkan Insight*, November 26, https://balkaninsight.com/2020/11/26/eu-envoy-criticises-kosovo-for-blocking-serbian-presidents-visit/ (accessed 2022, September 4).

Bami, Xhorxhina, and Adelina Ahmeti. 2020. "Kosovo Protests 'Illegal' Arrival of COVID-19 Vaccines in North." *Balkan Insight*, December 28, https://balkaninsight.com/2020/12/28/kosovo-protests-illegal-arrival-of-covid-19-vaccines-in-north/ (accessed 2022, September 4).

Banerji, Annie. 2012. "India to Allow FDI from Pakistan, Open Border Post." *Reuters*, April 13, https://www.reuters.com/article/india-pakistan-trade-fdi-investment-idINDEE83C04M20120413?edition-redirect=in (accessed 2022, June 30).

Barannikova, Anastasia. 2019. *United States-DPRK Relations: Is Normalization Possible?* Washington, D.C.: Center for Strategic and International Studies.

Barnett, Michael N., and Jack S. Levy. 1991. "Domestic Sources of Alliances and Alignments: The Case of Egypt, 1962–73." *International Organization* 45(3): 369–395.

Barrie, Douglas, Ben Barry, Lucie Béraud-Sudreau, Henry Boyd, Nick Childs, and Bastian Giegerich. 2019. *Defending Europe: Scenario-Based Capability Requirements for NATO's European Members*. London: International Institute for Strategic Studies.

Barry, Donald, and Duane Bratt. 2008. "Defense Against Help: Explaining Canada-U.S. Security Relations." *American Review of Canadian Studies* 38(1): 63–89.

Bartels, Frederico. 2020. *China's Defense Budget in Context: How Under-Reporting and Differing Standards and Economies Distort the Picture*. Washington, D.C.: Heritage Foundation.

Baynes, Chris. 2018. "Serbia Threatens Military Action After Kosovo Votes to Create Army." *Independent*, December 15, https://www.independent.co.uk/news/world/europe/kosovo-army-security-force-serbia-military-action-invasion-ana-brnabic-a8684861.html (accessed 2022, September 2).

BBC. 2015a. "Kosovo and Serbia Sign 'Landmark' Agreements." August 26, https://www.bbc.com/news/world-europe-34059497 (accessed 2022. September 1).

BBC. 2015b. "South Korea Evacuation After Shelling on Western Border." August 20, https://www.bbc.com/news/world-asia-34001126 (accessed 2022, July 15).

BBC. 2018. "Trump Kim Summit: Full Text of the Signed Statement." June 12, https://www.bbc.com/news/world-asia-44453330 (accessed 2022, July 11).

Bechev, Dimitar. 2021. "The Russian Challenge in Southeast Europe." In Mai'a K. Davis Cross and Ireneusz Paweł Karolewski (eds.), *European-Russian Power Relations in Turbulent Times*, 187–216. Ann Arbor: University of Michigan Press.

Beckley, Michael. 2018. *Unrivaled: Why America Will Remain the World's Sole Superpower.* Ithaca: Cornell University Press.

Beckley, Michael, Yusaku Horiuchi, and Jennifer M. Miller. 2018. "America's Role in the Making of Japan's Economic Miracle." *Journal of East Asian Studies* 18(1): 1–21.

Beech, Hannah. 2018. "Embracing China, Facebook and Himself, Cambodia's Ruler Digs In." *New York Times*, March 17, https://www.nytimes.com/2018/03/17/world/asia/hun-sen-cambodia-china.html (accessed 2022, June 11).

Bennett, Andrew, and Colin Elman. 2007. "Case Study Methods in the International Relations Subfield." *Comparative Political Studies* 40(2): 170–195.

Beta. 2016. "Serbia Makes Big Step Toward NATO." *B92*, February 17, https://www.b92.net/eng/news/politics.php?yyyy=2016&mm=02&dd=17&nav_id=97073 (accessed 2022, August 25).

Biddle, Tami Davis. 2020. "Coercion Theory: A Basic Introduction for Practitioners." *Texas National Security Review* 3(2): 94–109.

Blackwill, Robert D., and Jennifer M. Harris. 2016. *War by Other Means: Geoeconomics and Statecraft.* Cambridge: Harvard University Press.

Blagden, David, and Patrick Porter. 2021. "Desert Shield of the Republic? A Realist Case for Abandoning the Middle East." *Security Studies* 30(1): 5–48.

Blank, Stephen. 2021. "Silence of the Dragon: What Role Is China Playing in Korea?" *Global Asia* 16(1): 68–73.

Blankenship, Brian. 2020. "Promises Under Pressure: Statements of Reassurance in US Alliances." *International Studies Quarterly* 64(4): 1017–1030.

Blankenship, Brian. 2021. "The Price of Protection: Explaining Success and Failure of US Alliance Burden-Sharing Pressure." *Security Studies* 30(5): 691–724.

Blankenship, Brian, and Erik Lin-Greenberg. 2022. "Trivial Tripwires?: Military Capabilities and Alliance Reassurance." *Security Studies* 31(1): 92–117.

Blasko, Dennis J. 2021. "The PLA Army After 'Below the Neck' Reforms: Contributing to China's Joint Warfighting, Deterrence and MOOTW Posture." *Journal of Strategic Studies* 44(2): 149–183.

Blinnikov, Mikhail S. 2021. *A Geography of Russia and Its Neighbors*, 2nd ed. New York: Guilford Press.

Bne IntelliNews. 2019. "US Treasury's Big Stick Hits Armenia Sales Agent that 'Acts for Sanctioned Iranian Airline'." January 24, https://www.intellinews.com/us-treasury-s-big-stick-hits-armenia-sales-agent-that-acts-for-sanctioned-iranian-airline-155320/?source=armenia (accessed 2022, September 8).

Bohdan, Siarhei. 2014. *Belarusian Army: Its Capacities and Role in the Region.* London: Ostrogorski Centre.

Borger, Julian. 2014. "Vladimir Putin Moves to Strengthen Ties with Serbia at Military Parade." *Guardian*, October 16, https://www.theguardian.com/world/2014/oct/16/vladimir-putin-russia-serbia-alliance-military-parade (accessed 2022, August 24).

Borger, Julian, Andrew MacDowall, and Shaun Walker. 2016. "Serbia Deports Russians Suspected of Plotting Montenegro Coup." *Guardian*, November 11, https://www.theguardian.com/world/2016/nov/11/serbia-deports-russians-suspected-of-plotting-montenegro-coup (accessed 2022, August 23).

Bowen, Andrew S. 2019. "Coercive Diplomacy and the Donbas: Explaining Russian Strategy in Eastern Ukraine." *Journal of Strategic Studies* 42(3–4): 312–343.

Bowen, Tyler J. 2021. "The Logic of Escalation and the Benefits of Conventional Power Preponderance in the Nuclear Age." Ph.D. diss., Yale University.

Boulding, Kenneth E. 1963. "Towards a Pure Theory of Threat Systems." *American Economic Review* 53(2): 424–434.

Bracken, Paul. 1976. "Urban Sprawl and NATO Defence." *Survival* 18(6): 254–260.

Brown, Hayes. 2016. "That One Time Kim Jong Il Invited Bill Clinton to Vacation in North Korea." *BuzzFeed*, October 27, https://www.buzzfeednews.com/article/hayesbrown/this-memo-shows-what-bill-clinton-and-kim-jong-il-talked-abo (accessed 2022, July 16).

Brunnstrom, David. 2017. "North Korean Media Issues Rare Criticism of China over Nuclear Warnings." *Reuters*, May 4, https://www.reuters.com/article/us-northkorea-china-idUSKBN17Z1TA (accessed 2022, July 3).

Brunnstrom, David, and Idrees Ali. 2015. "Obama Urges Pakistan to Avoid Raising Nuclear Tensions with New Weapons." *Reuters*, October 23, https://www.reuters.com/article/us-usa-pakistan-idUSKCN0SG29020151023 (accessed 2022, June 30).

Buncombe, Andrew. 2013. "Aung San Suu Kyi Urges Support for Controversial Chinese-Backed Copper Mine." *Independent*, March 13, https://www.independent.co.uk/news/world/asia/aung-san-suu-kyi-urges-support-for-controversial-chinesebacked-copper-mine-8531508.html (accessed 2022, August 2).

Burgos, Sigfrido, and Sophal Ear. 2010. "China's Strategic Interests in Cambodia: Influence and Resources." *Asian Survey* 50(3): 615–639.

Butt, Ahsan I. 2013. "Anarchy and Hierarchy in International Relations: Examining South America's War-Prone Decade, 1932–41." *International Organization* 67(3): 575–607.

Buzan, Barry, and Ole Wæver. 2003. *Regions and Powers: The Structure of International Security*. Cambridge: Cambridge University Press.

Bytyci, Fatos. 2017. "Serbia Wants to Annex Part of Kosovo Using 'Crimea Model': President." *Reuters*, January 17, https://www.reuters.com/article/us-serbia-kosovo-president-idUSKBN15022Y (accessed 2022, August 29).

Byun, Duk-kun. 2023. "US Military Presence in S. Korea Does Not Bother N. Korea at All: Pompeo." *Yonhap*, January 25, https://en.yna.co.kr/view/AEN20230125000200325 (accessed 2023, July 9).

Byun, Joshua. 2022. "Regional Security Cooperation Against Hegemonic Threats: Theory and Evidence from France and West Germany (1945–65)." *European Journal of International Security* 7(2): 143–163.

Calabrese, John. 2015. "Balancing on 'the Fulcrum of Asia': China's Pakistan Strategy." *Indian Journal of Asian Affairs* 27–28(1–2): 1–21.

Carter, Brittnee. 2022. "Revisiting the Bandwagoning Hypothesis: A Statistical Analysis of the Alliance Dynamics of Small States." *International Studies* 59(1): 7–27.

Castillo, Jasen J., and Alexander B. Downes. 2023. "Loyalty, Hedging, or Exit: How Weaker Alliance Partners Respond to the Rise of New Threats." *Journal of Strategic Studies* 46(2): 227–268.

Center for Systemic Peace. 2019. "The Polity Project." https://www.systemicpeace.org/polityproject.html (accessed 2022, September 18).

Central Intelligence Agency. 2022. "The World Factbook." https://www.cia.gov/the-world-factbook/ (accessed 2022, October 10).

Cepurītis, Māris. 2017. "Belarusian Political Relations with Russia After the Annexation of Crimea." In Andis Kudors (ed.), *Belarusian Foreign Policy: 360°*, 73–86. Riga: University of Latvia Press.

Cha, Victor D. 2000. "Abandonment, Entrapment, and Neoclassical Realism in Asia: The United States, Japan, and Korea." *International Studies Quarterly* 44(2): 261–291.

Cha, Victor D. 2010. "Powerplay: Origins of the U.S. Alliance System in Asia." *International Security* 34(3): 158–196.

Chabbi, Mourad, and Yves-Heng Lim. 2013. "Équilibres régionaux et stratégies des non-puissances : Les cas du Golfe et de l'Asie du Sud-Est." *Études Internationales* 44(2): 227–249.

Chan, Steve. 2012. *Looking for Balance: China, the United States, and Power Balancing in East Asia*. Stanford: Stanford University Press.

Chance, Matthew, and Zahra Ullah. 2021. "Ukraine Spies Tried to Ensnare Alleged Russian War Criminals with a Fake Website, Promises of Riches and an International Sting." *CNN*, September 8, https://edition.cnn.com/2021/09/07/europe/ukraine-belarus-russia-mercenaries-sting/index.html (accessed 2022, June 2).

Chen, Ian Tsung-Yen, and Alan Hao Yang. 2013. "A Harmonized Southeast Asia? Explanatory Typologies of ASEAN Countries' Strategies to the Rise of China." *Pacific Review* 26(3): 265–288.

Cheunboran, Chanborey. 2017. "Cambodia-China Relations: What Do Cambodia's Past Strategic Directions Tell Us?" In Deth Sok Udom, Sun Suon, and Serkan Bulut (eds.), *Cambodia's Foreign Relations in Regional and Global Contexts*, 227–248. Phnom Penh: Konrad-Adenauer-Stiftung.

Chheang, Vannarith. 2021. "Cambodia's Embrace of China's Belt and Road Initiative: Managing Asymmetries, Maximizing Authority." *Asian Perspective* 45(2): 375–396.

Chheang, Vannarith. 2022. "Cambodia's Multifaceted Foreign Policy and Agency in the Making." *Pacific Review* 35(2): 342–367.

Chhengpor, Aun. 2021. "Vietnam's New Militia Unit a Response to Tensions with Cambodia, China: Analysts." *VOA*, June 28, https://www.voacambodia.com/a/vietnam-s-new-militia-unit-a-response-to-tensions-with-cambodia-china-analysts/5945532.html (accessed 2022, June 25).

Chiacu, Doina, and Lisa Lambert. 2020. "First U.S. Crude Oil Shipment Heads to Belarus This Week: Pompeo." *Reuters*, May 15, https://www.reuters.com/article/us-global-oil-usa-belarus/first-u-s-crude-oil-shipment-heads-to-belarus-this-week-pompeo-idUSKBN22R1Z5 (accessed May 21, 2022).

Choi, Barnard Ki Seong. 2021. "The Post-Power Shift Effectiveness of International Security Institutions." Ph.D. diss., University of Chicago.

Choi, Sung Eun, and Iordanka Alexandrova. 2020. "The Stable Peace Between France and Germany: The Role of the United States." *Journal of International Politics* 25(2): 253–289.

Chow, Jonathan T., and Leif-Eric Easley. 2019a. "Comparing Myanmar and North Korea's Resentful Reliance on China." *East Asia Forum*, November 6,

https://www.eastasiaforum.org/2019/11/07/comparing-myanmar-and-north
-koreas-resentful-reliance-on-china/ (accessed 2022, July 30).

Chow, Jonathan T., and Leif-Eric Easley. 2019b. "Renegotiating Pariah State Partnerships: Why Myanmar and North Korea Respond Differently to Chinese Influence." *Contemporary Security Policy* 40(4): 502–525.

Christensen, Thomas J., and Jack Snyder. 1990. "Chain Gangs and Passed Bucks: Predicting Alliance Patterns in Multipolarity." *International Organization* 44(2): 137–168.

Christie, Edward Hunter, Caroline Buts, and Cind Du Bois. 2023. "Demand for Military Expenditures and Security Alignment Choices in the Indo-Pacific." *Defence and Peace Economics* 34(5): 581–602.

Chung, Jae Ho. 2009. "East Asia Responds to the Rise of China: Patterns and Variations." *Pacific Affairs* 82(4): 657–675.

Chung, Jae Ho, and Hun Joon Kim. 2023. "East Asia's Strategic Positioning Toward China: Identifying and Accounting for Intra-Regional Variations." *Australian Journal of International Affairs* 77(2): 107–128.

Chung, Kuyoun. 2017. "Geopolitics and a Realist Turn of US Foreign Policy Toward North Korea." *Korea Observer* 48(4): 765–790.

Ciorciari, John D. 2015. "A Chinese Model for Patron–Client Relations? The Sino-Cambodian Partnership." *International Relations of the Asia-Pacific* 15(2): 245–278.

Clark, Wesley K. 2018. "Don't Wait for the Western Balkans to Blow Up Again. The U.S. and the E.U. Must Act." *Washington Post*, April 11, https://www.washingtonpost.com/news/global-opinions/wp/2018/04/11/dont-wait-for-the-western-balkans-to-blow-up-again-the-u-s-and-the-e-u-must-act/?noredirect=on (accessed 2022, September 2).

Colby, Elbridge A. 2021. *The Strategy of Denial: American Defense in an Age of Great Power Conflict*. New Haven: Yale University Press.

Cole, Bernard D. 2016. *China's Quest for Great Power: Ships, Oil, and Foreign Policy*. Annapolis: Naval Institute Press.

Collier, David. 2011. "Understanding Process Tracing." *Political Science and Politics* 44(4): 823–830.

Conley, Heather A., and Dejana Saric. 2021. "The Serbia-Kosovo Normalization Process." *CSIS*, May 27, https://www.csis.org/analysis/serbia-kosovo-normalization-process-temporary-us-decoupling (accessed 2022, August 24).

Connable, Ben, Abby Doll, Alyssa Demus et al. 2020. *Russia's Limit of Advance: Analysis of Russian Ground Force Deployment Capabilities and Limitations*. Santa Monica: RAND.

Connolly, Richard. 2019. *Russian Military Expenditure in Comparative Perspective: A Purchasing Power Parity Estimate*. Arlington: CNA.

Cooper, Zack. 2016. "Tides of Fortune: The Rise and Decline of Great Militaries." Ph.D. diss., Princeton University.

Cote, Owen R., Jr. 2019. "Invisible Nuclear-Armed Submarines, or Transparent Oceans? Are Ballistic Missile Submarines Still the Best Deterrent for the United States?" *Bulletin of the Atomic Scientists* 75(1): 30–35.

CountryReports. "Cambodia Geography." https://www.countryreports.org/country/Cambodia/geography.htm (accessed 2022, June 25).

Crawford, Timothy W. 2008. "Wedge Strategy, Balancing, and the Deviant Case of Spain, 1940–41." *Security Studies* 17(1): 1–38.

Crawford, Timothy W. 2011. "Preventing Enemy Coalitions: How Wedge Strategies Shape Power Politics." *International Security* 35(4): 155–189.

Crawford, Timothy W. 2014. "The Alliance Politics of Concerted Accommodation: Entente Bargaining and Italian and Ottoman Interventions in the First World War." *Security Studies* 23(1): 113–147.

Crawford, Timothy W. 2021. *The Power to Divide: Wedge Strategies in Great Power Competition*. Ithaca: Cornell University Press.

Creswell, Michael. 2002. "Between the Bear and the Phoenix: The United States and the European Defense Community, 1950–54." *Security Studies* 11(4): 89–124.

Croissant, Aurel. 2018. "Cambodia in 2017: Descending into Dictatorship?" *Asian Survey* 58(1): 194–200.

Cummings, William. 2019. "North Korea Gives Fiery Reply to Trump After President's 'Undesirable Remarks' at NATO Meeting." *USA Today*, December 5, https://www.usatoday.com/story/news/world/2019/12/05/north-korea-r esponse-trump-remark/2617148001/ (accessed 2022, July 14).

Cunningham, James, Hugo Llorens, Ronald Neumann, Richard Olson, and Earl Anthony Wayne. 2021. "Don't Lose Afghanistan." *Atlantic Council*, August 6, https://www.atlanticcouncil.org/blogs/new-atlanticist/dont-lose-afghanista n/ (accessed 2022, March 13).

Daily Sabah. 2021. "Russia, Azerbaijan, Armenia Hold 1st Meeting on Nagorno-Karabakh." January 31, https://www.dailysabah.com/world/europe/russia-azerbaijan-armenia-hold-1st-meeting-on-nagorno-karabakh (accessed 2022, September 8).

Danielyan, Emil. 2020. "Russian-Armenian Dispute over Railway 'Settled'." *Radio Free Europe*, September 3, https://www.azatutyun.am/a/30819063.html (accessed 2022, September 6).

David, Steven R. 1991. "Explaining Third World Alignment." *World Politics* 43(2): 233–256.

Davies, Christian. 2021. "North Korea Looks Across the Border for Its Biggest Threat." *Financial Times*, December 12, https://www.ft.com/content/4f4685 14-4336-4273-aaef-c427e920412c (accessed 2022, July 11).

Dawn. 2013. "Firing Injures Pakistani Civilian at Kashmir Border." August 8, https://www.dawn.com/news/1034973 (accessed 2022, June 30).

DeBardeleben, Joan. 2012. "Applying Constructivism to Understanding EU-Russian Relations." *International Politics* 49(4): 418–433.

Delcour, Laure, and Kataryna Wolczuk. 2015. "The EU's Unexpected 'Ideal Neighbour'? The Perplexing Case of Armenia's Europeanisation." *Journal of European Integration* 37(4): 491–507.

Deth, Sok Udom. 2017. "An Overview of Cambodia-Thailand Relations: From Hostility to Harmony?" In Deth Sok Udom, Sun Suon, and Serkan Bulut (eds.), *Cambodia's Foreign Relations in Regional and Global Contexts*, 27–44. Phnom Penh: Konrad-Adenauer-Stiftung.

Deudney, Daniel, and G. John Ikenberry. 1999. "The Nature and Sources of Liberal International Order." *Review of International Studies* 25(2): 179–196.

Devlin, Kat, and Christine Huang. 2020. "In Taiwan, Views of Mainland China Mostly Negative." *Pew Research Center*, May 12, https://www.pewresearch.org/global/2020/05/12/in-taiwan-views-of-mainland-china-mostly-negativ e/ (accessed 2022, January 20).

DNA. 2015. "Pakistan Provokes India Again, Kills Labourer on International Border." October 24, https://www.dnaindia.com/india/report-pakistan-prov okes-india-again-kills-labourer-on-international-border-2137893 (accessed 2022, June 30).

Dossi, Simone, and Giuseppe Gabusi. 2023. "Of Constraints and Opportunities. Dependent Asymmetry in China-Myanmar Relations, 2011–2021." *Pacific Review* 36(6): 1306–1336.

Doung, Chandy, William Kang, and Jaechun Kim. 2022. "Cambodia's Foreign Policy Choice During 2010 to 2020: From Strategic Hedging to Bandwagoning." *Korean Journal of International Studies* 20(1): 55–88.

Dyner, Anna Maria. 2020. "Belarus-Poland: Emphasis on Security." In Anatoly Pankovski and Valeria Kostyugova (eds.), *Belarusian Yearbook 2020*, 87–95. Vilnius: Logvino.

Eckstein, Arthur M. 2023. "'Jackal Bandwagoning'? The Achaean League Shifts Alliances from Macedon to Rome, Autumn 198 B.C." *International History Review* 45(1): 1–13.

Economic Times. 2018. "Obama Administration Proposes $860 Million in Aid for Pakistan." July 12, https://economictimes.indiatimes.com/news/defence /obama-administration-proposes-860-million-in-aid-for-pakistan/articlesh ow/50928170.cms?from=mdr (accessed 2022, June 30).

Economides, Spyros, and James Ker-Lindsay. 2015. "'Pre-Accession Europeanization': The Case of Serbia and Kosovo." *Journal of Common Market Studies* 53(5): 1027–1044.

Egreteau, Renaud, and Li Chenyang. 2018. "Neighbourhood." In Adam Simpson, Nicholas Farrelly, and Ian Holliday (eds.), *Routledge Handbook of Contemporary Myanmar*, 312–323. Abingdon: Routledge.

Einhorn, Robert, and W.P.S. Sidhu (eds.). 2017. *The Strategic Chain: Linking Pakistan, India, China, and the United States.* Washington: Brookings.

Elman, Colin. 2004. "Extending Offensive Realism: The Louisiana Purchase and America's Rise to Regional Hegemony." *American Political Science Review* 98(4): 563–576.

Embassy of the People's Republic of China in the Republic of Ghana. 2014. "Xi Jinping Meets with Prime Minister Nawaz Sharif of Pakistan." November 8, https://www.mfa.gov.cn/ce/cegh//eng/zgyw/t1209091.html (accessed 2022, July 1).

Embassy of the People's Republic of China in the United States of America. 2022. "Joint Statement Between the People's Republic of China and the Islamic Republic of Pakistan." February 6, http://us.china-embassy.gov.cn/e ng/zgyw/202202/t20220206_10639501.htm (accessed 2022, July 1).

Ergan, Uğur. 2015. "Ankara: Russia-Armenia Deal Heats Up Caucasus." *Hürriyet*, December 24, https://www.hurriyetdailynews.com/ankara-russia-armenia-deal-heats-up-caucasus-92995 (accessed 2022, September 6).

Estonian Foreign Intelligence Service. 2021. "International Security and Estonia 2021." https://www.valisluureamet.ee/assessment.html (accessed 2022, April 26).

Estonian Foreign Intelligence Service. 2022. "International Security and Estonia 2021." https://www.valisluureamet.ee/assessment.html (accessed 2022, April 29).

EURACTIV. 2010. "Russia Secures Military Presence in Armenia Until 2044." August 23, https://www.euractiv.com/section/global-europe/news/russia-sec ures-military-presence-in-armenia-until-2044/ (accessed 2022, September 5).

EURACTIV. 2021. "Serbian Minister Blasts US Human Rights Report." April 2, https://www.euractiv.com/section/politics/short_news/serbian-minister-bl asts-us-human-rights-report/ (accessed 2022, September 4).

Fareed, Rifat. 2021. "Villagers Along India-Pakistan Border Sceptical of Ceasefire Deal." *Al Jazeera*, March 5, https://www.aljazeera.com/news/2021/3/5/villagers -along-india-pakistan-border-skeptic-of-ceasefire-deal (accessed 2022, June 30).

Feinstein, Scott G., and Ellen B. Pirro. 2021. "Testing the World Order: Strategic Realism in Russian Foreign Affairs." *International Politics* 58(6): 817–834.

Fiammenghi, Davide. 2011. "The Security Curve and the Structure of International Politics: A Neorealist Synthesis." *International Security* 35(4): 126–154.

Fingar, Thomas, and David Straub. 2017. "Geography and Destiny: DPRK Concerns and Objectives with Respect to China." In Thomas Fingar (ed.), *Uneasy Partnerships: China's Engagement with Japan, the Koreas, and Russia in the Era of Reform*, 169–188. Stanford: Stanford University Press.

Flanagan, Stephen J., Jan Osburg, Anika Binnendijk, Marta Kepe, and Andrew Radin. 2019. *Deterring Russian Aggression in the Baltic States Through Resilience and Resistance*. Santa Monica: RAND.

Ford, Glyn. 2018. *Talking to North Korea: Ending the Nuclear Standoff*. London: Pluto.

Fox, Annette B. 1959. *The Power of Small States: Diplomacy in World War II*. Chicago: University of Chicago Press.

Frewer, Tim. 2016. "Cambodia's Anti-Vietnam Obsession." *Diplomat*, September 6, https://thediplomat.com/2016/09/cambodias-anti-vietnam-obsession/ (accessed 2022, June 11).

Frontier Myanmar. 2017. "Tatmadaw Chief Thanks China for 'Standing on Myanmar's Side'." November 27, https://www.frontiermyanmar.net/en/tatm adaw-chief-thanks-china-for-standing-on-myanmars-side-2/ (accessed 2022, August 2).

Fyodorov, Andrei. 2020. "Belarusian-American Relations: A Vicious Circle." In Anatoly Pankovski and Valeria Kostyugova (eds.), *Belarusian Yearbook 2020*, 96–103. Vilnius: Logvino.

Galeotti, Mark. 2018. "Do the Western Balkans Face a Coming Russian Storm?" *European Council on Foreign Relations*, April 4, https://ecfr.eu/publication/ do_the_western_balkans_face_a_coming_russian_storm/ (accessed 2022, September 2).

Gallarotti, Giulio M. 2011. "Soft Power: What It Is, Why It's Important, and the Conditions for Its Effective Use." *Journal of Political Power* 4(1): 25–47.

Garlick, Jeremy. 2018. "Deconstructing the China–Pakistan Economic Corridor: Pipe Dreams Versus Geopolitical Realities." *Journal of Contemporary China* 27(112): 519–533.

Garnaut, John. 2013. "China, North Korea - Close as Lips and Teeth." *Sydney Morning Herald*, February 13, https://www.smh.com.au/world/china-north-korea--close-as-lips-and-teeth-20130213-2ebzl.html (accessed 2022, July 11).

Gartzke, Erik. 2013. "The Myth of Cyberwar: Bringing War in Cyberspace Back Down to Earth." *International Security* 38(2): 41–73.

George, Alexander L., and Andrew Bennett. 2005. *Case Studies and Theory Development in the Social Sciences*. Cambridge: MIT Press.

Gettleman, Jeffrey, Hari Kumar, and Samir Yasir. 2019. "Deadly Shelling Erupts in Kashmir Between India and Pakistan After Pilot Is Freed." *New York Times*, March 2, https://www.nytimes.com/2019/03/02/world/asia/kashmir-shelling-india-pakistan.html (accessed 2022, June 30).

Gheorghe, Eliza. 2022. "Balance of Power Redux: Nuclear Alliances and the Logic of Extended Deterrence." *Chinese Journal of International Politics* 15(1): 87–109.

Gilpin, Robert. 1981. *War and Change in World Politics*. Cambridge: Cambridge University Press.

Goh, Evelyn, and David I. Steinberg. 2016. "Myanmar's Management of China's Influence." In Evelyn Goh (ed.), *Rising China's Influence in Developing Asia*, 55–79. Oxford: Oxford University Press.

Golts, Aleksandr. 2017. "Belarus and Russia: Military Cooperation but with Different Goals." In Andis Kudors (ed.), *Belarusian Foreign Policy: 360°*, 87–99. Riga: University of Latvia Press.

Götz, Elias. 2023. "Takeover by Stealth: The Curious Case of Russia's Belarus Policy." *Problems of Post-Communism*, advance online publication, https://doi.org/10.1080/10758216.2023.2224570.

Graef, Alexander, and Ulrich Kühn. 2022. "A Letter from Moscow: (In)Divisible Security and Helsinki 2.0." *War on the Rocks*, February 14, https://warontherocks.com/2022/02/a-letter-from-moscow-indivisible-security-and-helsinki-2-0/ (accessed 2022, February 14).

Grare, Frederic. 2014. "India–Pakistan Relations: Does Modi Matter?" *Washington Quarterly* 37(4): 101–114.

Gray, Colin S. 2006. *Strategy and History: Essays on Theory and Practice*. Abingdon: Routledge.

Green, Michael J. 2017. *By More Than Providence: Grand Strategy and American Power in the Asia Pacific Since 1783*. New York: Columbia University Press.

Grygiel, Jakub J. 2021. "The Limits of Sea Power." *Naval War College Review* 74(4): 101–116.

Guardian. 2010. "US Embassy Cables: US Fury at Armenia over Arms Transfers to Iran." November 28, https://www.theguardian.com/world/us-embassy-cables-documents/184879 (accessed 2022, September 7).

Haacke, Jürgen. 2015. "The United States and Myanmar: From Antagonists to Security Partners?" *Journal of Current Southeast Asian Affairs* 34(2): 55–83.

Haas, Mark L. 2005. *The Ideological Origins of Great Power Politics, 1789–1989*. Ithaca: Cornell University Press.

Hadden, R. Lee. 2008. *The Geology of Burma (Myanmar): An Annotated Bibliography of Burma's Geology, Geography and Earth Science.* Alexandria: Topographic Engineering Center.

Haidar, Suhasini. 2015. "3 Minutes that Changed India-Pak. Ties." *Hindu,* December 26, https://www.thehindu.com/news/national/3-minutes-that-changed-India-Pak.-ties/article60281621.ece (accessed 2022, June 30).

Han, Enze. 2018. "Under the Shadow of China-US Competition: Myanmar and Thailand's Alignment Choices." *Chinese Journal of International Politics* 11(1): 81–104.

Han, Zhen, and T. V. Paul. 2020. "China's Rise and Balance of Power Politics." *Chinese Journal of International Politics* 13(1): 1–26

Hancock, Kathleen J., and Steven E. Lobell. 2010. "Realism and the Changing International System: Will China and Russia Challenge the Status Quo?" *China and Eurasia Forum Quarterly* 8(4): 143–165.

Harris, Peter, and Iren Marinova. 2022. "American Primacy and US-China Relations: The Cold War Analogy Reversed." *Chinese Journal of International Politics* 15(4): 335–351.

Harutyunyan, Sargis. 2019. "U.S. Envoy Hails Democratic Change in Armenia." *Radio Free Europe,* May 15, https://www.azatutyun.am/a/29942778.html (accessed 2022, September 8).

Hashim, Asad. 2021. "Pakistan Urges Biden to Stick to Afghan Troop Withdrawal." *Al Jazeera,* January 21, https://www.aljazeera.com/news/2021/1/21/pakistan-calls-for-us-to-stay-course-on-afghan-peace-talks (accessed 2022, June 30).

He, Kai, and Huiyun Feng. 2008. "If not Soft Balancing, Then What? Reconsidering Soft Balancing and U.S. Policy Toward China." *Security Studies* 17(2): 363–395.

Hedenskog, Jakob. 2022. "Russia's 'Soft Annexation' of Belarus During Its Invasion of Ukraine." *SCEEUS,* March 1, https://www.ui.se/forskning/centrum-for-os teuropastudier/sceeus-commentary/russias-soft-annexation-of-belarus-durin g-its-invasion-of-ukraine/ (accessed 2022, June 2).

Heder, Steve. 2018. "Cambodia-Vietnam: Special Relationship Against Hostile and Unfriendly Forces." *Southeast Asian Affairs*: 113–132.

Heim, Jacob L., and Benjamin M. Miller. 2020. *Measuring Power, Power Cycles, and the Risk of Great-Power War in the 21st Century.* Santa Monica: RAND.

Heng, Kimkong. 2019. "Cambodia in 2019 and Beyond: Key Issues and Next Steps Forward." *Cambodian Journal of International Studies* 3(2): 121–143.

Heng, Kimkong. 2022. "Cambodia-Vietnam Relations: Key Issues and the Way Forward." *ISEAS Perspective,* April 12, https://www.iseas.edu.sg/articles-com mentaries/iseas-perspective/2022-36-cambodia-vietnam-relations-key-issu e s-and-the-way-forward-by-kimkong-heng/ (accessed 2022, June 9).

Herf, Jeffrey. 2014. "At War with Israel: East Germany's Key Role in Soviet Policy in the Middle East." *Journal of Cold War Studies* 16(3): 129–163.

Hindu. 2016. "Operation Ginger: Tit-For-Tat Across the Line of Control." November 3, https://www.thehindu.com/news/national/Operation-Ginger-Tit-for-tat-acr oss-the-Line-of-Control/article55913300.ece (accessed 2022, June 30).

Hiro, Dilip. 2015. *The Longest August: The Unflinching Rivalry Between India and Pakistan.* New York: Nation.

Hopf, Ted. 1991. "Soviet Inferences from Their Victories in the Periphery: Visions of Resistance or Cumulating Gains?" In Robert Jervis and Jack Snyder (eds.), *Dominoes and Bandwagons: Strategic Beliefs and Great Power Competition in the Eurasian Rimland*, 145–189. New York: Oxford University Press.

Hoyos, Dexter. 2015. "Carthage After 201 B.C.: African Prosperity and Roman Protection." *Classicum* 41(1): 25–32.

Hsiung, James C. 2009. "China's Second Ascent & International Relations (IR) Theory." *American Journal of Chinese Studies* 16: 19–39.

Hui, Victoria Tin-bor. 2004. "Toward a Dynamic Theory of International Politics: Insights from Comparing Ancient China and Early Modern Europe." *International Organization* 58(1): 175–205.

Hui, Victoria Tin-bor. 2005. *War and State Formation in Ancient China and Early Modern Europe*. New York: Cambridge University Press.

Hui, Victoria Tin-bor. 2018. "Confucian Pacifism or Confucian Confusion?" In Andreas Gofas, Inanna Hamati-Ataya, and Nicholas Onuf (eds.), *The SAGE Handbook of the History, Philosophy and Sociology of International Relations*, 148–161. Thousand Oaks: SAGE.

Hunt, Luke. 2016. "Vietnam Investment Plunges in Cambodia, Sparking Concerns." *VOA*, October 3, https://www.voanews.com/a/vietnam-investme nt-plunges-in-cambodia-sparking-concerns/3534422.html (accessed 2022, June 11).

Hussain, Iqtidar, Israr Hussain, and Iqrar Hussain Qambari. 2020. "History of Pakistan-China Relations: The Complex Interdependence Theory." *Chinese Historical Review* 27(2): 146–164.

Hutt, David. 2016. "How China Came to Dominate Cambodia," *Diplomat*, September 1, https://thediplomat.com/2016/09/how-china-came-to-domi nate-cambodia/ (accessed 2022, June 23).

Hwang, Joon-bum. 2019. "Trump Says He Received Letter from Kim Jong-un." *Hankyoreh*, June 12, https://english.hani.co.kr/arti/english_edition/e_north korea/897635.html (accessed 2022, July 14).

Indian Express. 2012. "Pak Willing to Resolve Bilateral Disputes with India: Hina Rabbani Khar." July 12, https://indianexpress.com/article/news-archive/pr int/pak-willing-to-resolve-bilateral-disputes-with-india-hina-rabbani-khar/ (accessed 2022, June 30).

Inhofe, Jim. 2021. "Combined China and Russian Defense Spending Exceeds U.S. Defense Budget." *Real Clear Defense*, May 3, https://www.realcleardefense. com/articles/2021/05/03/combined_china_and_russian_defense_spending_e xceeds_us_defense_budget_775323.html (accessed 2022, January 21).

Interfax-Ukraine. 2009. "Lukashenko Against Belarus Becoming Part of Russia." *Kyiv Post*, June 5, https://www.kyivpost.com/article/content/world/Lukashenko -against-belarus-becoming-part-of-russia-42860.html (accessed 2022, June 8).

International Crisis Group. 2018. "China-Pakistan Economic Corridor: Opportunities and Risks." *Asia Report*, June 29, https://www.crisisgroup.org/ asia/south-asia/pakistan/297-china-pakistan-economic-corridor-opportun ities-and-risks (accessed 2022, June 30).

International Institute for Strategic Studies. 2022. *The Military Balance, 2022.* Abingdon: Routledge.

Izumikawa, Yasuhiro. 2018. "Binding Strategies in Alliance Politics: The Soviet-Japanese-US Diplomatic Tug of War in the Mid-1950s." *International Studies Quarterly* 62(1): 108–120.

Jabri, Parvez. 2017. "No Room for Self-Proclaimed, Artificially Boosted States in South Asia Security Matrix." *Business Recorder*, September 20, https://www.brecorder.com/news/370376 (accessed 2022, July 1).

Jackson, Van. 2019. *On the Brink: Trump, Kim, and the Threat of Nuclear War*. Cambridge: Cambridge University Press.

Jagan, Larry. 2022. "Myanmar Reaches a Political Impasse." *Bangkok Post*, February 7, https://www.bangkokpost.com/opinion/opinion/2259727/mya nmar -reaches-a-political-impasse (accessed 2022, August 10).

Jakobsen, Jo. 2022. *The Geopolitics of U.S. Overseas Troops and Withdrawal*. Cham: Palgrave Macmillan.

Jervis, Robert. 1991. "Domino Beliefs and Strategic Behavior." In Robert Jervis and Jack Snyder (eds.), *Dominoes and Bandwagons: Strategic Beliefs and Great Power Competition in the Eurasian Rimland*, 20–50. New York: Oxford University Press.

Jesse, Neal G. 2020. *Learning from Russia's Recent Wars: Why, Where, and When Russia Might Strike Next*. Amherst: Cambria Press.

Jian, Chen. 2001. *Mao's China and the Cold War*. Chapel Hill: University of North Carolina Press.

Joffe, Josef. 1984. "Europe's American Pacifier." *Foreign Policy* 54: 64–82.

Jolliffe, Kim. 2016. *Ceasefires, Governance, and Development: The Karen National Union in Times of Change*. San Francisco: Asia Foundation.

Jonassen, Trine. 2021. "Russia Puts U.S. on List of 'Unfriendly Countries'." *High North News*, April 26, https://www.highnorthnews.com/en/russia-puts-us-list-unfriendly-countries (accessed 2021, April 27).

Jones, Lee, and Khin Ma Ma Myo. 2021. "Explaining Myanmar's Response to China's Belt and Road Initiative: From Disengagement to Embrace." *Asian Perspective* 45(2): 301–324.

Jovanovic, Igor. 2015. "Serbian Military Drill with Russia Annoys EU." *Balkan Insight*, August 19, https://balkaninsight.com/2015/08/19/eu-opposes-to-serbia-s-military-drills-with-russia-08-18-2015-1/ (accessed 2022, August 29).

Kaghzvantsian, Satenik. 2014. "Russian-Armenian War Games Target 'Ottomania'." *Radio Free Europe*, September 5, https://www.azatutyun.am/a/26568876.html (accessed 2022, September 6).

Kang, David C. 2003a. "Getting Asia Wrong: The Need for New Analytical Frameworks." *International Security* 27(4): 57–85.

Kang, David C. 2003b. "Hierarchy and Stability in Asian International Relations." In G. John Ikenberry and Michael Mastanduno (eds.), *International Relations Theory and the Asia-Pacific*, 163–190. New York: Columbia University Press.

Kang, David C. 2005. "Hierarchy in Asian International Relations: 1300–1900." *Asian Security* 1(1): 53–79.

Kang, David C. 2007. *China Rising: Peace, Power, and Order in East Asia*. New York: Columbia University Press.

Kania, Elsa B., and John Costello. 2021. "Seizing the Commanding Heights: The PLA Strategic Support Force in Chinese Military Power." *Journal of Strategic Studies* 44(2): 218–264.

Katagiri, Azusa, and Eric Min. 2019. "The Credibility of Public and Private Signals: A Document-Based Approach." *American Political Science Review* 113(1): 156–172.

Katz, Mark N. 2021. "Russia Secretly Feared the Iran Nuclear Deal. Here's Why." *Atlantic Council*, April 28. https://www.atlanticcouncil.org/blogs/iransource/russia -secretly-feared-the-iran-nuclear-deal-heres-why/ (accessed 2021, May 16).

Kaufman, Robert G. 1992. "'To Balance or to Bandwagon?' Alignment Decisions in 1930s Europe." *Security Studies* 1(3): 417–447.

Kaufman, Stuart J., Richard Little, and William C. Wohlforth (eds.). 2007. *The Balance of Power in World History.* Basingstoke: Palgrave Macmillan.

Keck, Zachary. 2014. "North Korea Slams Xi Jinping and the Chinese Dream." *Diplomat*, June 17, https://thediplomat.com/2014/06/north-korea-slams-xi-jinping-and-the-chinese-dream/ (accessed 2022, July 11).

Kesylytė-Alliks, Eglė. 2017. "Discursive Construction of Lithuania's 'Others': The Case of Belarus." *Nationalities Papers* 45(1): 80–95.

Khajuria, Ravi Krishnan. 2018. "109 Killed in Pakistan Firing on Jammu and Kashmir Borders Since 2016: RTI Reply." *Hindustan Times*, September 30, https://www.hindustantimes.com/india-news/109-killed-in-pakistan-firing -on-jammu-and-kashmir-borders-since-2016-rti-reply/story-DukZCdsgVdv qAt3FzxiQwI.html (accessed 2022, June 30).

Khan, Feroz Hassan. 2016. "Sino-Pakistani Relations: Axis or Entente Cordiale?" *Asia Policy* 21: 155–159.

Khan, Hafeez Ullah. 2020. "China, the Emerging Economic Power: Options and Repercussions for Pak–US Relations." *International Politics*, advance online publication, https://doi.org/10.1057/s41311-020-00265-1.

Khmer Times. 2021. "Thailand Says It Is Finally 'Ready' to Discuss Overlapping Claims Stretching 26,000 Sq Kms of Water with Cambodia." October 6, https ://www.khmertimeskh.com/50947431/thailand-says-it-is-finally-ready-to-d iscuss-overlapping-claims-stretching-26000-sq-kms-of-water-with-cambod ia/ (accessed 2022, June 23).

Khoo, Nicholas. 2011. *Collateral Damage: Sino-Soviet Rivalry and the Termination of the Sino-Vietnamese Alliance.* New York: Columbia University Press.

Kim, Jieun. 2018. "North Korea Stokes Anti-China Sentiment in Response to Tougher Sanctions." *Radio Free Asia*, January 4, https://www.rfa.org/english/ news/korea/north-korea-stokes-anti-china-sentiment-in-response-to-toug her-sanctions-01042018161757.html (accessed 2022, July 20).

Kim, Jina. 2022. "The Dilemma of North Korea's Foreign Policy: 10 Years of Diplomacy Under the Kim Jong-Un Regime." *Journal of Peace and Unification* 12(1): 53–78.

Kimseng, Men. 2019. "US House Passes Bill to Sanction Cambodia's Top Officials." *VOA*, July 18, https://www.voanews.com/a/east-asia-pacific_us-house-passes -bill-sanction-cambodias-top-officials/6172187.html (accessed 2022, June 9).

Kłysiński, Kamil. 2013. "No Other Choice but Co-Operation: The Background of Lithuania's and Latvia's Relations with Belarus." *OSW*, https://www.osw.waw.

pl/en/publikacje/osw-commentary/2013-01-07/no-other-choice-co-operati on-background-lithuanias-and-latvias (accessed 2022, May 8).

Knopf, Jeffrey W. 2012. "Varieties of Assurance." *Journal of Strategic Studies* 35(3): 375–399.

Knorr, Klaus. 1970. *Military Power and Potential.* Lexington: D. C. Heath.

Kobayashi, Yuka, and Josephine King. 2022. "Myanmar's Strategy in the China-Myanmar Economic Corridor: A Failure in Hedging?" *International Affairs* 98(3): 1013–1032.

Kofman, Michael. 2018. "The Collapsing Russian Defense Budget and Other Fairy Tales." *Russia Matters,* May 22, https://www.russiamatters.org/analysis/collapsi ng-russian-defense-budget-and-other-fairy-tales (accessed 2022, January 21).

Kofman, Michael, and Richard Connolly. 2019. "Why Russian Military Expenditure Is Much Higher Than Commonly Understood (as Is China's)." *War on the Rocks,* December 16, https://warontherocks.com/2019/12/why-r ussian-military-expenditure-is-much-higher-than-commonly-understoodas -is-chinas/ (accessed 2022, January 21).

Kong, Tat Yan. 2018. "China's Engagement-Oriented Strategy Towards North Korea: Achievements and Limitations." *Pacific Review* 31(1): 76–95.

Konitzer, Andrew. 2011. "Serbia Between East and West." *Russian History* 38(1): 103–124.

Kopalyan, Nerses, and Anna Ohanyan. 2022. "How to Train Your Dragon: Armenia's Velvet Revolution in an Authoritarian Orbit." *Communist and Post-Communist Studies* 55(1): 24–51.

Kraemer, Richard. 2022. *Serbia on the Edge.* Philadelphia: Foreign Policy Research Institute.

Kramer, Mark. 2017. "Stalin, the Split with Yugoslavia, and Soviet–East European Efforts to Reassert Control, 1948–53." In Svetozar Rajak, Konstantina E. Botsiou, Eirini Karamouzi, and Evanthis Hatzivassiliou (eds.), *The Balkans in the Cold War,* 29–63. London: Palgrave Macmillan.

Krepinevich, Andrew F. 2017. *Preserving the Balance: A U.S. Eurasia Defense Strategy.* Washington, D.C.: Center for Strategic and Budgetary Assessments.

Kroenig, Matthew. 2020. *The Logic of American Nuclear Strategy.* New York: Oxford University Press.

Krstic, Branislav. 2011. "Serbs Stop NATO Removing Roadblocks in North Kosovo." *Reuters,* October 22, https://www.reuters.com/article/uk-kosovo-tensions-idUKTRE79L0HZ20111022 (accessed 2022, August 25).

Kry, Suyheang, and Terith Chy. 2017. "Cambodia's Relations with Vietnam: Prospects and Challenges." In Deth Sok Udom, Sun Suon, and Serkan Bulut (eds.), *Cambodia's Foreign Relations in Regional and Global Contexts,* 63–82. Phnom Penh: Konrad-Adenauer-Stiftung.

Kucera, Joshua. 2023. "Is Armenia Turning to the West?" *Radio Free Europe/Radio Liberty,* September 13, https://www.rferl.org/a/armenia-pashinian-united-state s-west-relations-russia-analysis/32591327.html (accessed 2023, October 30).

Kudors, Andis. 2017. "Introduction." In Andis Kudors (ed.), *Belarusian Foreign Policy: 360°,* 5–8. Riga: University of Latvia Press.

Kurita, Masahiro. 2022. "China's Kashmir Policy Since the Mid-2010s: Ramifications of CPEC and India's Kashmir Reorganization." *Asian Security* 18(1): 56–74.

Kurlantzick, Joshua. 2022. "China's Support for Myanmar Further Shows the World Dividing into Autocracy Versus Democracy." *Council on Foreign Relations*, April 4, https://www.cfr.org/blog/chinas-support-myanmar-further-shows-world-dividing-autocracy-versus-democracy (accessed 2022, August 12).

Kynge, James, Leila Haddou, and Michael Peel. 2016. "FT Investigation: How China Bought Its Way into Cambodia." *Financial Times*, September 9, https://www.ft.com/content/23968248-43a0-11e6-b22f-79eb4891c97d (accessed 2022, June 7).

Labs, Eric J. 1992. "Do Weak States Bandwagon?" *Security Studies* 1(3): 383–416.

Labs, Eric J. 1997. "Beyond Victory: Offensive Realism and the Expansion of War Aims." *Security Studies* 6(4): 1–49.

Lake, David A. 2007. "Escape from the State of Nature: Authority and Hierarchy in World Politics." *International Security* 32(1): 47–79.

Larson, Deborah W. 1997. "Trust and Missed Opportunities in International Relations." *Political Psychology* 18(3): 701–734.

Layne, Christopher. 1993 "The Unipolar Illusion: Why New Great Powers Will Rise." *International Security* 17(4): 5–51.

Lee, Do Young. 2021. "Strategies of Extended Deterrence: How States Provide the Security Umbrella." *Security Studies* 30(5): 761–796.

Lee, Hsi-Min, and Michael A. Hunzeker. 2022. "The View of Ukraine from Taiwan: Get Real About Territorial Defense." *War on the Rocks*, March 15, https://warontherocks.com/2022/03/the-view-of-ukraine-from-taiwan-get-real-about-territorial-defense/ (accessed 2022, March 19).

Lee, Ji-Young. 2017. *China's Hegemony: Four Hundred Years of East Asian Domination*. New York: Columbia University Press.

Lee, Sang-Man, Sang-Sook Lee, and Dae-Keun Moon. 2021. *Bukjung gwanggye: 1945–2020* [North Korea-China Relations: 1945–2020]. Seoul: Institute for Far Eastern Studies.

Legro, Jeffrey W., and Andrew Moravcsik. 1999. "Is Anybody Still a Realist?" *International Security* 24(2): 5–55.

Leng, Thearith. 2017. "Small State Diplomacy: Cambodia's Foreign Policy Towards Vietnam." *Pacific Review* 30(3): 328–347.

Leng, Thearith, and Vannarith Chheang. 2021. "Are Cambodia-U.S. Relations Mendable?" *Asia Policy* 16(4): 124–133.

Levy, Jack S. 1989. "The Causes of War: A Review of Theories and Evidence." In Philip E. Tetlock et al. (eds.), *Behavior, Society, and Nuclear War*, 209–333. New York: Oxford University Press.

Levy, Jack S. 2008. "Case Studies: Types, Designs, and Logics of Inference." *Conflict Management and Peace Science* 25(1): 1–18.

Levy, Jack S., and William R. Thompson. 2005. "Hegemonic Threats and Great-Power Balancing in Europe, 1495–1999." *Security Studies* 14(1): 1–33.

Levy, Jack S., and William R. Thompson. 2010. "Balancing on Land and at Sea: Do States Ally Against the Leading Global Power?" *International Security* 35(1): 7–43.

Liberman, Peter. 1996. *Does Conquest Pay? The Exploitation of Occupied Industrial Societies*. Princeton: Princeton University Press.

Lieber, Keir A., and Gerard Alexander. 2005. "Waiting for Balancing: Why the World Is Not Pushing Back." *International Security* 30(1): 109–139.

Lieber, Keir A., and Daryl G. Press. 2017. "The New Era of Counterforce: Technological Change and the Future of Nuclear Deterrence." *International Security* 41(4): 9–49.

Lieber, Keir A., and Daryl G. Press. 2020. *The Myth of the Nuclear Revolution: Power Politics in the Atomic Age*. Ithaca: Cornell University Press.

Lim, Darren J., and Zack Cooper. 2015. "Reassessing Hedging: The Logic of Alignment in East Asia." *Security Studies* 24(4): 696–727.

Lintner, Bertil. 2019. "The United Wa State Army and Burma's Peace Process." *United States Institute of Peace*, April, https://www.usip.org/publications/2019/0 4/united-wa-state-army-and-burmas-peace-process (accessed 2022, August 11).

Lintner, Bertil. 2021. "China, the Geopolitical Winner of Myanmar's Coup." *Asia Times*, February 4, https://asiatimes.com/2021/02/china-the-geopolitical-winner-of-myanmars-coup/ (accessed 2022, August 10).

Lobell, Steven E. 2018. "A Granular Theory of Balancing." *International Studies Quarterly* 62(3): 593–605.

Lobell, Steven E. 2023. "Preventive Military Strike or Preventive War? The Fungibility of Power Resources." *Cambridge Review of International Affairs* 36(5): 607–624.

Luttwak, Edward. 2012. *The Rise of China vs. the Logic of Strategy*. Cambridge: Harvard University Press.

Machiavelli, Niccolò. 1985. *The Prince*, 2nd ed., trans. Harvey C. Mansfield. Chicago: University of Chicago Press.

Macias, Amanda. 2021. "Biden Administration Slaps Sanctions on Belarus After It Forcibly Diverted Passenger Jet to Arrest Opposition Journalist." *CNBC*, June 21, https://www.cnbc.com/2021/06/21/belarus-sanctioned-after-diver sion-of-ryanair-flight-to-arrest-journalist.html (accessed 2022, June 3).

Mahnken, Thomas G. (ed.). 2020. *Net Assessment and Military Strategy: Retrospective and Prospective Essays*. Amherst: Cambria.

Mahoney, James. 2012. "The Logic of Process Tracing Tests in the Social Sciences." *Sociological Methods & Research* 41(4): 570–597.

Maley, William. 2021. "Joe Biden Failed Afghanistan's People and Tarnished U.S. Credibility." *UPI*, August 16, https://www.upi.com/Voices/2021/08/16/Joe-Biden-failed-Afghanistan/8731629118160/ (accessed 2022, March 13).

Malik, J. Mohan. 2018. "Myanmar's Role in China's Maritime Silk Road Initiative." *Journal of Contemporary China* 27(111): 362–378.

Manić, Emilija, Vladimir Nikitović, and Predrag Djurović (eds.). 2022. *The Geography of Serbia: Nature, People, Economy*. Cham: Springer.

Mares, David R. 1988. "Middle Powers Under Regional Hegemony: To Challenge or Acquiesce in Hegemonic Enforcement." *International Studies Quarterly* 32(4): 453–471.

Markey, Daniel. 2016. "The Strange Tale of Sino-Pakistani Friendship." *Asia Policy* 21: 151–155.

Martin, Susan B. 2003. "From Balance of Power to Balancing Behavior: The Long and Winding Road." In Andrew K. Hanami (ed.), *Perspectives on Structural Realism*, 61–82. New York: Palgrave Macmillan.

Maschmeyer, Lennart. 2021. "The Subversive Trilemma: Why Cyber Operations Fall Short of Expectations." *International Security* 46(2): 51–90.

Masood, Bashaarat. 2021. "Pulwama Attack Prime Accused, Kin of Jaish's Masood Azhar, Killed in Encounter." *Indian Express*, August 1, https://indianexpress.com/article/india/two-militants-killed-in-encounter-with-securit y-forces-in-jammu-kashmir-pulwama-7431294/ (accessed 2022, June 30).

Mearsheimer, John J. 1983. *Conventional Deterrence*. Ithaca: Cornell University Press.

Mearsheimer, John J. 1990. "Back to the Future: Instability in Europe After the Cold War." *International Security* 15(1): 5–56.

Mearsheimer, John J. 2001. *The Tragedy of Great Power Politics*. New York: W. W. Norton.

Mearsheimer, John J. 2010. "The Gathering Storm: China's Challenge to US Power in Asia." *Chinese Journal of International Politics* 3(4): 381–396.

Mearsheimer, John J. 2014. *The Tragedy of Great Power Politics*, updated ed. New York: W. W. Norton.

Mearsheimer, John J. 2018. *The Great Delusion: Liberal Dreams and International Realities*. New Haven: Yale University Press.

Mearsheimer, John J. 2019. "Bound to Fail: The Rise and Fall of the Liberal International Order." *International Security* 43(4): 7–50.

Mearsheimer, John J. 2021. "The Inevitable Rivalry: America, China, and the Tragedy of Great-Power Politics." *Foreign Affairs* 100(6): 48–58.

Medeiros, Evan S. 2005. "Strategic Hedging and the Future of Asia-Pacific Stability." *Washington Quarterly* 29(1): 145–167.

Meijer, Hugo, and Stephen G. Brooks. 2021. "Illusions of Autonomy: Why Europe Cannot Provide for Its Security if the United States Pulls Back." *International Security* 45(4): 7–43.

Melyantsou, Dzianis, and Andrej Kazakevich. 2008. "Belarus' Relations with Ukraine and Lithuania Before and After the 2006 Presidential Elections." *Lithuanian Foreign Policy Review* 20: 47–78.

Meng, Weizhan, and Weixing Hu. 2020. "Reacting to China's Rise Throughout History: Balancing and Accommodating in East Asia." *International Relations of the Asia-Pacific* 20(1): 119–148.

Miller, Drew. 1985. "Fortifications and Underground Nuclear Defense Shelters for NATO Troops." Ph.D. diss., Harvard University.

Min, Kyung-tae. 2023. "Navigating Geopolitical Change in Northeast Asia: A Realist Approach to Analyze the Matrix Scenario of US-China Conflict and US-North Korea Relations." *Pacific Focus*, advance online publication, https://doi.org/10.1111/pafo.12236.

Ministry of Foreign Affairs, Islamic Republic of Pakistan. 2015. "Joint Statement Between the Islamic Republic of Pakistan and the People's Republic of China on Establishing the All-Weather Strategic Cooperative Partnership." April 20, https://mofa.gov.pk/joint-statement-between-the-islamic-republic-of-pakis tan-and-the-peoples-republic-of-china-on-establishing-the-all-weather-stra tegic-cooperative-partnership/ (accessed 2022, June 30).

Ministry of Foreign Affairs, Republic of Armenia. 2022. "Bilateral Relations." March 11, https://www.mfa.am/en/bilateral-relations/us (accessed 2022, September 9).

Ministry of Foreign Affairs, Republic of Korea. 2018. "Panmunjom Declaration for Peace, Prosperity and Unification of the Korean Peninsula (2018.4.27)." September 11, https://www.mofa.go.kr/eng/brd/m_5478/view.do?seq=3191 30&srchFr=&srchTo=&srchWord=&srchTp=&multi_itm_seq=0&itm_seq_1=0 &itm_seq_2=0&company_cd=&company_nm=&page=1&titleNm= (accessed 2022, July 3).

Ministry of Foreign Affairs and International Cooperation, Kingdom of Cambodia. 2021. "Cambodia's Foreign Policy Direction." https://www.mfaic .gov.kh/Page/2021-02-08-Cambodia-s-Foreign-Policy-Direction (2022, June 25).

Mir, Nazir Ahmad. 2021. "Issues and Mistrust in US-Pakistan Relations." *Atlantic Council*, November 9, https://www.atlanticcouncil.org/blogs/southasiasour ce/issues-and-mistrust-in-us-pakistan-relations/ (accessed 2022, June 30).

Mirski, Sean. 2013. "Stranglehold: The Context, Conduct and Consequences of an American Naval Blockade of China." *Journal of Strategic Studies* 36(3): 385–421.

Mishali-Ram, Meirav. 2022. "International Crisis in the Midst of Civil War." *International Relations* 36(2): 307–326.

Mistry, Dinshaw. 2020. "Divergence and Convergence in U.S.-Pakistan Security Relations." *Asian Security* 16(2): 243–262.

Mitchell, A. Wess. 2018. *The Grand Strategy of the Habsburg Empire*. Princeton: Princeton University Press.

Montgomery, Evan B. 2013. "Competitive Strategies Against Continental Powers: The Geopolitics of Sino-Indian-American Relations." *Journal of Strategic Studies* 36(1): 76–100.

Montgomery, Evan B. 2016. *In the Hegemon's Shadow: Leading States and the Rise of Regional Powers*. Ithaca: Cornell University Press.

Moore, Gregory J. 2013. "Constructing Cooperation in Northeast Asia: Historical Northeast Asian Dyadic Cultures and the Potential for Greater Regional Cooperation." *Journal of Contemporary China* 22(83): 887–904.

Morrow, James D. 1993. "Arms Versus Allies: Trade-Offs in the Search for Security." *International Organization* 47(2): 207–233.

Moscow Times. 2016. "Russia and Armenia to Create Joint Military Forces." November 14, https://www.themoscowtimes.com/2016/11/14/russia-and-armenia-to-create-joint-military-forces-a56121 (accessed 2022, September 6).

Motin, Dylan. 2021. "South America Off Balance? Aggregate and Military Power in International Politics." *Journal of Social Sciences* 60(2): 31–54.

Motin, Dylan. 2022a. "Great Power Politics in World History: Balance of Power and Central Wars Since Antiquity." *Korean Journal of International Studies* 20(2): 175–212.

Motin, Dylan. 2022b. "Not in My Backyard, But in Yours: Containment Realism, Restraint Realism, and China-U.S. Competition." *Irish Studies in International Affairs* 33(1): 27–47.

Motin, Dylan. 2022c. "On Containing China: A Realist Case for American Engagement with North Korea." *Journal of East Asian Affairs* 35(2): 95–154.

Motin, Dylan. 2022d. "Stir Up the Hornet's Nest: How to Exploit the Friction Between China and North Korea." In National Committee on American Foreign Policy (ed.), *The Future of the Korean Peninsula and Beyond: Next Generation Policy Perspectives*, 148–158. New York: NCAFP.

Motin, Dylan. 2022e. "The Fault in Our Stars? Korea's Strategy for Survival and Germany's Rise, 1876–1910." *Seoul Journal of Korean Studies* 35(1): 131–161.

Motin, Dylan. 2023. "The Last Stake to the Palisade: How to Engage with North Korea." *Marcellus Policy Analysis*, https://jqas.org/the-last-stake-to-the-palisade-how-to-engage-with-north-korea-marcellus-policy-analysis/ (accessed 2023, July 9).

Mrachek, Alexis. 2019. "U.S. Relations with Belarus and the Russia Effect." *Heritage Foundation*, August 12, https://www.heritage.org/europe/report/us-relations-belarus-and-the-russia-effect (accessed 2022, May 21).

Mrachek, Alexis. 2021. "How the Biden Administration Should Approach Belarus." *Heritage Foundation*, March 22, https://www.heritage.org/sites/default/files/2021-03/IB6070.pdf (accessed 2022, June 3).

Mukherjee, Anit. 2009. "A Brand New Day or Back to the Future? The Dynamics of India-Pakistan Relations." *India Review* 8(4): 404–445.

Munir, Muhammad. 2018. "Pakistan-China Strategic Interdependence." *Strategic Studies* 38(2): 21–42.

Murg, Bradley J. 2022. "Walking a Fine Line: How Cambodia Navigates Its Way Between China and Vietnam." *Southeast Asian Affairs*: 126–137.

Muzyka, Konrad. 2021. *The Belarusian Armed Forces: Structures, Capabilities, and Defence Relations with Russia.* Tallinn: International Centre for Defence and Security.

Myanmar Peace Monitor. "KIO/KIA." https://www.mmpeacemonitor.org/1529/ (accessed 2022, August 12).

Naimark, Norman M. 2019. *Stalin and the Fate of Europe: The Postwar Struggle for Sovereignty.* Cambridge: Harvard University Press.

Nakazawa, Katsuji. 2017. "Pyongyang Missile Footage Is a Dagger to Xi's Throat." *Nikkei Asia*, August 21, https://asia.nikkei.com/Politics/Pyongyang-missile-footage-is-a-dagger-to-Xi-s-throat2 (accessed 2022, July 11).

Nanto, Dick K., and Mark E. Manyin. 2011. "China-North Korea Relations." *North Korean Review* 7(2): 94–101.

Narizny, Kevin. 2017. "On Systemic Paradigms and Domestic Politics: A Critique of the Newest Realism." *International Security* 42(2): 155–190.

NDTV. 2008. "Forward Deployment of Pak Air Force Planes Detected." December 24, http://www.ndtv.com/convergence/ndtv/story.aspx?id=NEWEN20080077643&ch=12%2F24%2F2008%209%3A23%3A00%20PM (accessed 2022, June 30).

Nexon, Daniel H., and Thomas Wright. 2007. "What's at Stake in the American Empire Debate." *American Political Science Review* 101(2): 253–271.

Nguyen, Vu Tung. 2017. "Vietnam-Cambodia Relations: An Analysis from a Vietnamese Perspective." In Deth Sok Udom, Sun Suon, and Serkan Bulut (eds.), *Cambodia's Foreign Relations in Regional and Global Contexts*, 85–99. Phnom Penh: Konrad-Adenauer-Stiftung.

Nikkei Asia. 2021. "Cambodia's Hun Sen: 'If I Don't Rely on China, Who Will I Rely On?'." May 20, https://asia.nikkei.com/Spotlight/The-Future-of-Asia/-Future-of-Asia-2021/Cambodia-s-Hun-Sen-If-I-don-t-rely-on-China-who-will-I-rely-on (accessed 2022, June 25).

Nikolic, Ivana. 2014. "Serbian President Demands Kosovo Referendum." *Balkan Insight*, December 29, https://balkaninsight.com/2014/12/29/serbia n-president-calls-for-kosovo-referendum/ (accessed 2022, September 1).

Nizhnikau, Ryhor, and Arkady Moshes. 2020. "Belarus in Search of a New Foreign Policy: Why Is It So Difficult?" In Kristian Fischer and Hans Mouritzen (eds.), *Danish Foreign Policy Review, 2020*, 48–72. Copenhagen: Danish Institute for International Studies.

Nouwens, Meia, and Lucie Béraud-Sudreau. 2020. *Assessing Chinese Defence Spending: Proposals for New Methodologies*. London: IISS.

Nye, Joseph S. 2004. "Soft Power and American Foreign Policy." *Political Science Quarterly* 119(2): 255–270.

Obe, Charles Parton, and James Byrne. 2021. "China's Only Ally." *RUSI Newsbrief*, July 2, https://rusi.org/explore-our-research/publications/rusi-newsbrief/chinas-only-ally (accessed 2022, July 3).

Olson, Mancur, and Richard Zeckhauser. 1966. "An Economic Theory of Alliances." *Review of Economics and Statistics* 48(3): 266–279.

Online Burma/Myanmar Library. 2011. "President U Thein Sein Delivers Inaugural Address to Pyidaungsu Hluttaw." March 30, https://www.burma library.org/en/president-u-thein-sein-delivers-inaugural-address-to-pyidau ngsu-hluttaw (accessed 2022, August 2).

O'Rourke, Lindsey, and Joshua Shifrinson. 2022. "Squaring the Circle on Spheres of Influence: The Overlooked Benefits." *Washington Quarterly* 45(2): 105–124.

O'Rourke, Ronald. 2022. "China Naval Modernization: Implications for U.S. Navy Capabilities—Background and Issues for Congress." *Congressional Research Service*, March 8, https://sgp.fas.org/crs/row/RL33153.pdf (accessed 2022, July 25).

Owen, John M. 2001. "Transnational Liberalism and U.S. Primacy." *International Security* 26(3): 117–152.

Owen, John M. 2005. "When Do Ideologies Produce Alliances? The Holy Roman Empire, 1517–1555." *International Studies Quarterly* 49(1): 73–99.

Panda, Ankit. 2016. "A Great Leap to Nowhere: Remembering the US-North Korea 'Leap Day' Deal." *Diplomat*, February 29, https://thediplomat.com/2016/02/a-great-leap-to-nowhere-remembering-the-us-north-korea-leap-d ay-deal/ (accessed 2022, July 12).

Pande, Aparna. 2021. "Is a US-Pakistan Reset Possible?" *Hill*, February 17, https://thehill.com/opinion/international/539175-is-a-us-pakistan-reset-p ossible/ (accessed 2022, July 2).

Pankovski, Anatoly. 2020. "Belarus — Russia: Two Decades of Regressive Integration." In Anatoly Pankovski and Valeria Kostyugova (eds.), *Belarusian Yearbook 2020*, 70–79. Vilnius: Logvino.

Papayoanou, Paul A. 1996. "Interdependence, Institutions, and the Balance of Power: Britain, Germany, and World War I." *International Security* 20(4): 42–76.

Pape, Robert A. 1996. *Bombing to Win: Air Power and Coercion in War*. Ithaca: Cornell University Press.

Pape, Robert A. 2005. "Soft Balancing Against the United States." *International Security* 30(1): 7–45.

Parent, Joseph M., and Sebastian Rosato. 2015. "Balancing in Neorealism." *International Security* 40(2): 51–86.

Park, Chan-kyong. 2019. "North Korea Offers Support for Beijing over Hong Kong Protests, Condemning Foreign Forces." *South China Morning Post*, August 12, https://www.scmp.com/news/asia/east-asia/article/3022399/north-korea-offers-support-beijing-over-hong-kong-protests (accessed 2022, July 12).

Park, Ju-min. 2017. "South Korea Finds Apparent North Korean Drone Near Border." *Reuters*, June 9, https://www.reuters.com/article/us-northkorea-southkorea-drone-idUSKBN1900WR (accessed 2022, July 15).

Passeri, Andrea. 2020. "'A Tender Gourd Among the Cactus'. Making Sense of Myanmar's Alignment Policies Through the Lens of Strategic Culture." *Pacific Review* 33(6): 931–957.

Paul, T. V. 2005. "Soft Balancing in the Age of U.S. Primacy." *International Security* 30(1): 46–71.

Paul, T. V. 2018. *Restraining Great Powers: Soft Balancing from Empires to the Global Era*. New Haven: Yale University Press.

Paul, T. V. 2019. "When Balance of Power Meets Globalization: China, India and the Small States of South Asia." *Politics* 39(1): 50–63.

Peng, Nian. 2018. "Myanmar's China Policy Since 1988: A Neoclassical Realist Approach." Ph.D. diss., Hong Kong Baptist University.

Peng, Nian. 2021. "Hedging Against the Dragon: Myanmar's Tangled Relationship with China Since 1988." *Pacific Focus* 36(2): 179–201.

Perović, Jeronim. 2007. "The Tito-Stalin Split: A Reassessment in Light of New Evidence." *Journal of Cold War Studies* 9(2): 32–63.

Petit, Brian. 2023. "Should I Stay or Should I Go? Stay-Behind Force Decision-Making." *War on the Rocks*, November 8, https://warontherocks.com/2023/11/should-i-stay-or-should-i-go-stay-behind-force-decision-making/ (accessed 2023, November 10).

Po, Sovinda, and Christopher B. Primiano. 2020a. "An 'Ironclad Friend': Explaining Cambodia's Bandwagoning Policy Towards China." *Journal of Current Southeast Asian Affairs* 39(3): 444–464.

Po, Sovinda, and Christopher B. Primiano. 2020b. "It's All About the Coalition: Explaining the Cambodian Government's Alignment with China's Belt and Road Initiative and the Impact It Is Having." *European Journal of East Asian Studies* 19: 325–354.

Polovyi, Taras. 2021. "Deterioration of Polish-Belarusian Relations After the 2020 Political Crisis in Belarus." *Ukrainian Policymaker* 9: 93–100.

Popescu, Ionut. 2017. *Emergent Strategy and Grand Strategy: How American Presidents Succeed in Foreign Policy*. Baltimore: Johns Hopkins University Press.

Popescu, Ionut. 2018. "Grand Strategy vs. Emergent Strategy in the Conduct of Foreign Policy." *Journal of Strategic Studies* 41(3): 438–460.

Posen, Barry R. 1993. "Nationalism, the Mass Army, and Military Power." *International Security* 18(2): 80–124.

Posen, Barry R. 2006. "European Union Security and Defense Policy: Response to Unipolarity?" *Security Studies* 15(2): 149–186.

Potjomkina, Diāna, and Dovilė Šukytė. 2017. "Belarus and the Baltics: Did Crisis Really Become an Opportunity?" In Andis Kudors (ed.), *Belarusian Foreign Policy: 360°*, 139–158. Riga: University of Latvia Press.

Powell, Robert. 1999. *In the Shadow of Power: States and Strategies in International Politics*. Princeton: Princeton University Press.

President of Russia. 2008. "Press Statements and Answers to Journalists' Questions Following Russian-Armenian Talks." October 21, http://en.kremlin.ru/event s/president/transcripts/1810 (accessed 2022, September 9).

President of the Republic of Belarus. 2014. "Session of Belarus' Security Council." December 16, https://president.gov.by/en/events/session-of-belarus-securi ty-council-10448#block-after-media-scroll (accessed 2022, May 24).

President of the Republic of Belarus. 2022a. "Belarus' Role on the International Arena." https://president.gov.by/en/quotes/category/belarus-role-on-the-i nternational-arena (accessed 2022, May 24).

President of the Republic of Belarus. 2022b. "Peace Initiatives." https://presi dent.gov.by/en/quotes/category/peace-initiatives (accessed 2022, May 24).

President of the Republic of Belarus. 2022c. "Sovereignty and Independence." https://president.gov.by/en/quotes/category/sovereignty-and-independence (accessed 2022, May 24).

Rabbi, Fazal, Mahar Munawar, and Syed Hamid Mehmood Bukhari. 2022. "Donald Trump's Policy and Posture Towards Pakistan: The Emerging Dynamics and Drivers of the Bilateral Ties." *Pakistan Journal of Social Research* 4(2): 194–207.

Radio Free Asia. 2020. "Joint Cambodia-China 'Golden Dragon' Military Drills to Proceed, Despite Threat of Coronavirus." March 2, https://www.rfa.org/en glish/news/cambodia/drills-03022020170333.html#:~:text=This%20year's%2 0exercise%2C%20held%20under,Kampuchea%20Press%20(AKP)%20reporte d (accessed 2022, June 9).

Radio Free Europe. 2009. "Russian President Deepens Balkan Ties on Belgrade Visit." October 20, https://www.rferl.org/a/Russian_President_Seeks_To_De epen_Ties_In_Belgrade/1856602.html (accessed 2022, August 24).

Radio Free Europe. 2011. "U.S., Armenian Militaries Plan First-Ever Joint Drills." July 25, https://www.rferl.org/a/us_armenian_militaries_plan_first_ever_joi nt_drills/24275683.html (accessed 2022, September 7).

Radio Free Europe. 2013. "Russia, Serbia Sign Military Pact." November 13, https://www.rferl.org/a/russia-serbia-military-pact-/25167365.html (accessed 2022, August 23).

Radio Free Europe. 2019a. "Armenian Speaker Rules Out Support for U.S. Sanctions Against Iran." July 16, https://www.azatutyun.am/a/30058646.html (accessed 2022, April 21).

Radio Free Europe. 2019b. "Serbia Signs Trade Agreement with Russia-Led Eurasian Economic Union." October 25, https://www.rferl.org/a/serbia-to-ink -trade-agreement-with-russia-led-eurasian-economic-union/30235917.html (accessed 2022, August 23).

Radio Free Europe. 2020. "Kosovo Lifts 100 Percent Tariff on Serbia; Belgrade Calls It 'Fake News'." April 1, https://www.rferl.org/a/kosovo-lifts-serbia-tarif fs-belgrade/30521305.html (accessed 2022, September 1).

Radio Free Europe. 2021. "Armenia Won't Join U.S.-Led Military Drills." April 27, https://www.azatutyun.am/a/31225472.html (accessed 2022, September 7).

Radovanovic, Radul. 2008. "Peacekeepers Battle Serbs in Kosovo." *Associated Press*, March 17, https://web.archive.org/web/20080322011032/http://news.yahoo.com/s/ap/20080317/ap_on_re_eu/kosovo_serbs (accessed 2022, August 24).

Rattanasengchanh, P. Michael. 2017. "The Role of Preah Vihear in Hun Sen's Nationalism Politics, 2008–2013." *Journal of Current Southeast Asian Affairs* 36(3): 63–89.

Rauch, Carsten. 2017. "Challenging the Power Consensus: GDP, CINC, and Power Transition Theory." *Security Studies* 26(4): 642–664.

Reaksmey, Hul. 2019. "Cambodian King Supports Belt and Road Initiative: Chinese Media." *VOA*, May 16, https://www.voacambodia.com/a/cambodian-king-supports-belt-and-road-initiative-chinese-media/4918977.html (accessed 2022, June 11).

Reeves, Philip. 2015. "Pakistanis View Obama's India Visit with a Touch of Irritation." *NPR*, January 27, https://www.npr.org/sections/parallels/2015/01/27/381946495/pakistanis-view-obamas-india-visit-with-a-touch-of-irritation (accessed 2022, June 30).

Rehman, Zia Ur. 2020. "Pakistan Bans Political Party Critical of China's Belt and Road." *Nikkei Asia*, May 21, https://asia.nikkei.com/Spotlight/Belt-and-Road/Pakistan-bans-political-party-critical-of-China-s-Belt-and-Road (accessed 2022, June 29).

Reiter, Dan. 1999. "Military Strategy and the Outbreak of International Conflict: Quantitative Empirical Tests, 1903–1992." *Journal of Conflict Resolution* 43(3): 366–387.

Resende-Santos, João. 1996. "Anarchy and the Emulation of Military Systems: Military Organization and Technology in South America, 1870–1930." *Security Studies* 5(3): 193–260.

Reuters. 2008. "Serbia Says Working with Russia on Kosovo Response." March 18, https://www.reuters.com/article/latestCrisis/idUSL17760221 (accessed 2022, August 24).

Reuters. 2014. "North, South Korea Exchange Artillery Fire Off West Coast." *CNBC*, March 31, https://www.cnbc.com/2014/03/31/north-korea-starts-firing-drill-off-west-coast-media.html (accessed 2022, July 15).

Reuters. 2021. "U.S. Ends Military Academy Programme for Cambodia Amid Strained Ties." July 1, https://www.reuters.com/world/asia-pacific/us-ends-military-academy-progamme-cambodia-amid-strained-ties-2021-07-01/ (accessed 2022, June 25).

Riker, William H. 1962. *The Theory of Political Coalitions*. New Haven: Yale University Press.

Ripsman, Norrin M., and Jean-Marc F. Blanchard. 1996. "Commercial Liberalism Under Fire: Evidence from 1914 and 1936." *Security Studies* 6(2): 4–50.

Ripsman, Norrin M. 2021. "Globalization, Deglobalization and Great Power Politics." *International Affairs* 97(5): 1317–1333.

Robertson, Peter E. 2022. "The Real Military Balance: International Comparisons of Defense Spending." *Review of Income and Wealth* 68(3): 797–818.

Roche, James G., and Barry D. Watts. 1991. "Choosing Analytic Measures." *Journal of Strategic Studies* 14(2): 165–209.

Rosato, Sebastian. 2011. *Europe United: Power Politics and the Making of the European Community*. Ithaca: Cornell University Press.

Rosato, Sebastian. 2021. *Intentions in Great Power Politics: Uncertainty and the Roots of Conflict*. New Haven: Yale University Press.

Rosecrance, Richard, and Chih-Cheng Lo. 1996. "Balancing, Stability, and War: The Mysterious Case of the Napoleonic International System." *International Studies Quarterly* 40(4): 479–500.

Ross, Robert S. 2006. "Balance of Power Politics and the Rise of China: Accommodation and Balancing in East Asia." *Security Studies* 15(3): 355–395.

Ross, Robert S. 2013. "US Grand Strategy, the Rise of China, and US National Security Strategy for East Asia." *Strategic Studies Quarterly* 7(2): 20–40.

Ross, Robert S. 2018. "Nationalism, Geopolitics, and Naval Expansionism: From the Nineteenth Century to the Rise of China." *Naval War College Review* 71(4): 10–44.

Ross, Robert S. 2021. "China-Vietnamese Relations in the Era of Rising China: Power, Resistance, and Maritime Conflict." *Journal of Contemporary China* 30(130): 613–629.

Rothstein, Robert L. 1968. *Alliances and Small Powers*. New York: Columbia University Press.

Rowe, David M. 2005. "The Tragedy of Liberalism: How Globalization Caused the First World War." *Security Studies* 14(3): 407–447.

Roy, Denny. 2019. "Assertive China: Irredentism or Expansionism?" *Survival* 61(1): 51–74.

Rudic, Filip. 2017a. "Serbia Seeks Russian Role in Kosovo Talks." *Balkan Insight*, December 20, https://balkaninsight.com/2017/12/20/vucic-russia-willing-to-mediate-serbia-kosovo-talks-12-20-2017/ (accessed 2022, August 25).

Rudic, Filip. 2017b. "Serbian Officials Divided on Foreign Policy 'Balancing Act'." *Balkan Insight*, October 24, https://balkaninsight.com/2017/10/24/serbian-off icials-divided-over-yee-statement-10-24-2017/ (accessed 2022, August 23).

Safi, Michael, and Julian Borger. 2020. "US Silence on Armenia-Azerbaijan Conflict Reflects International Disengagement." *Guardian*, October 4, https://www.theguardian.com/world/2020/oct/04/us-armenia-azerbaijan-nagaon -karabakh (accessed 2022, September 9).

Sahakian, Nane. 2015. "U.S., Armenia Set to Sign New Trade Deal." *Radio Free Europe*, May 5, https://www.azatutyun.am/a/26995978.html (accessed 2022, September 9).

Salter, Christopher L. 2007. *North Korea*, 2nd ed. New York: Infobase.

Samorukov, Maxim. 2022. "Last Friend in Europe: How Far Will Russia Go to Preserve Its Alliance with Serbia?" *Carnegie*, June 10, https://carnegieendow ment.org/eurasiainsight/87303 (accessed 2022, August 25).

Schinella, Anthony M. 2019. *Bombs Without Boots: The Limits of Airpower*. Washington, D.C.: Brookings.

Schneider, Jacquelyn, Benjamin Schechter, and Rachael Shaffer. 2022. "A Lot of Cyber Fizzle But not a Lot of Bang: Evidence About the Use of Cyber Operations from Wargames." *Journal of Global Security Studies* 7(2), https://doi.org/10. 1093/jogss/ogac005.

Schroeder, Paul. 1994. "Historical Reality vs. Neo-Realist Theory." *International Security* 19(1): 108–148.

Schuessler, John M., and Joshua Shifrinson. 2019. "The Shadow of Exit from NATO." *Strategic Studies Quarterly* 13(3): 38–51.

Schuessler, John M., Joshua Shifrinson, and David Blagden. 2021. "Revisiting Insularity and Expansion: A Theory Note." *Perspectives on Politics*, advance online publication, https://doi.org/10.1017/S153759272100222X.

Schweller, Randall L. 1994. "Bandwagoning for Profit: Bringing the Revisionist State Back In." *International Security* 19(1): 72–107.

Schweller, Randall L. 2004. "Unanswered Threats: A Neoclassical Realist Theory of Underbalancing." *International Security* 29(2): 159–201.

Sechser, Todd S., and Elizabeth N. Saunders. 2010. "The Army You Have: The Determinants of Military Mechanization, 1979–2001." *International Studies Quarterly* 54(2): 481–511.

Selden, Zachary. 2016. *Alignment, Alliance, and American Grand Strategy*. Ann Arbor: University of Michigan Press.

Selth, Andrew. 2018. "The Defence Services." In Adam Simpson, Nicholas Farrelly, and Ian Holliday (eds.), *Routledge Handbook of Contemporary Myanmar*, 25–34. Abingdon: Routledge.

Shah, Rahat. 2022. "Pakistan's Quest for Balance in the Context of the Indo-Pacific Strategy." *Australian Journal of Maritime & Ocean Affairs* 14(1): 39–52.

Shah, Syed Ali. 2016. "RAW Involved in Destabilizing Pakistan, Says General Raheel." *Dawn*, April 12, https://www.dawn.com/news/1251654 (accessed 2022, June 29).

Sherwin, Emily. 2017. "Serbia Balances Between Russia and the West." *Deutsche Welle*, December 19, https://www.dw.com/en/serbia-balances-between-russia-and-the-west/a-41854351 (accessed 2022, August 25).

Shirinyan, Anahit. 2019. *Armenia's Foreign Policy Balancing in an Age of Uncertainty*. London: Chatham.

Shlapak, David A., and Michael W. Johnson. 2016. *Reinforcing Deterrence on NATO's Eastern Flank: Wargaming the Defense of the Baltics*. Santa Monica: RAND.

Simón, Luis, Linde Desmaele, and Jordan Becker. 2021. "Europe as a Secondary Theater? Competition with China and the Future of America's European Strategy." *Strategic Studies Quarterly* 15(1): 90–115.

Singh, Sushant. 2016. "What Signal Is Obama Administration Sending by Selling More F-16 Jets to Pakistan?" *Indian Express*, February 13, https://india nexpress.com/article/explained/what-signal-is-obama-administration-sending-by-selling-more-f-16-fighter-jets-to-pakistan/ (accessed 2022, June 30).

Sinnreich, Richard H. 2014. "Victory by Trial and Error: Britain's Struggle Against Napoleon." In Williamson Murray and Richard H. Sinnreich (eds.), *Successful Strategies: Triumphing in War and Peace from Antiquity to the Present*, 155–188. Cambridge: Cambridge University Press.

Sinoruka, Fjori. 2021. "Russia Dismisses Albanian Spying Reports as 'NATO Propaganda'." *Balkan Insight*, July 9, https://balkaninsight.com/2021/07/09/russia-dismisses-albanian-spying-reports-as-nato-propaganda/ (accessed 2021, November 20).

SIPRI. 2021. "Military Expenditure by Country, in Local Currency, 1988–2020." https://sipri.org/sites/default/files/Data%20for%20all%20countries%20from%201988%E2%80%932020%20in%20local%20currency%20%28pdf%29.pdf (accessed 2022, January 21).

Slater, Jerome. 1987. "Dominos in Central America: Will They Fall? Does It Matter?" *International Security* 12(2): 105–134.

Small, Andrew. 2015. *The China-Pakistan Axis: Asia's New Geopolitics*. New York: Oxford University Press.

Small, Andrew. 2020. "India and the China-Pakistan Relationship: De-Hyphenation and Re-Hyphenation." In Kanti Bajpai, Selina Ho, and Manjari Chatterjee Miller (eds.), *Routledge Handbook of China-India Relations*, 410–419. Abingdon: Routledge.

Smetana, Michal, and Jan Ludvik. 2019. "Theorising Indirect Coercion: The Logic of Triangular Strategies." *International Relations* 33(3): 455–474.

Smith, Alexander, and Andy Eckardt. 2018. "Austria's Tilt Toward Russia Worries Intelligence Experts." *NBC*, May 22, https://www.nbcnews.com/news/world/austria-s-tilt-toward-russia-worries-intelligence-experts-n870711 (accessed 2021, November 21).

Snyder, Glenn H. 1984. "The Security Dilemma in Alliance Politics." *World Politics* 36(4): 461–495.

Snyder, Glenn H. 1990. "Alliance Theory: A Neorealist First Cut." *Journal of International Affairs* 44(1): 103–123.

Snyder, Glenn H. 1991. "Alliances, Balance, and Stability." *International Organization* 45(1): 121–142.

Snyder, Jack. 1991. "Introduction." In Robert Jervis and Jack Snyder (eds.), *Dominoes and Bandwagons: Strategic Beliefs and Great Power Competition in the Eurasian Rimland*, 3–19. New York: Oxford University Press.

Sochan, Ry. 2021. "Thai Diplomat's Visit Focused on Economy Plans." *Phnom Penh Post*, December 21, https://www.phnompenhpost.com/national-politics/thai-diplomats-visit-focused-economy-plans (accessed 2022, June 23).

Sokhean, Ben. 2019. "Cambodia, Vietnam Ratify Border Work." *Khmer Times*, October 7, https://www.khmertimeskh.com/648486/cambodia-vietnam-ratify-border-work/ (accessed 2022, June 25).

Sondhaus, Lawrence. 2009. "Planning for the Endgame: The Central Powers, September 1916–April 1917." In Ian F. W. Beckett (ed.), *1917: Beyond the Western Front*, 1–24. Leiden: Brill.

Sothirak, Pou. 2013. "Cambodia's Border Conflict with Thailand." *Southeast Asian Affairs*: 87–100.

Spate, O.H.K., and A.T.A. Learmonth. 2017. *India and Pakistan: A General and Regional Geography*. Abingdon: Routledge.

Sputnik. 2011. "Armenia, Azerbaijan Fail to Reach Agreement on Nagorny Karabakh." June 24, https://sputniknews.com/20110624/164831341.html (accessed 2022, September 8).

Spykman, Nicholas J. 1942. *America's Strategy in World Politics: The United States and the Balance of Power*. New York: Harcourt, Brace.

Steinberg, David I. 2015. "Myanmar and the United States, Closing and Opening Doors: An Idiosyncratic Analysis." *Social Research* 82(2): 427–452.

Steinberg, David I. 2018. "The World." In Adam Simpson, Nicholas Farrelly, and Ian Holliday (eds.), *Routledge Handbook of Contemporary Myanmar*, 291–299. Abingdon: Routledge.

Strangio, Sebastian. 2011. "Hun Sen's War Calculations." *Asia Times Online*, May 2, https://www.sebastianstrangio.com/2011/05/02/hun-sens-war-calculations/ (accessed 2022, June 13).

Stringer, Kevin D. 2021. "Survival in the Russian Occupied Zone: Command and Organization in Resistance Underground Operations." *Military Review* 101(4): 125–132.

Strüver, Georg. 2016. "What Friends Are Made of: Bilateral Linkages and Domestic Drivers of Foreign Policy Alignment with China." *Foreign Policy Analysis* 12(2): 170–191.

Subhan, Arief. 2018. "Lesser Known Border Tensions Between Cambodia and Vietnam." *ASEAN Post*, April 9, https://theaseanpost.com/article/lesser-known-border-tensions-between-cambodia-and-vietnam-0 (accessed 2022, June 25).

Subramanian, Nirupama. 2008. "McCain Warns Pakistan of Indian Air Strikes." *Hindu*, December 7, https://web.archive.org/web/20081207224014/http:/www.hindu.com/2008/12/07/stories/2008120757500100.html (accessed 2022, June 30).

Sullivan, Becky. 2022. "Why Belarus Is so Involved in Russia's Invasion of Ukraine." *NPR*, March 11, https://www.npr.org/2022/03/11/1085548867/belarus-ukraine-russia-invasion-lukashenko-putin (accessed 2022, March 14).

Sullivan, Patricia L. 2007. "War Aims and War Outcomes: Why Powerful States Lose Limited Wars." *Journal of Conflict Resolution* 51(3): 496–524.

Sweeney, Kevin, and Paul Fritz. 2004. "Jumping on the Bandwagon: An Interest-Based Explanation for Great Power Alliances." *Journal of Politics* 66(2): 428–449.

Taliaferro, Jeffrey W. 2006. "State Building for Future Wars: Neoclassical Realism and the Resource-Extractive State." *Security Studies* 15(3): 464–495.

Tanjug. 2016. "PM: We Need NATO as Ally to Protect People in Kosovo." *B92*, February 16, https://www.b92.net/eng/news/politics.php?yyyy=2016&mm=02&dd=16&nav_id=97059 (accessed 2022, August 25).

TASS. 2021. "Containment of Russia to Continue Since It Is Unwanted by Opponents, Putin Says." May 20. https://tass.com/politics/1292065 (accessed 2021, June 6).

Tecott, Rachel, and Andrew Halterman. 2021. "The Case for Campaign Analysis: A Method for Studying Military Operations." *International Security* 45(4): 44–83.

Telhami, Shibley. 2003. "An Essay on Neorealism and Foreign Policy." In Andrew K. Hanami (ed.), *Perspectives on Structural Realism*, 105–118. New York: Palgrave Macmillan.

Ter-Matevosyan, Vahram, Anna Drnoian, Narek Mkrtchyan, and Tigran Yepremyan. 2017. "Armenia in the Eurasian Economic Union: Reasons for Joining and Its Consequences." *Eurasian Geography and Economics* 58(3): 340–360.

Thayer, Carlyle A. 2009. "Cambodia: The Cambodian People's Party Consolidates Power." *Southeast Asian Affairs*: 85–101.

Thayer, Carlyle A. 2010. "US Rapprochement with Laos and Cambodia." *Contemporary Southeast Asia* 32(3): 442–459.

Thucydides. 2009. *The Peloponnesian War*, trans. Martin Hammond. Oxford: Oxford University Press.

Thompson, William R. 1992. "Dehio, Long Cycles, and the Geohistorical Context of Structural Transition." *World Politics* 45(1): 127–152.

Tsarik, Yuri. 2021. "Belarus Goes Nuclear: Context and Prospects of the Astravyets NPP." *International Centre for Defence and Security*, https://forst rategy.org/en/posts/20210329 (accessed 2022, May 3).

Ullah, Shakir, Usman Khan, Khalil Ur Rahman, and Aman Ullah. 2021. "Problems and Benefits of the China-Pakistan Economic Corridor (CPEC) for Local People in Pakistan: A Critical Review." *Asian Perspective* 45(4): 861–876.

Um, Khatharya. 2011. "Cambodia: Hopes, Trials, and Tribulations." *Southeast Asian Affairs*: 53–70.

United Nations Comtrade. 2022. https://comtrade.un.org/ (accessed 2022, September 17).

United States Department of Defense. 2018. *Summary of the 2018 National Defense Strategy of the United States of America: Sharpening the American Military's Competitive Edge.* Washington, D.C.: Office of the Secretary of Defense.

United States Government. 2017. *National Security Strategy of the United States of America.* Washington, D.C.: White House.

Van Evera, Stephen. 1999. *Causes of War: Power and the Roots of Conflict.* Ithaca: Cornell University Press.

Vanaga, Nora. 2017. "The Defence Policy of Belarus: A Regional Perspective." In Andis Kudors (ed.), *Belarusian Foreign Policy: 360°*, 57–69. Riga: University of Latvia Press.

Var, Veasna. 2017. "Cambodia-Thailand Sovereignty Disputes: Implications for Cambodia's Strategic Environment and Defence Organization." *Strategic Analysis* 41(2): 152–172.

Vasilyan, Syuzanna. 2017. "'Swinging on a Pendulum': Armenia in the Eurasian Economic Union and with the European Union." *Problems of Post-Communism* 64(1): 32–46.

Vasovic, Aleksandar. 2016. "With Russia as an Ally, Serbia Edges Toward NATO." *Reuters*, July 3, https://www.reuters.com/article/us-serbia-nato-idUSKCN0Z J 06S (accessed 2022, August 23).

V-Dem Institute. 2022. "Varieties of Democracy." https://www.v-dem.net/ (accessed 2022, September 19).

Vieira, Alena Vysotskaya Guedes. 2014. "The Politico-Military Alliance of Russia and Belarus: Re-Examining the Role of NATO and the EU in Light of the Intra-Alliance Security Dilemma." *Europe-Asia Studies* 66(4): 557–577.

VNA. 2018. "Thailand, Cambodia Agree to Elevate Relations." *Vietnam Plus*, March 23, https://en.vietnamplus.vn/thailand-cambodia-agree-to-elevate-relations/128362.vnp (accessed 2022, June 25).

VOA. 2009. "US Furious over Belgrade Embassy Attack." October 27, https://www. voanews.com/a/a-13-2008-02-22-voa1-66806062/374100.html (accessed 2022, August 25).

VOA. 2019. "US, South Korea Postpone Joint Military Drills as 'Act of Goodwill' Toward North Korea." November 17, https://www.voanews.com/a/east-asia-pacific_us-south-korea-postpone-joint-military-drills-act-goodwill-toward-north-korea/6179574.html (accessed 2022, July 14).

Volgy, Thomas J., Paul Bezerra, Jacob Cramer, and J. Patrick Rhamey. 2017. "The Case for Comparative Regional Analysis in International Politics." *International Studies Review* 19(3): 452–480.

Vuksanovic, Vuk. 2019. "Why Serbia Won't Stop Playing the Russia Card Any Time Soon." *Carnegie*, October 28, https://carnegie.ru/commentary/80188 (accessed 2022, August 23).

Vuksanovic, Vuk. 2021. "Systemic Pressures, Party Politics and Foreign Policy: Serbia Between Russia and the West, 2008–2020." Ph.D. diss., London School of Economics and Political Science.

Walker, Shaun. 2018. "Now Is Chance for Kosovo Deal, Says Serbian President — but at What Cost?" *Guardian*, April 26, https://www.theguardian.com/world/2018/apr/26/now-chance-kosovo-deal-serbian-president-what-cost-aleksandar-vucic (accessed 2022, August 23).

Walker, Shaun. 2019a. "Putin Gets Puppy and Hero's Welcome on Serbia Trip." *Guardian*, January 17, https://www.theguardian.com/world/2019/jan/17/putin-attacks-west-role-in-balkans-ahead-of-lavish-serbia-visit (accessed 2022, August 23).

Walker, Shaun. 2019b. "Serbian President Accuses Russia of Spy Plot Involving Army." *Guardian*, November 21, https://www.theguardian.com/world/2019/nov/21/serbia-investigates-video-claiming-to-show-russian-spy-paying-off-official (accessed 2022, August 23).

Walsh, P. G. 1965. "Massinissa." *Journal of Roman Studies* 55: 149–160.

Walt, Stephen M. 1985. "Alliance Formation and the Balance of World Power." *International Security* 9(4): 3–43.

Walt, Stephen M. 1987. *The Origins of Alliances*. Ithaca: Cornell University Press.

Walt, Stephen M. 1988. "Testing Theories of Alliance Formation: The Case of Southwest Asia." *International Organization* 42(2): 275–316.

Walt, Stephen M. 2018. "US Grand Strategy After the Cold War: Can Realism Explain It? Should Realism Guide It?" *International Relations* 32(1): 3–22.

Waltz, Kenneth N. 1959. *Man, the State, and War: A Theoretical Analysis*. New York: Columbia University Press.

Waltz, Kenneth N. 1979. *Theory of International Politics*. Boston: Addison-Wesley.

Waltz, Kenneth N. 1993. "The Emerging Structure of International Politics." *International Security* 18(2): 44–79.

Waltz, Kenneth N. 1997. "Evaluating Theories." *American Political Science Review* 91(4): 913–917.

Webb, Kieran. 2007. "The Continued Importance of Geographic Distance and Boulding's Loss of Strength Gradient." *Comparative Strategy* 26(4): 295–310.

Weisiger, Alex. 2014. "Victory Without Peace: Conquest, Insurgency, and War Termination." *Conflict Management and Peace Science* 31(4) 357–382.

Wendt, Alexander. 1999. *Social Theory of International Politics*. Cambridge: Cambridge University Press.

Wertz, Daniel. 2018. "The U.S., North Korea, and Nuclear Diplomacy." *National Committee on North Korea*, October, https://www.ncnk.org/resources/briefing-papers/all-briefing-papers/history-u.s.-dprk-relations (accessed 2022, July 13).

Williams, Martyn. 2013. "Full Text of KCNA Announcement on Execution of Jang." *North Korea Tech*, December 13, www.northkoreatech.org/2013/12/13/full-text-of-kcna-announcement-on-execution-of-jang/ (accessed 2022, July 3).

Woehrel, Steven. 2010. "Belarus: Background and U.S. Policy Concerns." *Congressional Research Service*, April 15, https://apps.dtic.mil/sti/pdfs/ADA 520772.pdf (accessed 2022, June 3).

Wolfers, Arnold. 1962. *Discord and Collaboration: Essays on International Politics*. Baltimore: Johns Hopkins Press.

WorldData. "Russian Speaking Countries." https://www.worlddata.info/langu ages/russian.php (accessed 2022, September 17).

Wuthnow, Joel. 2021. "A New Era for Chinese Military Logistics." *Asian Security* 17(3): 279–293.

Wuthnow, Joel. 2022. "Chinese Perspectives on US Strategy in Asia, 2017–2021." *Asian Perspective* 46(3): 401–422.

Wuthnow, Joel, and M. Taylor Fravel. 2022. "China's Military Strategy for a 'New Era': Some Change, More Continuity, and Tantalizing Hints." *Journal of Strategic Studies*, advance online publication, https://doi.org/10.1080/01 402390.2022.2043850.

Xia, Lili, Alan Robock, Kim Scherrer et al. 2022. "Global Food Insecurity and Famine from Reduced Crop, Marine Fishery and Livestock Production Due to Climate Disruption from Nuclear War Soot Injection." *Nature Food* 3(8): 586–596.

Xiao, Ren. 2015. "Toward a Normal State-to-State Relationship? China and the DPRK in Changing Northeast Asia." *North Korean Review* 11(2): 63–78.

Xinhua. 2016. "Cambodia not to Support Arbitration Court's Decision over South China Sea: PM." *China Daily*, June 28, https://www.chinadaily.com.cn/world/2016-06/28/content_25889328.htm (accessed 2022, June 11).

Yarhi-Milo, Keren, Alexander Lanoszka, and Zack Cooper. 2016. "To Arm or to Ally? The Patron's Dilemma and the Strategic Logic of Arms Transfers and Alliances." *International Security* 41(2): 90–139.

Yeliseyeu, Andrei. 2017. "The Poland-Belarus Relationship: Geopolitics Gave New Impetus, but no Breakthrough." In Andis Kudors (ed.), *Belarusian Foreign Policy: 360°*, 159–174. Riga: University of Latvia Press.

Yonhap. 2021. "7 out of 10 S. Koreans See China as Biggest Threat: Poll." December 29, https://en.yna.co.kr/view/AEN20211229004900325 (accessed 2022, January 20).

Yoo, Hyon Joo. 2022. "Political Vulnerability and Alliance Restraint in Foreign Policy: South Korea's Territorial Issue." *Australian Journal of International Affairs* 76(4): 452–472.

Yordanov, Radoslav. 2021. "Fishing in the Desert: Unravelling the Soviet Bloc's Economic Activities and Intelligence Gathering in Ethiopia in the 1960s, with Particular Reference to Bulgaria." *International History Review* 43(1): 109–121.

Zakaria, Fareed. 1998. *From Wealth to Power: The Unusual Origins of America's World Role*. Princeton: Princeton University Press.

Zaman, Aly. 2015. "Compliance and Defiance in Patron-Client State Relationships: A Case Study of Pakistan's Relationship with the United States, 1947–2013." Ph.D. diss., Australian National University.

Zhou, Laura. 2021. "In Japan, the View of China Is Gloomier as Perceptions of Threat Grow." *South China Morning Post,* October 21, https://www.scmp.com/news/china/diplomacy/article/3153163/japan-view-china-gloomier-perceptions-threat-grow (accessed 2022, January 20).

Zhu, Zhiqun. 2016. "Comrades in Broken Arms: Shifting Chinese Policies Toward North Korea." *Asian Politics & Policy* 8(4): 575–592.

Zimmerman, William. 1972. "Hierarchical Regional Systems and the Politics of System Boundaries." *International Organization* 26(1): 18–36.

Zin, Min. 2012. "Burmese Attitude Toward Chinese: Portrayal of the Chinese in Contemporary Cultural and Media Works." *Journal of Current Southeast Asian Affairs* 31(1): 115–131.

Zivanovic, Maja, and Die Morina. 2018. "Kosovo Imposes Customs Tariffs on Serbia, Bosnia." *Balkan Insight,* November 6, https://balkaninsight.com/2018/11/06/kosovo-imposes-customs-tariffs-for-serbia-and-bosnia-and-herzegovina-11-06-2018/ (accessed 2022, September 1).

Zogiani, Nektar. 2014. "Kosovo Opposition Hand Serbia Talks to Nationalists." *Balkan Insight,* September 10, https://balkaninsight.com/2014/09/10/kosovo-nationalist-party-might-run-belgrade-pristina-dialogue-1/ (accessed 2022, September 1).

Index

175

9798881900700